NE능률 영어교과서

대한민국 고등학생 **10** 명 중 **4.7** 명이 보는 교과서

영어 고등 교과서 점유율 1위

(7차, 2007 개정, 2009 개정, 2015 개정)

리딩튜터

그동안 판매된
리딩튜터 1,900만 부
차곡차곡 쌓으면 19만 미터

에베레스트 21 배 높이

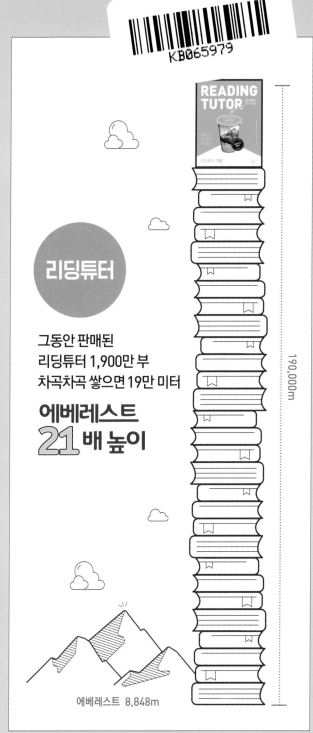

190,000m

에베레스트 8,848m

능률보카

그동안 판매된
능률VOCA 1,100만 부

대한민국 박스오피스
**천만명을 넘은 영화
단 28개**

VOCA

그래머존

그동안 판매된 450만 부의 그래머존을 바닥에 쭉 ~ 깔면
1000km 서울 - 부산 왕복가능

서울

부산

READING

Inside

LEVEL 1

지은이	NE능률 영어교육연구소
선임연구원	조은영
연구원	이선영, 유소영
영문교열	Curtis Thompson, Angela Lan, Olk Bryce Barrett
디자인	김연주
내지 일러스트	최주석, 박응식, 김동현, 양경미
맥편집	김재민

Let's grow together

NE능률이
미래를
창조합니다.

건강한 배움의 고객가치를 제공하겠다는 꿈을 실현하기 위해
40년이 넘는 시간 동안 열심히 달려왔습니다.

앞으로도 끊임없는 연구와 노력을 통해
당연한 것을 멈추지 않고

고객, 기업, 직원 모두가 함께 성장하는 NE능률이 되겠습니다.

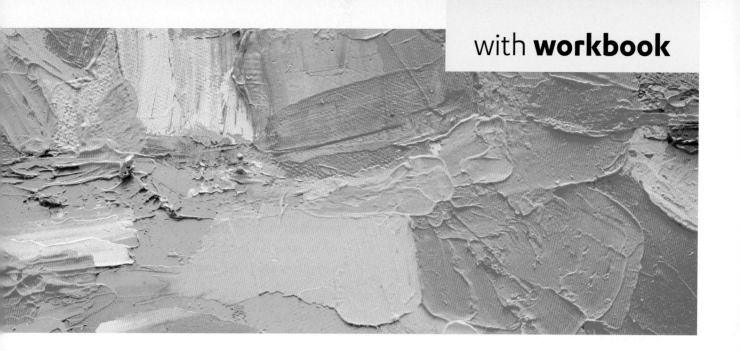

with **workbook**

READING
Inside

LEVEL 1

STRUCTURES

● This shows how each reading passage is related to the topic and the school subject.

● Reading Comprehension

The students' understanding of the passage is checked through a series of multiple-choice and descriptive questions. This also helps to strengthen students' reading accuracy.

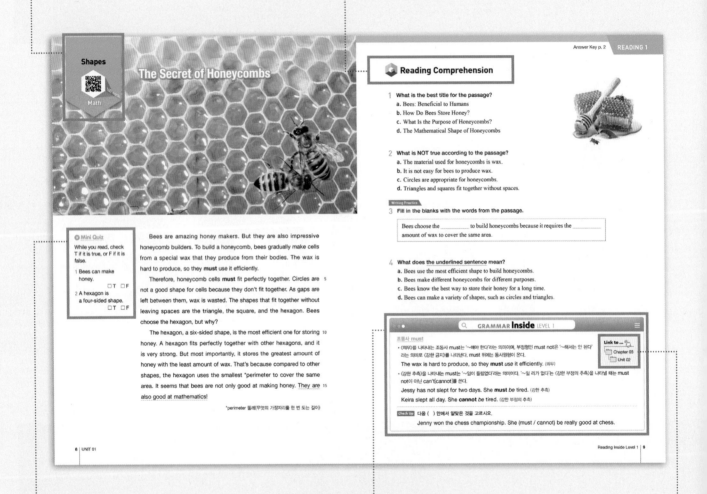

● Mini Quiz

While learners are reading the passage, they are asked to do some simple tasks. Through these simple activities, students can understand the information in the passage more easily and get ready to answer the Reading Comprehension questions.

● GRAMMAR Inside

This helps learners grasp the key structures of sentences and strengthens their understanding of the passage. It is also related to the best-selling grammar series *Grammar Inside*.

🗎 From the **Link to...**, ●

learners can see which chapter and unit of the *Grammar Inside* series are directly related to this section.

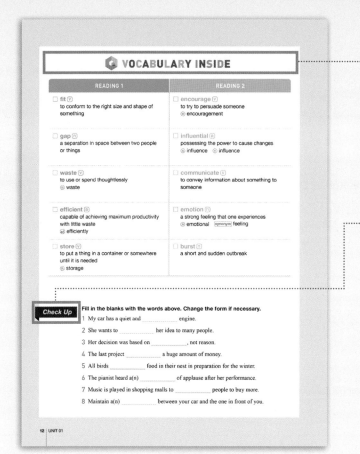

VOCABULARY INSIDE

This presents content words in context and provides synonyms, antonyms, and related parts of speech to improve students' vocabulary. Learners should check if they know the words first before proceeding with the further learning.

Through Check Up ,

students can better understand the practical usage of words by filling in the blanks with words from the chart.

Workbook

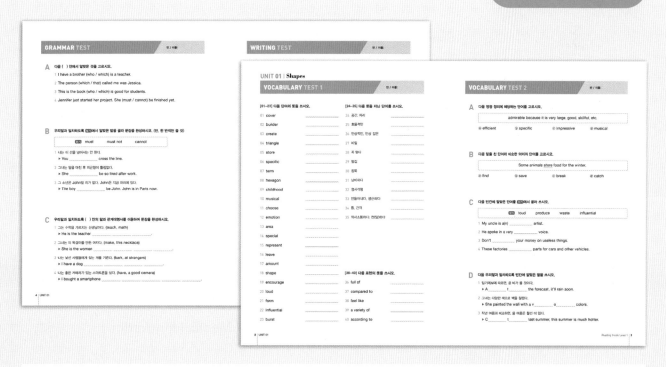

The workbook, which is composed of four pages of vocabulary tests, grammar tests, and writing tests helps reinforce what students have learned in the main text.

◆ CONTENTS

Link to GRAMMAR Inside

Grammar Points in *Reading Inside Level 1*		Grammar Inside Series	
Unit 01	1. 조동사 must	Level 1 Ch.03	Unit 02 must, have to, should
	2. 주격 관계대명사	Level 2 Ch.11	Unit 01 관계대명사
Unit 02	1. 이유, 결과를 나타내는 접속사	Level 2 Ch.10	Unit 01 시간, 이유, 결과의 접속사
	2. 사역동사 + 목적어 + 동사원형	Level 2 Ch.01	Unit 02 목적격 보어를 가지는 동사
Unit 03	1. 원급 비교	Level 1 Ch.08	Unit 03 원급, 비교급, 최상급
	2. 수동태 「be + v-ed(+ by + 행위자)」	Level 2 Ch.07	Unit 01 능동태와 수동태
Unit 04	1. 목적어가 두 개 필요한 동사	Level 1 Ch.05	Unit 02 목적어가 두 개 필요한 동사
	2. 부사적 용법의 to부정사	Level 1 Ch.09	Unit 02 to부정사의 형용사적, 부사적 용법
Unit 05	1. 조동사 can, have to	Level 1 Ch.03	Unit 01 can, may Unit 02 must, have to, should
	2. 목적격 보어로 형용사를 쓰는 동사	Level 1 Ch.05	Unit 03 목적격 보어가 필요한 동사
Unit 06	1. 조건을 나타내는 접속사 if	Level 1 Ch.11	Unit 03 because, if, that
	2. 형용사적 용법의 to부정사	Level 1 Ch.09	Unit 02 to부정사의 형용사적, 부사적 용법
Unit 07	1. 목적격 관계대명사의 생략	Level 2 Ch.11	Unit 02 관계대명사 that, what / 관계대명사의 생략
	2. 현재분사와 과거분사	Level 2 Ch.06	Unit 01 현재분사와 과거분사
Unit 08	1. 접속사 that	Level 1 Ch.11	Unit 03 because, if, that
	2. 재귀대명사	Level 1 Ch.07	Unit 01 인칭대명사, 재귀대명사
Unit 09	1. 감각동사 + 형용사	Level 1 Ch.05	Unit 01 감각동사 + 형용사
	2. 시간의 접속사	Level 1 Ch.11	Unit 02 when, before, after, until
Unit 10	1. 동사 + 목적어 + to-v	Level 1 Ch.05	Unit 03 목적격 보어가 필요한 동사
	2. 현재완료	Level 2 Ch.02	Unit 02 현재완료
Unit 11	1. 비교급과 최상급	Level 1 Ch.08	Unit 03 원급, 비교급, 최상급
	2. 비교급 강조	Level 1 Ch.08	Unit 03 원급, 비교급, 최상급
Unit 12	1. 목적격 보어가 있는 문장의 수동태	Level 2 Ch.07	Unit 02 수동태의 여러 가지 형태
	2. 조동사의 수동태	Level 2 Ch.07	Unit 02 수동태의 여러 가지 형태
Unit 13	1. 「수여동사 + 직접목적어 + to/for/of + 간접목적어」	Level 1 Ch.05	Unit 02 목적어가 두 개 필요한 동사
	2. 부사의 역할	Level 1 Ch.08	Unit 02 부사
Unit 14	1. 〈정도〉를 나타내는 to부정사의 관용 표현	Level 2 Ch.04	Unit 04 to부정사의 의미상의 주어, too ~ to-v, enough to-v
	2. to부정사의 명사적 용법	Level 1 Ch.09	Unit 01 to부정사의 명사적 용법
Unit 15	1. 가주어 it과 진주어 to부정사	Level 1 Ch.09	Unit 01 to부정사의 명사적 용법
	2. 시간을 나타내는 전치사	Level 1 Ch.10	Unit 02 시간을 나타내는 전치사
Unit 16	1. 동명사	Level 1 Ch.09	Unit 03 동명사의 역할
	2. 뒤에서 명사를 수식하는 분사구	Level 2 Ch.06	Unit 01 현재분사와 과거분사

UNIT
01 | Shapes

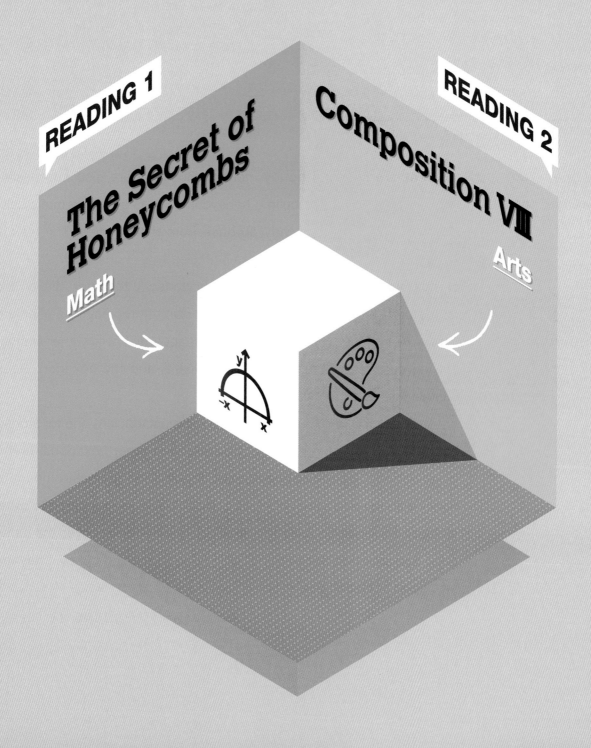

READING 1

The Secret of Honeycombs

Math

READING 2

Composition VIII

Arts

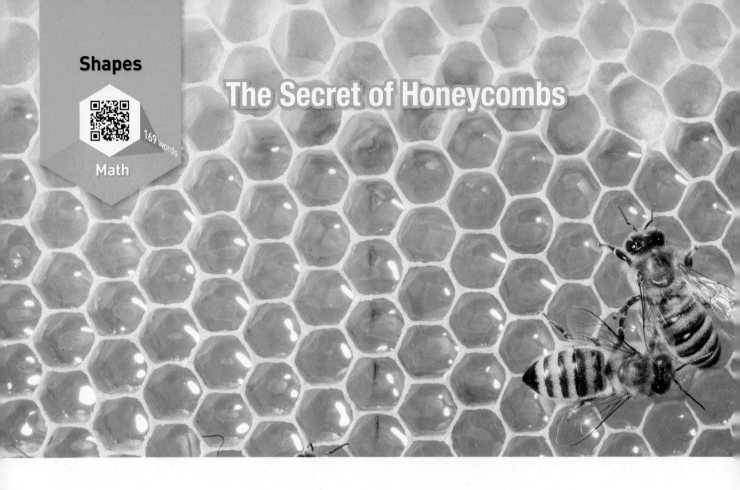

Shapes

Math

169 words

The Secret of Honeycombs

▼ Mini Quiz

While you read, check T if it is true, or F if it is false.

1 Bees can make honey.
□ T □ F

2 A hexagon is a four-sided shape.
□ T □ F

Bees are amazing honey makers. But they are also impressive honeycomb builders. To build a honeycomb, bees gradually make cells from a special wax that they produce from their bodies. The wax is hard to produce, so they **must** use it efficiently.

Therefore, honeycomb cells **must** fit perfectly together. Circles are 5 not a good shape for cells because they don't fit together. As gaps are left between them, wax is wasted. The shapes that fit together without leaving spaces are the triangle, the square, and the hexagon. Bees choose the hexagon, but why?

The hexagon, a six-sided shape, is the most efficient one for storing 10 honey. A hexagon fits perfectly together with other hexagons, and it is very strong. But most importantly, it stores the greatest amount of honey with the least amount of wax. That's because compared to other shapes, the hexagon uses the smallest *perimeter to cover the same area. It seems that bees are not only good at making honey. They are 15 also good at mathematics!

*perimeter 둘레(무엇의 가장자리를 한 번 도는 길이)

Reading Comprehension

1 **What is the best title for the passage?**

  a. Bees: Beneficial to Humans

  b. How Do Bees Store Honey?

  c. What Is the Purpose of Honeycombs?

  d. The Mathematical Shape of Honeycombs

2 **What is NOT true according to the passage?**

  a. The material used for honeycombs is wax.

  b. It is not easy for bees to produce wax.

  c. Circles are appropriate for honeycombs.

  d. Triangles and squares fit together without spaces.

Writing Practice

3 **Fill in the blanks with the words from the passage.**

> Bees choose the _____ to build honeycombs because it requires the _____ amount of wax to cover the same area.

4 **What does the underlined sentence mean?**

  a. Bees use the most efficient shape to build honeycombs.

  b. Bees make different honeycombs for different purposes.

  c. Bees know the best way to store their honey for a long time.

  d. Bees can make a variety of shapes, such as circles and triangles.

🔍 **GRAMMAR Inside** LEVEL 1

조동사 must

- 〈의무〉를 나타내는 조동사 must는 '~해야 한다'라는 의미이며, 부정형인 must not은 '~해서는 안 된다'라는 의미로 〈강한 금지〉를 나타낸다. must 뒤에는 동사원형이 온다.

  The wax is hard to produce, so they **must** *use* it efficiently. (의무)

- 〈강한 추측〉을 나타내는 must는 '~임이 틀림없다'라는 의미이다. '~일 리가 없다'는 〈강한 부정의 추측〉을 나타낼 때는 must not이 아닌 can't[cannot]를 쓴다.

  Jessy has not slept for two days. She **must** *be* tired. (강한 추측)

  Keira slept all day. She **cannot** *be* tired. (강한 부정의 추측)

Link to ...
- Chapter 03
- Unit 02

Check Up 다음 ( ) 안에서 알맞은 것을 고르시오.

  Jenny won the chess championship. She (**must** / **cannot**) be really good at chess.

Shapes

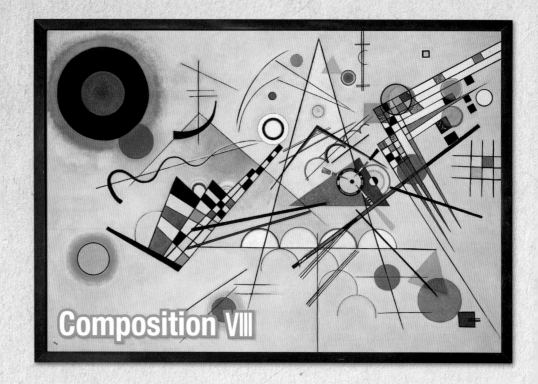

Composition VIII

168 words

Arts

○ Mini Quiz

Paragraph 3
What did Kandinsky want people who viewed his paintings to feel? Find and underline the answer.

Wassily Kandinsky was born in Moscow in 1866. In his early childhood, his parents encouraged him to listen to music, and he grew to love it. This love became very influential in his art. He even named his works after musical terms such as *Impressions, Improvisations,* and *Compositions.*

▲ Wassily Kandinsky (1866~1944)

Kandinsky believed that shapes and colors could communicate the different sounds and emotions of music. One example is *Composition VIII*. He painted it in 1923. (①) It is a painting **that** is full of shapes, such as triangles and circles. (②) And these shapes all work together to create a variety of *geometric forms on the canvas. (③) According to Kandinsky, black represents silence and yellow represents loud bursts of sound, such as those made by trumpets or horns. (④)

Kandinsky wanted people **who** viewed his paintings to feel like they were listening to music. He hoped this would cause them to feel strong emotions. What kind of music do you hear when you look at *Composition VIII*? How does it make you feel?

*geometric 기하학적인

Reading Comprehension

1 **What is the best title for the passage?**
   a. The Achievements of Wassily Kandinsky
   b. The Influence of Music on Famous Painters
   c. How Forms and Colors Are Used in Modern Art
   d. The Shapes and Colors of Music in Kandinsky's Art

2 **What is NOT mentioned in the passage?**
   a. where Kandinsky was born
   b. what influenced Kandinsky's work
   c. when *Composition VIII* was produced
   d. the kind of music Kandinsky preferred

3 **Where would the following sentence best fit?**

   > He painted these forms in specific colors, such as black, yellow, and pink.

   a. ①   **b.** ②   **c.** ③   **d.** ④

Writing Practice
4 **According to the passage, what does yellow represent in *Composition VIII*?**
   It represents _____, such as those made by trumpets or horns.

Q   **GRAMMAR Inside** LEVEL 2   ☰

주격 관계대명사
- 관계대명사는 「대명사＋접속사」 역할을 하며, 그것이 이끄는 절은 앞의 명사인 선행사를 수식한다.
- 주격 관계대명사는 절 안에서 주어의 역할을 하며, 선행사가 사람이면 who[that], 사물이면 that[which]을 쓴다.

I know a girl. She wants to be a singer.
→ I know *a girl* [**who[that]** wants to be a singer].

It is a painting. It is full of shapes, ...
→ It is *a painting* [**that[which]** is full of shapes], ...

Link to ...
📁 Chapter 11
📁 Unit 01

Check Up 빈칸에 who 또는 which 중 적절한 것을 골라 쓰시오.

   1 Ben is a doctor _____ works in a hospital.
   2 Sophie wrote a story _____ is about her mother.

◈ VOCABULARY INSIDE

READING 1	READING 2
☐ **fit** Ⓥ to conform to the right size and shape of something	☐ **encourage** Ⓥ to try to persuade someone ⓝ encouragement
☐ **gap** ⓝ a separation in space between two people or things	☐ **influential** ⓐ possessing the power to cause changes ⓝ influence Ⓥ influence
☐ **waste** Ⓥ to use or spend thoughtlessly ⓝ waste	☐ **communicate** Ⓥ to convey information about something to someone
☐ **efficient** ⓐ capable of achieving maximum productivity with little waste ⓐⅾ efficiently	☐ **emotion** ⓝ a strong feeling that one experiences ⓐ emotional [synonym] feeling
☐ **store** Ⓥ to put a thing in a container or somewhere until it is needed ⓝ storage	☐ **burst** ⓝ a short and sudden outbreak

Check Up

Fill in the blanks with the words above. Change the form if necessary.

1 My car has a quiet and _____ engine.

2 She wants to _____ her idea to many people.

3 Her decision was based on _____, not reason.

4 The last project _____ a huge amount of money.

5 All birds _____ food in their nest in preparation for the winter.

6 The pianist heard a(n) _____ of applause after her performance.

7 Music is played in shopping malls to _____ people to buy more.

8 Maintain a(n) _____ between your car and the one in front of you.

UNIT 02 | Origins

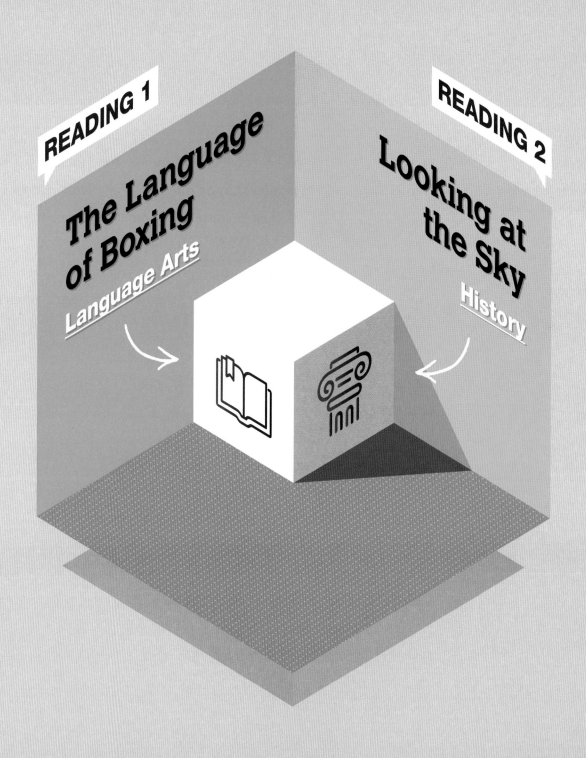

READING 1
The Language of Boxing
Language Arts

READING 2
Looking at the Sky
History

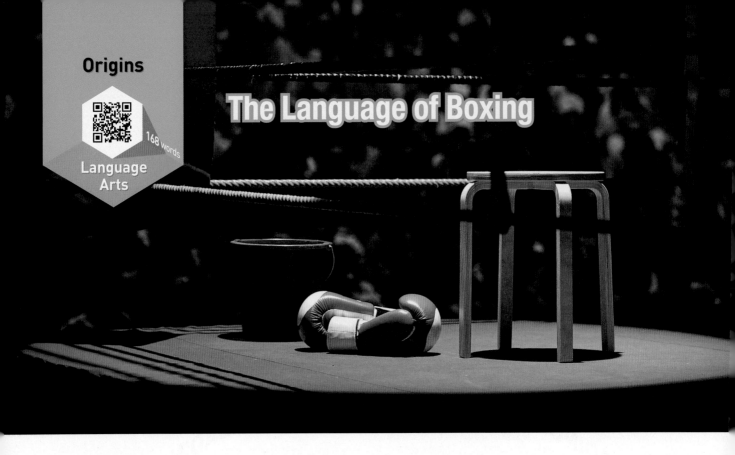

The Language of Boxing

V Mini Quiz

Do you know any of the
following expressions?
Look and check.

☐ in my corner
☐ throw in the towel
☐ on the ropes

Q: I read the following sentences but couldn't understand them.

"I argued with my classmate, but no one was *in my corner*. I *threw in the towel* and apologized first **because** I was totally *on the ropes*."

Can you explain them?

A: Actually, those expressions are from boxing. Over a century ago in 5 England, boxing was **so** popular **that** several boxing terms entered the English language.

1. "In my corner"

Between rounds of a boxing match, boxers rest in opposite corners of the ring while their coaches encourage them. **So** "in my corner" 10 means that someone is on my side.

2. "Throw in the towel"

Traditionally, boxers' coaches admitted defeat by throwing a towel into the ring, **so** "throw in the towel" means to give up.

3. "On the ropes" 15

There are four ropes around the edge of a boxing ring. When a boxer is driven onto the ropes by the opponent, he or she is nearly defeated. **So** "on the ropes" means to be in _____.

Now do you understand the sentences?

Reading Comprehension

1   **What is the best title for the passage?**
   a. The Ancient Rules of Boxing
   b. Boxing Terms in the English Language
   c. What Special Signals Are Used by Boxers?
   d. Finding the Meaning of Difficult Sports Terms

Writing Practice

2   **According to the passage, why did some boxing terms become part of the English language?**
   It is because _____ was very _____ in _____ over a century ago.

3   **What is the best choice for the blank?**
   a. debt   b. shape   c. trouble   d. control

4   **Who used the underlined expressions from the passage correctly?**

   • Jessica: My parents don't support me. I have no one in my corner.
   • Holden: When our team was winning 5-0, I felt we were on the ropes.
   • Max: I knew I would win, so I threw in the towel.

   a. no one   b. Jessica   c. Holden   d. Max

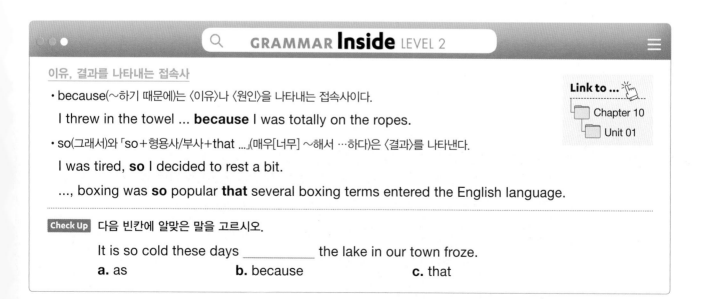

○ ○ ○ •   🔍   GRAMMAR **Inside** LEVEL 2   ≡

이유, 결과를 나타내는 접속사

• because(~하기 때문에)는 〈이유〉나 〈원인〉을 나타내는 접속사이다.
   I threw in the towel ... **because** I was totally on the ropes.

• so(그래서)와 「so＋형용사/부사＋that ...」(매우[너무] ~해서 …하다)은 〈결과〉를 나타낸다.
   I was tired, **so** I decided to rest a bit.
   ..., boxing was **so** popular **that** several boxing terms entered the English language.

Link to ... 👆
   📁 Chapter 10
   📁 Unit 01

Check Up 다음 빈칸에 알맞은 말을 고르시오.

   It is so cold these days _____ the lake in our town froze.
   a. as   **b.** because   **c.** that

Looking at the Sky

V Mini Quiz

Paragraph 2

When was the first telescope built? Find and underline the answer.

▲ Galileo Galilei
(1564~1642)

Prior to the 1600s, people looked at the night sky, but this only **let** them **imagine** what was happening. Beyond the clouds was an unknown world. But this all changed with the invention of the telescope.

The first telescope was built in 1608. People usually think Galileo   5
Galilei, the Italian scientist, invented it. But, in fact, it was Hans Lippershey, a German eyeglass maker. His telescope, however, was very basic—it could only **make** things **appear** three times bigger.

Galileo heard about Lippershey's device and decided to make his own version. Galileo greatly improved Lippershey's design. His   10
telescope was much stronger than Lippershey's. With more lenses in it, his telescope allowed him to magnify things up to thirty times. And he was the first person to use a telescope to study the stars. Through his observations, he realized that the Sun was the center of our solar system.   15

The invention of the telescope helped us _____. The creativity and effort of Lippershey and Galileo allowed science to take a great leap forward.

Reading Comprehension

1   **What is the passage mainly about?**
   a. different types of telescopes
   b. the invention of the telescope
   c. technologies used to observe the sky
   d. the great discoveries of Galileo Galilei

2   **What is NOT true according to the passage?**
   a. Galileo Galilei made the first telescope.
   b. The first telescope could magnify an object three times.
   c. Galileo Galilei was the first to observe the stars with a telescope.
   d. Galileo Galilei discovered that the Sun is the center of our solar system.

3   **Write T if the statement is true or F if it's false.**
   (1) Lippershey's telescope could magnify things up to thirty times. _____
   (2) Galileo added more lenses to Lippershey's telescope design. _____

4   **What is the best choice for the blank?**
   a. see close things clearly   b. understand space better
   c. confirm our previous theories   d. change our religious perspectives

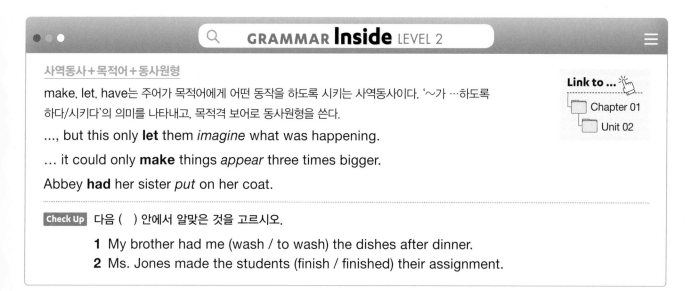

Q   **GRAMMAR Inside** LEVEL 2

사역동사＋목적어＋동사원형

make, let, have는 주어가 목적어에게 어떤 동작을 하도록 시키는 사역동사이다. '~가 …하도록 하다/시키다'의 의미를 나타내고, 목적격 보어로 동사원형을 쓴다.

..., but this only **let** them *imagine* what was happening.

… it could only **make** things *appear* three times bigger.

Abbey **had** her sister *put* on her coat.

Link to …
   Chapter 01
   Unit 02

Check Up   다음 ( ) 안에서 알맞은 것을 고르시오.

   1 My brother had me (wash / to wash) the dishes after dinner.
   2 Ms. Jones made the students (finish / finished) their assignment.

VOCABULARY INSIDE

READING 1	READING 2
☐ **apologize** ⓥ to express regret for something one did or said ⓝ apology	☐ **unknown** ⓐ unfamiliar or not known antonym famous
☐ **expression** ⓝ a meaningful word or phrase ⓥ express	☐ **invention** ⓝ the act of creating something completely new ⓥ invent
☐ **match** ⓝ a contest between two or more people or parties synonym game	☐ **basic** ⓐ extremely simple or lowest in level ⓝ base
☐ **opposite** ⓐ situated at the other side of something or across from something	☐ **device** ⓝ a machine used for a special purpose synonym equipment
☐ **edge** ⓝ the part farthest from the center of something antonym center	☐ **observation** ⓝ the act of watching and taking note of someone or something ⓥ observe

Check Up   **Fill in the blanks with the words above. Change the form if necessary.**

1 We truly _____ for the delay in your delivery.

2 He enjoys exploring _____ areas in the forest.

3 She sat on the _____ side of the table from me.

4 They will build a new park on the _____ of town.

5 The rugby team will play an important _____ this Friday.

6 Close _____ of nature often leads to new scientific insights.

7 I bought the _____ model of this car, so it wasn't too expensive.

8 The _____ of the telephone has made communication easier for people.

UNIT
03 | Sports

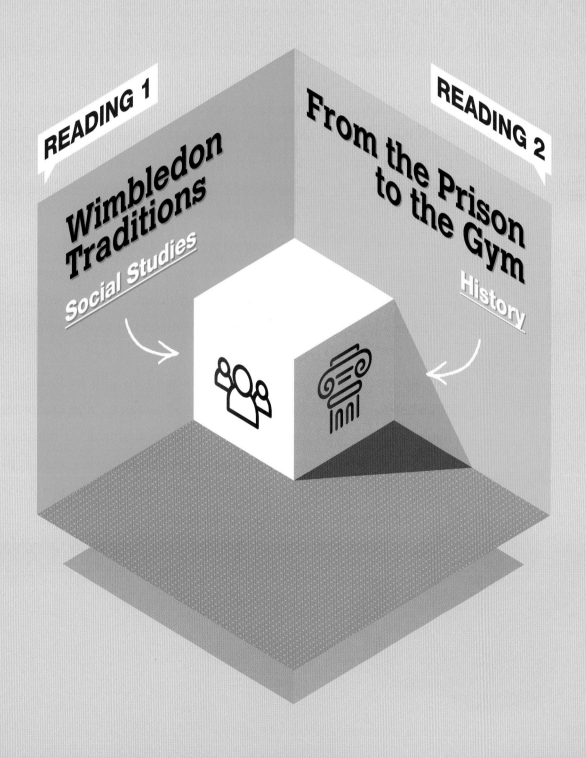

READING 1
Wimbledon Traditions
Social Studies

READING 2
From the Prison to the Gym
History

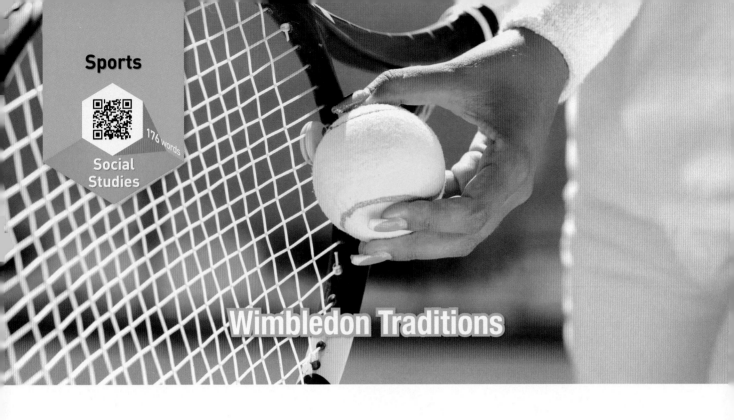

Wimbledon Traditions

⊙ Mini Quiz

Find and underline the
main idea sentences
of the 2nd and the 3rd
paragraph.

For thirteen days this June and July, thousands of tennis fans will attend an event almost **as old as** tennis itself: Wimbledon. The tournament began in 1877. It is named after the area of London where it takes place. As fans enjoy this year's competition, they will also experience two interesting traditions.   5

First, the players must wear all white. Today, this is a strict dress code rule, but, originally, white clothes were a way for players to look better for their fans. White clothing doesn't show sweat stains **as clearly as** dark clothing, so early Wimbledon players wore white

_____.   10

Second, fans will consume a stunning 28,000 kilograms of strawberries and 7,000 liters of cream. Strawberries and cream has been served at Wimbledon since the first tournament. At that time, it was a fashionable dessert. Since English strawberries grow in the summer, the season of the competition, strawberries and cream 15 remains the perfect snack at Wimbledon.

If you plan to watch Wimbledon this summer, try taking part in these traditions, and cheer for your favorite player!

Reading Comprehension

1   **What is the passage mainly about?**
   a. what to do in London in the summer
   b. the origin of the Wimbledon tournament
   c. interesting traditions of the Wimbledon tournament
   d. why people love to eat strawberries and cream together

2   **What CANNOT be answered about the Wimbledon tournament according to the passage?**
   a. When did it first start?   **b.** Where is it held?
   c. What is its dress code?   **d.** How many players participate?

3   **What is the best choice for the blank?**
   a. to keep the tradition
   b. to attract fans' attention
   c. to avoid looking sweaty
   d. to protect themselves from the summer sun

Writing Practice

4   **According to the passage, why are strawberries the perfect snack for Wimbledon?**
   It is because English strawberries grow _____.

Q   GRAMMAR Inside LEVEL 1   ≡

원급 비교

「as+형용사/부사+as」는 '~만큼 …한/하게'의 의미이다.

... will attend an event almost **as old as** tennis itself: Wimbledon.

White clothing doesn't show sweat stains **as clearly as** dark clothing, ...

My mother came home **as early as** my father.

Link to ...
Chapter 08
Unit 03

Check Up 우리말과 일치하도록 ( ) 안에 주어진 말을 바르게 배열하시오.

   Emily는 Ann만큼 키가 크다. (as / Ann / tall / as)
   → Emily is _____.

From the Prison to the Gym

Mini Quiz

Paragraph 3

Q: Why were treadmills banned in 1898?

A: They were banned for _____
_____.

Running on a treadmill at the gym is hard work. Just fifteen minutes can feel like hours. For some people, it feels like punishment. In fact, punishment was the reason for the invention of the first treadmill.

In 19th-century England, the treadmill **was invented** to punish prisoners. They **were forced** to *tread on the steps of a large, moving 5 wheel. The rotation of the wheel **was used** to power a mill. And that's the origin of the name "treadmill." Prisoners spent around six hours a day on treadmills. That's like climbing a mountain every day! Unsurprisingly, many prisoners became exhausted from walking on treadmills. 10

(A) In 1898, they **were banned** for being too cruel. (B) However, the treadmill made a surprising comeback as sports equipment in the 1950s. (C) Treadmills **were used** in prisons until the late 19th century. For fitness fans, the new treadmill was an easy and convenient way to exercise, and it remains popular today. 15

*tread 발을 디디다, 걷다

Reading Comprehension

1 **What is the passage mainly about?**
a. how the treadmill works
b. where treadmills came from
c. the life of prisoners in England
d. why running on a treadmill is painful

Writing Practice

2 **According to the passage, what was the original purpose of the treadmill?**
It was invented to _____.

Writing Practice

3 **Fill in the blanks using the words from the passage.**

Q: How did the treadmill in the 19th century work?
A: Prisoners trod on the steps of a large, moving _____, and its _____ was
used to _____ a mill.

4 **What is the best order of the sentences (A) ~ (C)?**
a. (A) – (B) – (C)   b. (B) – (A) – (C)
c. (C) – (A) – (B)   d. (C) – (B) – (A)

🔍 **GRAMMAR Inside** LEVEL 2   ☰

수동태 「be+v-ed(+by+행위자)」

수동태는 주어가 동사의 영향을 받거나 동작을 당하는 것을 나타낼 때 쓰며, '(~에 의해) …되다'라는 의미이다.
행위자가 막연한 일반인일 때, 분명하지 않거나 중요하지 않을 때 「by+행위자」는 생략할 수 있다.

..., the treadmill **was invented** to punish prisoners.

This problem **was solved by** Jack.

Sandra **was chosen** as the Best Actress of the Year.

Link to ... 👆
📁 Chapter 07
📁 Unit 01

Check Up 밑줄 친 부분을 어법에 맞게 고쳐 쓰시오.
1 Cars are use by many people all over the world.   _____
2 The class president is electing by the students.   _____

VOCABULARY INSIDE

READING 1	READING 2
☐ **attend** ⓥ to be in present in a meeting, event or something ⓝ attendance	☐ **punishment** ⓝ the act of disciplining someone for doing something wrong ⓥ punish [antonym] reward
☐ **competition** ⓝ an event where people try to be the best at something ⓥ compete	☐ **power** ⓥ to give something the energy to work ⓝ power ⓐ powerful
☐ **strict** ⓐ controlling people to obey rules or act in a certain way [antonym] generous	☐ **exhausted** ⓐ completely out of physical or mental energy ⓥ exhaust [antonym] energetic
☐ **sweat** ⓝ a clear liquid from your skin due to being hot or nervous ⓥ sweat ⓐ sweaty	☐ **ban** ⓥ to block people from doing or using something [synonym] prohibit [antonym] allow
☐ **stunning** ⓐ very surprising and shocking ⓥ stun	☐ **convenient** ⓐ easy to use or without difficulty ⓝ convenience

Check Up   **Fill in the blanks with the words above. Change the form if necessary.**

1 She won the first prize in the _____ .

2 I've been on the run all day, so I'm so _____ .

3 I hurried to _____ the meeting and wasn't late.

4 They made her clean up the mess as a(n) _____ .

5 For me, online shopping is both cheap and _____ .

6 She is on a(n) _____ diet. She never eats bread or rice.

7 I was covered in _____ when I reached the top of the hill.

8 This movie is so violent. Teenagers should be _____ from watching it.

UNIT
04 | Jobs

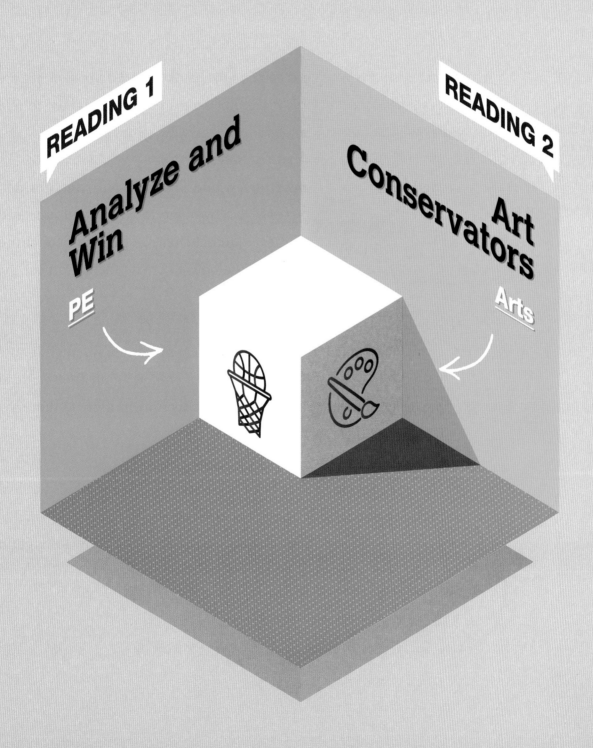

READING 1

Analyze and Win

PE

READING 2

Art Conservators

Arts

Analyze and Win

Ⓥ Mini Quiz

Paragraph 1

Q: What do sports performance analysts help teams do?

A: They help sports teams make

_____

that allows them

_____ .

In sports, small advantages can bring huge rewards. Sports performance analysts help sports teams make a game plan that allows them to win. But how? Let's ask sports performance analyst James Parker.

Q: What do sports performance analysts do?

A: We look at teams and athletes, and identify their strengths and 5
   weaknesses. We _____(A)_____ by going to games and practices,
   and watching videos of the games. Then we **give the coaching
   staff our analysis**. They use the data to create tactics to beat the
   opposition.

Q: Could you **give me an example**? 10

A: Okay. Think about baseball. After watching games, we might notice
   that a hitter has a higher hitting percentage against left-handed
   pitchers. We **tell the coaching staff this information** so that they
   can change their tactics.

Q: _____(B)_____ 15

A: First, you need to be very interested in sports. You also need excellent
   math, research, and analytical skills to create databases. Finally,
   good communication skills are important to explain
   complex data to the coaching staff.

Reading Comprehension

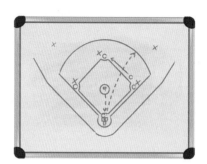

1 **What is the interview mainly about?**
   a. the duties of sports performance analysts
   b. different game plans that sports teams use
   c. the history of sports performance analysts
   d. why tactics are important for sports teams

2 **What is the best choice for blank (A)?**
   a. play games
   b. collect data
   c. train players
   d. cheer for teams

Writing Practice

3 **According to the passage, how do coaching staffs use the data from sports analysts?**
   They use it to _____.

4 **What is the best choice for blank (B)?**
   a. How do you analyze player performance?
   b. What is the hardest part about doing your job?
   c. What is needed to become a sports performance analyst?
   d. Why did you decide to become a sports performance analyst?

GRAMMAR Inside LEVEL 1

목적어가 두 개 필요한 동사

수여동사 give, tell, send, write, lend, show, teach, cook, buy, make, ask 등은 간접목적어 (~에게)와 직접목적어(…을) 모두를 필요로 하며, 「수여동사＋간접목적어＋직접목적어」는 '~에게 …을 (해)주다'로 해석한다.

Link to ...
☐ Chapter 05
☐ Unit 02

Then we **give** *the coaching staff* *our analysis*.(= Then we **give** our analysis *to* the coaching staff.)
      간접목적어   직접목적어

Mia **bought** *her mother* *some flowers*. (= Mia **bought** some flowers *for* her mother.)
       간접목적어   직접목적어

Check Up 우리말과 일치하도록 ( ) 안에 주어진 말을 바르게 배열하시오.

   Peter는 어제 나에게 메시지를 보냈다. (a message / sent / Peter / me)

   → _____ yesterday.

Art Conservators

✔ Mini Quiz

Paragraph 2

What is a conservator an expert at? Find and underline the answer.

People go to the doctor's office **to get** checkups or treatment. But did you know that works of art need treatment too? Conservators take care of artwork just like doctors take care of patients.

A conservator is an expert at keeping artwork in good condition and repairing any damage. _____(A)_____, in 1990 someone threw acid 5 on Rembrandt's *The Night Watch*. Although the guards quickly added water **to weaken** the acid, the *varnish was still ruined. Conservators restored the painting by carefully removing the damaged varnish and recoating it.

(①) Conservators have different specialties, just as doctors do. 10 (②) They are experts in different types of art and materials, such as oil painting, photography, or sculpture. (③) For example, conservators can adjust the humidity **to provide** the best environment for a wooden sculpture. (④)

_____(B)_____ the conservators, 15 the works of Leonardo da Vinci, Raphael, and other great artists will be enjoyed for many more years. Their time and effort helps protect our valuable cultural history. 20

▲ *The Night Watch*(1642)
by Rembrandt van Rijn

*varnish 광택제, 니스

Reading Comprehension

1 What is the best title for the passage?

a. Who Works at a Museum?

b. Conservators: Doctors for Artwork

c. Rembrandt's Greatest Work: *The Night Watch*

d. How to Keep Different Artwork in the Best Condition

2 What is the best pair for blanks (A) and (B)?

	(A)	(B)		(A)	(B)
a.	However	— Because of	b.	However	— Thanks to
c.	For example	— Thanks to	d.	For example	— In addition to

Writing Practice

3 According to the passage, how did conservators restore Rembrandt's *The Night Watch* when it was damaged?

They restored it by _____ .

4 Where would the following sentence best fit?

> They also know the safest ways to display each material.

a. ①   b. ②   c. ③   d. ④

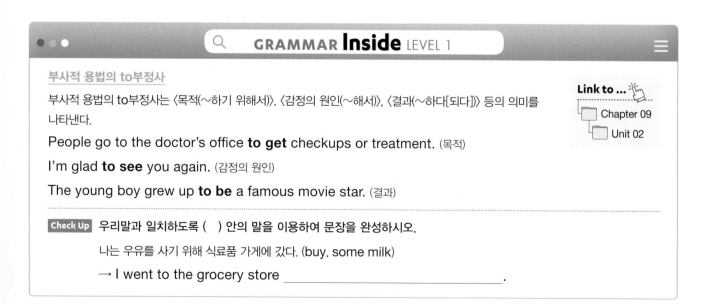

GRAMMAR **Inside** LEVEL 1

부사적 용법의 to부정사

부사적 용법의 to부정사는 〈목적(~하기 위해서)〉, 〈감정의 원인(~해서)〉, 〈결과(~하다[되다])〉 등의 의미를 나타낸다.

Link to ...

Chapter 09
Unit 02

People go to the doctor's office **to get** checkups or treatment. (목적)

I'm glad **to see** you again. (감정의 원인)

The young boy grew up **to be** a famous movie star. (결과)

Check Up 우리말과 일치하도록 ( ) 안의 말을 이용하여 문장을 완성하시오.

나는 우유를 사기 위해 식료품 가게에 갔다. (buy, some milk)

→ I went to the grocery store _____ .

VOCABULARY INSIDE

READING 1	READING 2
☐ analyze ⓥ to examine or study something carefully ⓝ analysis ⓝ analyst ⓐ analytical	☐ expert ⓝ a person who specializes in something or is trained in it ⓐ expert synonym specialist
☐ reward ⓝ something you get as an award for hard work or doing something good ⓥ reward ⓐ rewarding	☐ restore ⓥ to repair something so that it looks like it originally did ⓝ restoration
☐ identify ⓥ to recognize and be able to say who someone is or what something is ⓝ identification	☐ specialty ⓝ an area of work or study that a person is best at or knows a lot about ⓥ specialize
☐ tactic ⓝ a particular way to achieve something synonym strategy	☐ adjust ⓥ to change something slightly to make it more effective or suitable ⓝ adjustment
☐ communication ⓝ the activity of expressing ideas and feelings or giving information ⓥ communicate	☐ valuable ⓐ very important or helpful ⓝ value antonym worthless

Check Up

Fill in the blanks with the words above. Change the form if necessary.

1 She is a(n) _____ on ancient Egypt.

2 Her job is to _____ antique furniture.

3 Brian is a(n) _____ member of our staff.

4 He deserves a(n) _____ for working so hard.

5 I don't have any _____ with my sister these days.

6 If you want to _____ the volume, use these buttons.

7 The students were asked to _____ the research data.

8 The coach suggested a new _____ for the next game.

UNIT
05 | Solutions

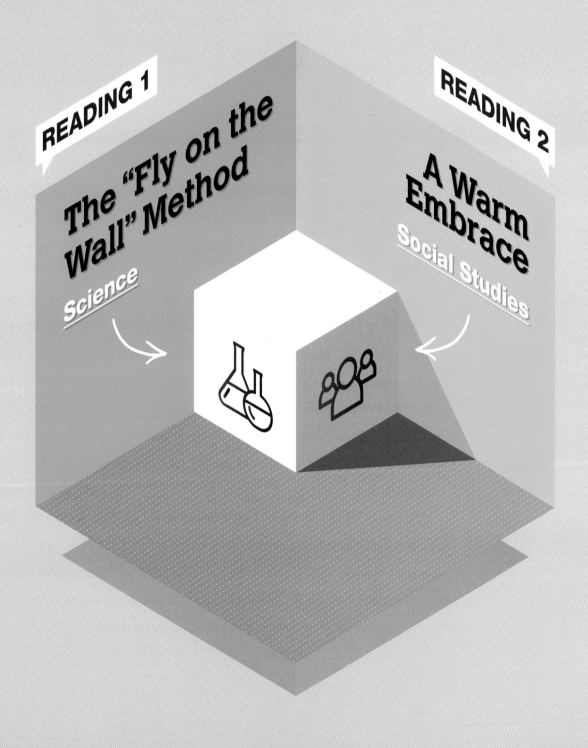

READING 1

The "Fly on the Wall" Method

Science

READING 2

A Warm Embrace

Social Studies

The "Fly on the Wall" Method

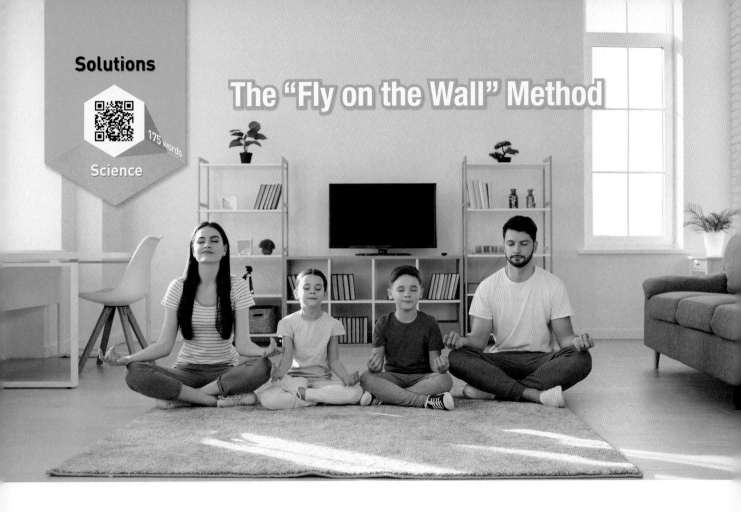

We live in a high-stress society, so stress seems unavoidable. As a result, methods of stress relief have become a requirement in our daily lives. We constantly look for the latest techniques and hope they work.

However, stress relief **doesn't have to** be complicated. In fact, 5 according to a study conducted at Ohio University, relieving stress is quite simple. You just **have to** become a fly on the wall. It may sound strange, but the results of the study proved the effectiveness of the "fly on the wall" technique. In the experiment, participants who used this method **were able to** reduce their anger in stressful situations. 10 Furthermore, their performance in given tasks improved by 30%.

The key is _____. By looking at it from an outsider's point of view, like that of a fly on the wall, you **can** separate your emotions from your experiences. This is important because intense emotions prevent you from making calm, clear 15 decisions. But having an outside perspective allows you to control these emotions, make better decisions, and lower stress.

Reading Comprehension

1 **What is the best title for the passage?**
   a. Interesting Facts about flies
   b. A Simple Way to Relieve Stress
   c. Common Ways to Test Stress Levels
   d. How Emotions Cause Bad Decisions

2 **Write T if the statement is true or F if it's false.**
   (1) Following the "fly on the wall" method sounds complicated. _____
   (2) In the "fly on the wall" experiment, participants showed improved performances. _____

3 **What is the best choice for the blank?**
   a. to face the problem and solve it
   b. to see your situation objectively
   c. to try to forget the past and move on
   d. to let other people handle the situation

Writing Practice

4 **According to the passage, why is it important to separate your emotions from your experiences?**
   It is important because intense emotions _____.

Q **GRAMMAR Inside** LEVEL 1 ≡

<u>조동사 can, have to</u>

• 조동사 can은 〈능력〉, 〈허가〉를 나타내며 '~할 수 있다'의 의미이다. can 대신에 「be+able+to-v」를 쓸 수 있다. 부정형 can't는 '~할 수 없다'의 의미이다.

..., you **can** *separate* your emotions from your experiences.

..., participants ... **were able to** *reduce* their anger in stressful situations.

• 조동사 have/has to는 〈의무〉를 나타내며 '~해야 한다'의 의미이다. 부정형인 don't/doesn't have to는 〈필요〉를 나타내며 '~할 필요 없다'의 의미이다.

You just **have to** *become* a fly on the wall.

..., stress relief **doesn't have to** *be* complicated.

Link to ...
☐ Chapter 03
☐ Unit 01
☐ Unit 02

Check Up 다음 ( ) 안에서 알맞은 것을 고르시오.

I can help you more. You don't have (to worry / worry) about that.

A Warm Embrace

When babies are born too early, they have little body fat to **keep them warm**. They are too small to regulate their body temperature, and this can lead to major health problems, such as heart disease or poor brain function. However, such problems can be prevented by **keeping premature babies warm**.　　　　　　　　　　　　　　　　　5

That's what incubators are for. Unfortunately, the price of incubators and their electricity costs are too high for most developing countries. Jane Chen, a young MBA student with a passion for healthcare, wanted to solve this problem. She knew that hospital staffs and parents needed a low-cost solution that didn't use electricity. Chen had a smart 10 but simple idea: the Embrace Warmer.

(①) The Embrace Warmer is a tiny sleeping bag that **keeps premature babies warm**. (②) The wax melts at 37 degrees Celsius— human body temperature. (③) Users simply melt the wax with hot

▲ the Embrace Warmer

water and place it back inside the 15 Embrace Warmer. (④) The Embrace Warmer can then **keep a baby warm** for four to six hours at a time. Now this simple invention is **keeping thousands of premature babies** 20 **warm**.

Reading Comprehension

1 **What is the best title for the passage?**
   a. The Origin of Incubators
   b. The Health Problems of Premature Babies
   c. A Simple but Great Invention to Keep Babies Warm
   d. Incubators: The Best Invention for Premature Babies

2 **What is NOT mentioned about the Embrace Warmer in the passage?**
   a. who invented it
   b. how much it costs
   c. how people can use it
   d. how long it can keep babies warm

Writing Practice

3 **According to the passage, what does the underlined this problem refer to?**
   _____ for most developing countries.

4 **Where would the following sentence best fit?**

   | There is a pouch of wax inside. |

   a. ①   **b.** ②   **c.** ③   **d.** ④

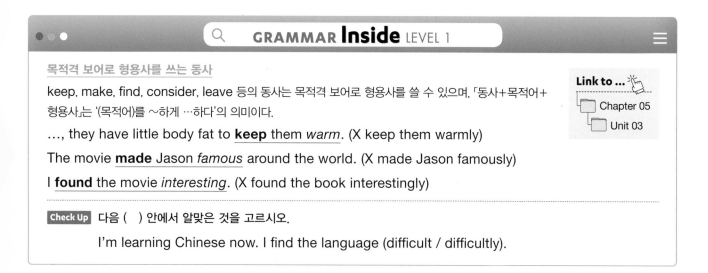

GRAMMAR **Inside** LEVEL 1

목적격 보어로 형용사를 쓰는 동사
keep, make, find, consider, leave 등의 동사는 목적격 보어로 형용사를 쓸 수 있으며, 「동사+목적어+형용사」는 '(목적어)를 ~하게 …하다'의 의미이다.

…, they have little body fat to **keep** them _warm_. (X keep them warmly)
The movie **made** Jason _famous_ around the world. (X made Jason famously)
I **found** the movie _interesting_. (X found the book interestingly)

Link to ...
Chapter 05
Unit 03

Check Up 다음 ( ) 안에서 알맞은 것을 고르시오.

   I'm learning Chinese now. I find the language (difficult / difficultly).

VOCABULARY INSIDE

READING 1	READING 2
☐ **unavoidable** ⓐ not able to stop from happening	☐ **regulate** ⓥ to control or maintain the amount, degree, or rate of something ⓝ regulation [synonym] control
☐ **relief** ⓝ a feeling of happiness with the removal of pain ⓥ relieve	☐ **disease** ⓝ an illness that affects people, animals, or plants
☐ **requirement** ⓝ something that someone needs or must do ⓥ require	☐ **function** ⓝ the action that something is designed to do ⓥ function ⓐ functional
☐ **complicated** ⓐ hard to understand or deal with ⓥ complicate [antonym] simple	☐ **prevent** ⓥ to stop a situation or action from happening or existing ⓝ prevention [antonym] allow
☐ **reduce** ⓥ to become or make smaller in amount, degree, or size [synonym] decrease [antonym] increase	☐ **electricity** ⓝ a form of energy used to power machines ⓐ electric, electrical

Check Up

Fill in the blanks with the words above. Change the form if necessary.

1 Put on good footwear to _____ injuries.

2 Your diet can increase the risk of heart _____.

3 It became totally dark when all the _____ was off.

4 The car accident was _____ due to the heavy snow.

5 What is the minimum education _____ for this position?

6 The medicine is known for temporary but fast pain _____.

7 These instructions are quite _____ and hard to understand.

8 Many countries have set goals to _____ greenhouse gas emissions.

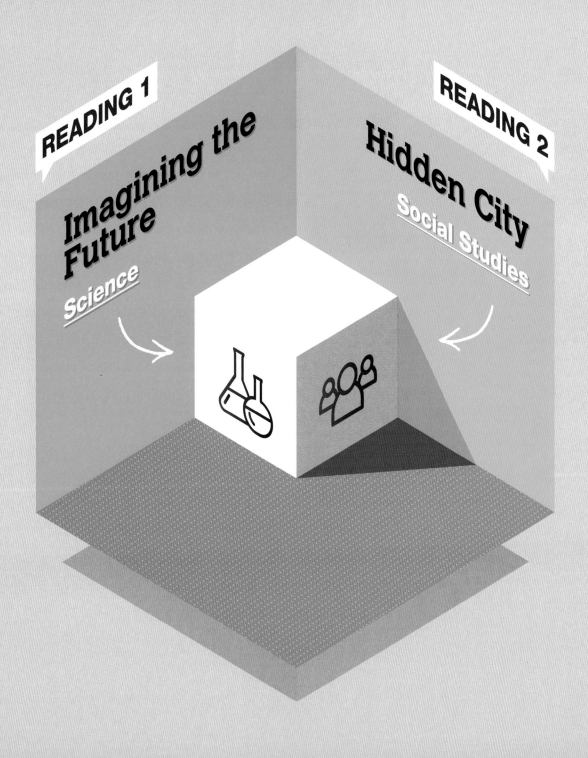

READING 1

Imagining the Future

Science

READING 2

Hidden City

Social Studies

Imagining the Future

Mini Quiz

While you read, write T if it is true, or F if it's false.

1 Humans' brains have been gradually getting smaller. _____

2 People with larger eyes could see better on planets farther from the sun. _____

What will humans look like in 100,000 years? Researchers looked at the human body, Earth's climate, and technology. Then they made predictions about the appearance of humans in the future.

First, some researchers predict that the shape and size of people's bodies will change in the future. Since the 14th century, humans have ⁵ been gradually developing larger brains and heads. **If** this continues, future people may have larger foreheads than people today. Earth's climate has also gotten warmer. **If** global temperatures keep rising, people may eventually have taller, thinner bodies that can release heat more efficiently. ¹⁰

(①) Second, future humans could have darker skin and bigger eyes. (②) **If** that happens, darker skin could help protect them from UV radiation outside of Earth's atmosphere. (③) Also, larger eyes would help them see on planets farther from the sun. (④)

Other influences may also change people. Perhaps parents will be ¹⁵ able to design healthy bodies or even specific faces for their children. Only time will prove these predictions right or wrong.

Reading Comprehension

1 **What is the passage mainly about?**
a. predictions about the future appearance of humans
b. the possible impact of global warming in the future
c. how people's bodies have changed throughout history
d. predictions about how people on other planets might look

2 **What is NOT predicted in the passage?**
a. People will have bigger foreheads, as their brains will get bigger.
b. People will have darker skin to protect them on other planets.
c. People's eyes will get smaller to protect them from strong sunlight.
d. The bodies and faces of children will be designed by their parents.

Writing Practice
3 **According to the passage, why will people be taller and thinner in the future?**
It is because taller and thinner bodies can _____.

4 **Where would the following sentence best fit?**

> People might create technology that will allow them to live on other planets.

a. ①   b. ②   c. ③   d. ④

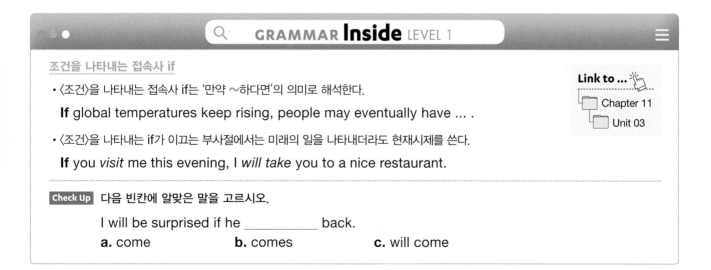

GRAMMAR Inside LEVEL 1

조건을 나타내는 접속사 if

• 〈조건〉을 나타내는 접속사 if는 '만약 ~하다면'의 의미로 해석한다.
If global temperatures keep rising, people may eventually have … .

• 〈조건〉을 나타내는 if가 이끄는 부사절에서는 미래의 일을 나타내더라도 현재시제를 쓴다.
If you *visit* me this evening, I *will take* you to a nice restaurant.

Link to …
Chapter 11
Unit 03

Check Up 다음 빈칸에 알맞은 말을 고르시오.
I will be surprised if he _____ back.
a. come   **b.** comes   **c.** will come

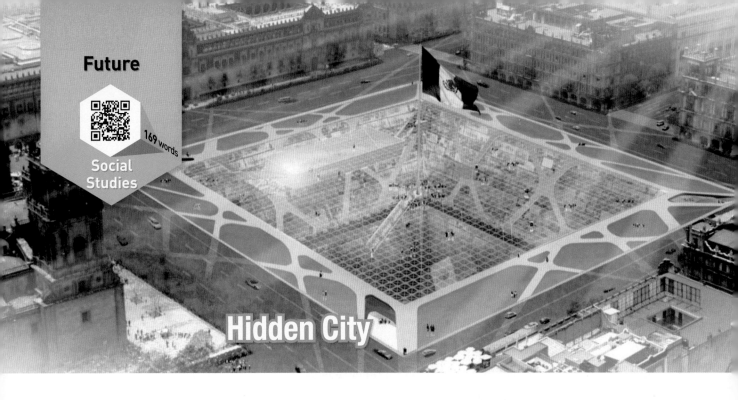

Hidden City

Move over, skyscrapers! The "Earthscraper" is here! This upside-down pyramid is the groundbreaking idea of architects in Mexico City. Currently, Mexico has a fast-growing population but little space. Also, tall buildings are forbidden in order to preserve the city's cultural heritage. As a way **to deal with** these issues, architects suggested digging under Zócalo, Mexico City's main square. 10

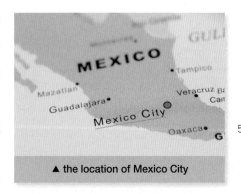

▲ the location of Mexico City 5

Because it will be hidden underground, the 65-floor Earthscraper will maintain the city's historical look and public spaces. And the square will still be able to hold events, such as concerts and parades, on the structure's massive glass roof. Furthermore, natural light will come through the glass and brighten the entire building — even the 15 lowest floor! The Earthscraper will include a museum as well as provide space for offices, stores, and homes. In addition, every tenth floor will be a garden floor. The plants there will work as natural air filters.

The Earthscraper is still in the planning stages, but it could be an important type of building in the future. 20

Reading Comprehension

1 **What is the best title for the passage?**
   a. Slowing Population Growth
   b. An Underground Skyscraper
   c. A Building Designed by Nature
   d. Mexico City's Rich Cultural Heritage

Writing Practice
2 **What does the underlined these issues refer to in the passage? Write two.**
   (1) _____
   (2) _____

3 **What is NOT true about the Earthscraper?**
   a. It will be under Mexico City's main square.
   b. It will maintain the city's historical look.
   c. The natural light will brighten the lowest floor.
   d. Its construction is in the final stage.

4 **What is NOT going to be included in the Earthscraper?**
   a. a sports stadium   **b.** a museum
   c. a massive glass roof   **d.** garden floors

GRAMMAR **Inside** LEVEL 1

형용사적 용법의 to부정사
형용사적 용법의 to부정사는 명사, 대명사를 꾸미는 역할을 한다. 이때 to부정사는 꾸미는 말 뒤에 위치하며, '~하는[할]'으로 해석한다.

As *a way* [**to deal with** these issues], architects suggested digging ... .

I have *something* [**to tell** you].

Link to ...
Chapter 09
Unit 02

Check Up 다음 밑줄 친 to부정사구가 꾸미는 말에 동그라미 하시오.

I don't have time to do this.

VOCABULARY INSIDE

READING 1	READING 2
☐ **predict** Ⓥ to say or guess what is going to happen ⓝ prediction ⟨synonym⟩ forecast	☐ **groundbreaking** ⓐ showing a new idea or way of doing something ⟨synonym⟩ innovative
☐ **develop** Ⓥ to make something grow and become bigger, stronger, or better ⓝ development ⟨synonym⟩ evolve	☐ **preserve** Ⓥ to keep something in good condition ⓝ preservation ⟨synonym⟩ conserve
☐ **release** Ⓥ to allow something to come out of a place ⓝ release	☐ **dig** Ⓥ to make a hole in the ground
☐ **atmosphere** ⓝ the gases and air surrounding a planet ⓐ atmospheric	☐ **maintain** Ⓥ to keep the same ⓝ maintenance ⟨antonym⟩ change
☐ **prove** Ⓥ to show that something is true ⓝ proof	☐ **entire** ⓐ including all of something ⟨ad⟩ entirely ⟨synonym⟩ whole

Check Up   **Fill in the blanks with the words above. Change the form if necessary.**

1 Rabbits _____ holes to make their homes.

2 The _____ building was destroyed by the fire.

3 It is important to _____ peace among countries.

4 We should _____ our valuable natural resources.

5 The level of pollution in the _____ is increasing.

6 It was a good opportunity to _____ my English skills.

7 I need to find some evidence that will _____ him innocent.

8 Animal behavior can help us _____ when natural disasters will happen.

UNIT
07 | Environment

READING 1
Tiny but Fatal
Science

READING 2
A New Kind of Sportswear
Social Studies

Tiny but Fatal

v Mini Quiz

Fill in the blanks using the words from the passage.

Paragraph 2
Microbeads are even _____ than sand.

Paragraph 4
We should _____ the amount of microbeads in _____ habitats.

Nowadays, we rely on plastic to make many things, including bottles, pens, and bags. The list goes on and on. Unfortunately, plastic is polluting our oceans. And now a new type of plastic trash called microbeads is making the situation even worse.

Microbeads are a type of microplastic. They are plastic beads 5 that are even smaller than sand. These microbeads are used in health care products and cosmetics **we use** every day, such as shampoo, face scrubs, and toothpastes.

Because these products are washed down drains and into the sewer system, the microbeads get into our rivers and oceans. 10 This is a problem because microbeads carry harmful chemicals. When sea creatures eat the microbeads, the toxic chemicals build up and are passed up the food chain. These chemicals might even be found in some of the seafood **we eat**.

(①) We need to reduce the amount of microbeads in marine 15 habitats. (②) One thing **we can do** is buy products more wisely. (③) Through smarter choices, we can help our oceans and ourselves. (④)

▲ microbeads

Reading Comprehension

1 **What is the best title for the passage?**
　a. Plastic: Is It Good or Bad for People?
　b. The Environmental Impact of Microbeads
　c. How to Protect Marine Habitats from Pollution
　d. Microbeads: New Plastic that Improves Consumer Products

2 **What is NOT mentioned about microbeads?**
　a. what they are
　b. where they can be found
　c. how they reach rivers and oceans
　d. what happens when humans eat them

Writing Practice
3 **According to the passage, what happen to sea creatures when they eat microbeads?**
The _____ _____ in the microbeads build up and are passed up
the _____ _____.

4 **Where would the following sentence best fit?**

> For example, we can buy organic toothpaste and use sugar as a natural skin scrub.

　a. ①　　　　　　**b.** ②　　　　　　**c.** ③　　　　　　**d.** ④

● ● ●　🔍 **GRAMMAR Inside** LEVEL 2　　　≡

목적격 관계대명사의 생략
목적격 관계대명사 who(m), that, which는 생략할 수 있다. 그러나 전치사가 관계대명사 앞에 오면
그 관계대명사를 생략할 수 없다.

Link to ...👆
📁 Chapter 11
　📁 Unit 02

These chemicals … in some of the seafood (**that[which]**) we eat.

One thing (**that[which]**) we can do is buy products more wisely.

This is the friend (**who(m)[that]**) I went to Paris with.

This is the friend *with* **whom** I went to Paris. (생략 불가)

- -

Check Up 다음 밑줄 친 관계대명사가 생략 가능하면 O, 아니면 X 표시를 하시오.
　1 This is a classroom in which I take classes.　　_____
　2 He is the person that I love the most in the world.　_____

A New Kind of Sportswear

ⓥ Mini Quiz

Paragraph 2

Q: What does the underlined the process indicate?

A: It indicates processing _____ into _____ for the jersey.

Many people love soccer. Some fans also love buying nice football jerseys. However, did you know that football jerseys are often produced with environmentally harmful materials?

Consider how football jerseys are made: First, a team of designers and engineers need to see their initial ideas in physical form. (①) 5 They do this by making the jersey out of *polyester, the most common **synthetic material. (②) This means oil must be processed into polyester for the jerseys. (③) But the process requires great amounts of energy. (④) And, as a result, very large amounts of **damaging** CO_2 are released into the atmosphere. 10

Luckily, sports brands and football clubs are beginning to fight back against this environmentally unfriendly practice. For instance, an English football club recently released a jersey made partially from coffee beans. Additionally, a famous sportswear company even started making clothing and footwear from **upcycled** marine plastic. These 15 innovations are reducing the environmental impact of jerseys by using less polyester.

*polyester 폴리에스터(가구·섬유 등을 만드는 데 쓰이는 화합물의 한 종류)
**synthetic 합성의

Reading Comprehension

1 **What is the best title for the passage?**
 a. Polyester: A Wonderful Fabric
 b. The Rising Costs of Making Sportswear
 c. Football Teams That Are Saving the Earth
 d. A Need for Environmentally Friendly Jerseys

2 **Where would the following sentence best fit?**

> Unfortunately, polyester is a plastic, and plastic is made from oil.

 a. ①　　　　　**b.** ②　　　　　**c.** ③　　　　　**d.** ④

Writing Practice

3 **According to the passage, what does the process of making new jerseys release into the atmosphere?**
 It releases _____ into the atmosphere.

4 **What are mentioned as examples of eco-friendly football jerseys? (Choose two.)**
 a. jerseys made with coffee beans
 b. jerseys made with processed oil
 c. jerseys made from CO_2 and plastic
 d. jerseys made from upcycled marine plastic

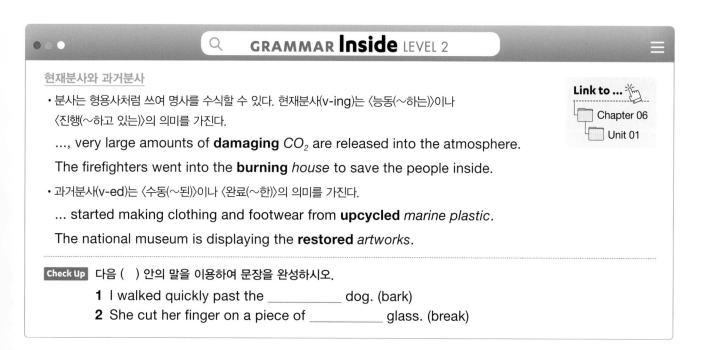

GRAMMAR **Inside** LEVEL 2

현재분사와 과거분사

• 분사는 형용사처럼 쓰여 명사를 수식할 수 있다. 현재분사(v-ing)는 〈능동(~하는)〉이나 〈진행(~하고 있는)〉의 의미를 가진다.

..., very large amounts of **damaging** *CO_2* are released into the atmosphere.

The firefighters went into the **burning** *house* to save the people inside.

• 과거분사(v-ed)는 〈수동(~된)〉이나 〈완료(~한)〉의 의미를 가진다.

... started making clothing and footwear from **upcycled** *marine plastic*.

The national museum is displaying the **restored** *artworks*.

Link to ...
Chapter 06
Unit 01

Check Up 다음 ( ) 안의 말을 이용하여 문장을 완성하시오.
 1 I walked quickly past the _____ dog. (bark)
 2 She cut her finger on a piece of _____ glass. (break)

VOCABULARY INSIDE

READING 1	READING 2
☐ **pollute** Ⓥ	☐ **jersey** ⓝ
to make the land, air, or water dirty	a shirt worn by somebody playing a sport
ⓝ pollution	
[antonym] purify, clean	
☐ **harmful** ⓐ	☐ **environmentally** ⓐⓓ
causing harm, injury, or damage to something	in a way that affects the natural world
or someone	ⓝ environment ⓐ environmental
Ⓥ harm [synonym] dangerous [antonym] safe	
☐ **chemical** ⓝ	☐ **physical** ⓐ
a substance used in chemistry or made by	relating to things that can be seen touched,
a chemical process	or felt
ⓐ chemical	ⓐⓓ physically
☐ **marine** ⓐ	☐ **process** Ⓥ
having to do with the sea or the plants and	to treat natural materials or food for the
animals that live in it	purpose of changing it, preserving it, etc.
	ⓝ process
☐ **habitat** ⓝ	☐ **innovation** ⓝ
the place where an animal or plant lives	a new idea or way to do something that has
	been discovered or introduced
	Ⓥ innovate ⓐ innovative

Check Up   **Fill in the blanks with the words above. Change the form if necessary.**

1 These toxic gases can _____ the air.

2 _____ bacteria can grow in spoiled food.

3 Snorkeling is a great way to see _____ life.

4 This soap is made with _____ safe materials.

5 The spotted owl's favorite _____ is old forests.

6 The researchers made a(n) _____ model with a 3D printer.

7 He put the blueberries into the machine to _____ them into juice.

8 The technological _____ of the company improved their products.

UNIT
08 | Health

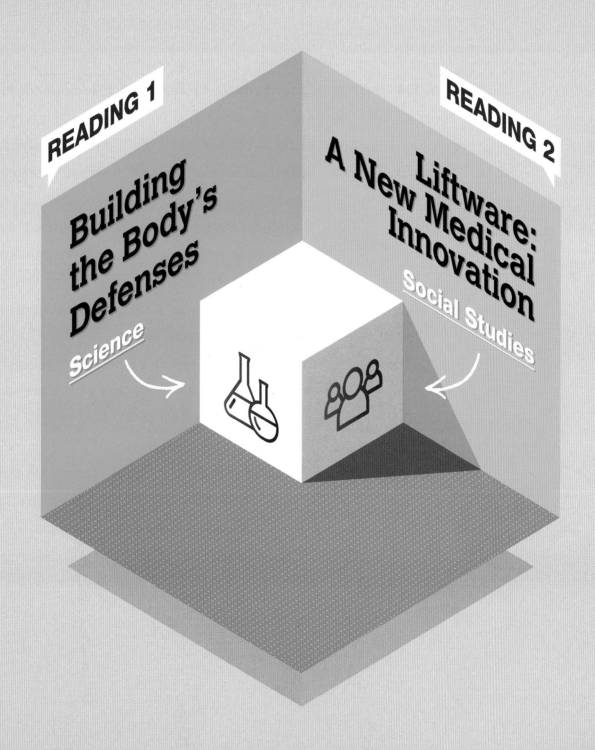

READING 1

Building the Body's Defenses

Science

READING 2

Liftware: A New Medical Innovation

Social Studies

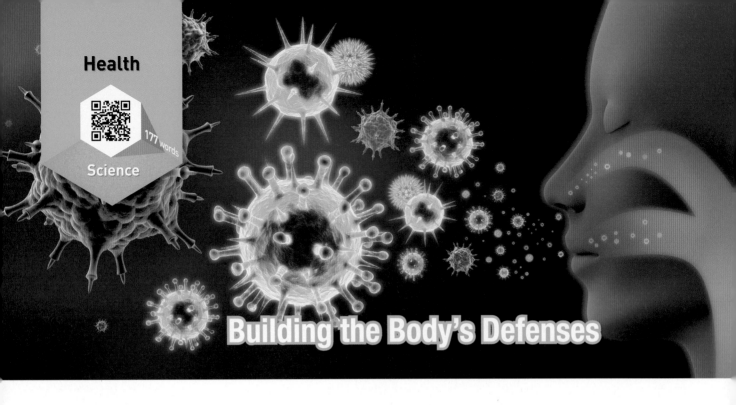

Building the Body's Defenses

V Mini Quiz

Paragraph 1

Q: When was the first vaccine invented? Who invented it?

A: In _____,
scientist _____
_____ invented
the first vaccine.

In 1796, scientist Edward Jenner injected an 8-year-old boy with *cowpox. Jenner correctly believed **that** surviving the weak cowpox virus would protect the boy from the much more dangerous virus, **smallpox. This was the first vaccine in the world. It worked because of the body's immune system. 5

The immune system protects the body. When a virus attacks, we get symptoms such as a cough or fever. This means **that** the immune system is fighting the virus. The immune system tries to remove the virus, and records information about it. So if the same virus attacks again, the immune system remembers how to beat it. 10

The vaccine contains weak or even dead virus cells, so the infection won't develop into a disease. However, the body thinks it's a serious threat. This builds the body's defense system so it will be ready if the full-strength virus actually invades in the future.

There are still some diseases that we can't make vaccines for, but 15 scientists hope **that** one day we will be able to make vaccines for every dangerous virus!

*cowpox 우두(사람에게 전염될 수 있는 소의 바이러스성 질병)
**smallpox 천연두

Reading Comprehension

1　What is the best title for the passage?

a. Smallpox: A Fatal Disease

b. Vaccines: How Do They Work?

c. Ways to Improve the Immune System

d. Edward Jenner: The Inventor of Vaccines

2　Write T if the statement is true or F it's false.

(1) The cowpox virus is less dangerous than the smallpox virus.　_____

(2) A vaccine contains weak or dead virus cells.　_____

(3) Scientists can now make vaccines for every disease.　_____

Writing Practice

3　According to the passage, what does it mean by getting symptoms such as a cough or fever when a virus attacks?

It means that _____.

Writing Practice

4　Fill in the blanks using the words from the passage.

> A virus attacks the body.
> → The immune system tries to _____ it.
> → The immune system _____ information about it.
> → If the virus attacks again, the immune system remembers how to _____ it.

Q　**GRAMMAR Inside** LEVEL 1　　　　≡

접속사 that

that은 명사절을 이끄는 접속사로, '~이라는 것'의 의미이다. that이 이끄는 명사절은 문장에서 주어, 보어, 목적어의 역할을 한다.

This means [**that** the immune system is fighting the virus]. (that절 목적어)

It is obvious [**that** he is lying]. (It 가주어, that절 진주어)

My problem is [**that** I worry too much]. (that절 보어)

Link to ... 👆
　🗂 Chapter 11
　🗂 Unit 03

Check Up　다음 ( ) 안에서 알맞은 것을 고르시오.

　I think (that / because) friendship is very important in life.

Liftware: A New Medical Innovation

Ⓥ Mini Quiz

Paragraph 4
What does Liftware allow people with Parkinson's disease to do? Find and underline the answer.

Meals are an important part of our lives. They are an opportunity to spend time with friends or family. Some people, unfortunately, are not able to fully enjoy this experience. This is because they suffer from Parkinson's disease. 5

(①) Parkinson's disease affects the nervous system, so it causes people to shake uncontrollably. (②) In the past, special devices were used to stop their hands from shaking. (③) But they weren't very effective. (④) 10

A new electronic spoon called Liftware, _____ (A) _____, is different. Instead of trying to stop the hand from shaking, Liftware stops the spoon **itself**. This device uses the same anti-shake technology as digital cameras. When a person's hand shakes, tiny motors in its handle move the spoon's bowl in the opposite direction. _____ (B) _____, 15 shaking is reduced by about 75%.

This is important because people with Parkinson's disease often have to be fed by others. But Liftware allows them to feed **themselves**. This makes them more independent and allows them to enjoy their meals again. 20

Reading Comprehension

1 What is the passage mainly about?

   a. the symptoms of Parkinson's disease

   b. how our body's nervous system works

   c. the social meaning of having meals together

   d. technology for people with Parkinson's disease

2 Where would the following sentence best fit?

> This makes it extremely difficult for them to lift food from their plates to their mouths.

   a. ①   **b.** ②   **c.** ③   **d.** ④

3 What is the best pair for blanks (A) and (B)?

	(A)	(B)		(A)	(B)
a.	however	– As a result	**b.**	for example	– As a result
c.	however	– On the contrary	**d.**	for example	– On the contrary

Writing Practice

4 Fill in the blanks using the words from the passage.

> Liftware moves the spoon in the _____ direction of the shaking, so it allows Parkinson's sufferers to _____ themselves.

GRAMMAR Inside LEVEL 1

재귀대명사

• 동작을 하는 주체와 그 동작이 가해지는 대상이 같을 때, 목적어로 재귀대명사(myself, yourself, himself, herself, itself, ourselves, themselves)를 쓴다. 이 경우, 재귀대명사는 '~ 자신'으로 해석하며, 생략할 수 없다.

  But Liftware allows them to feed **themselves**. (동사 feed의 주체와 대상이 같음)

• 주어, 보어, 목적어 등의 (대)명사를 강조하기 위해 재귀대명사를 사용하기도 한다. 이 경우, 재귀대명사는 '직접', '스스로' 또는 '그 자체'의 의미이며 생략할 수 있다.

  ..., Liftware stops the spoon **itself**. (목적어인 the spoon 강조)

Link to ...

Chapter 07
Unit 01

Check Up 다음 빈칸에 알맞은 말을 고르시오.

  When she has something to think about, she usually talks to _____.

  a. she   **b.** her   **c.** herself

VOCABULARY INSIDE

READING 1	READING 2
☐ **inject** ⓥ to force a liquid medicine into someone or something by using a special needle ⓝ injection	☐ **suffer** ⓥ to experience pain in the body or mind
☐ **symptom** ⓝ a sign of sickness [synonym] sign	☐ **opportunity** ⓝ a situation when it is easy for you to do something [antonym] chance
☐ **fever** ⓝ a higher body temperature than normal	☐ **effective** ⓐ successful in doing what you wanted ⓝ effect [synonym] efficient
☐ **beat** ⓥ to defeat something [synonym] win	☐ **handle** ⓝ a part that is made to be held by a person's hand
☐ **invade** ⓥ to enter a place using force ⓝ invasion	☐ **feed** ⓥ to give food to someone or something [antonym] starve

Check Up   **Fill in the blanks with the words above. Change the form if necessary.**

1 Aspirin helps reduce _____.

2 Give me a(n) _____ to explain my ideas.

3 Police officers have worked to _____ crime.

4 This sunscreen isn't _____, so I got a sunburn.

5 You can _____ small worms to your pet lizard.

6 The main _____ of asthma is difficulty in breathing.

7 I often _____ from back pain, so I'm going to buy a new bed.

8 The country is planning to _____ a small neighboring country.

UNIT
09 | Colors

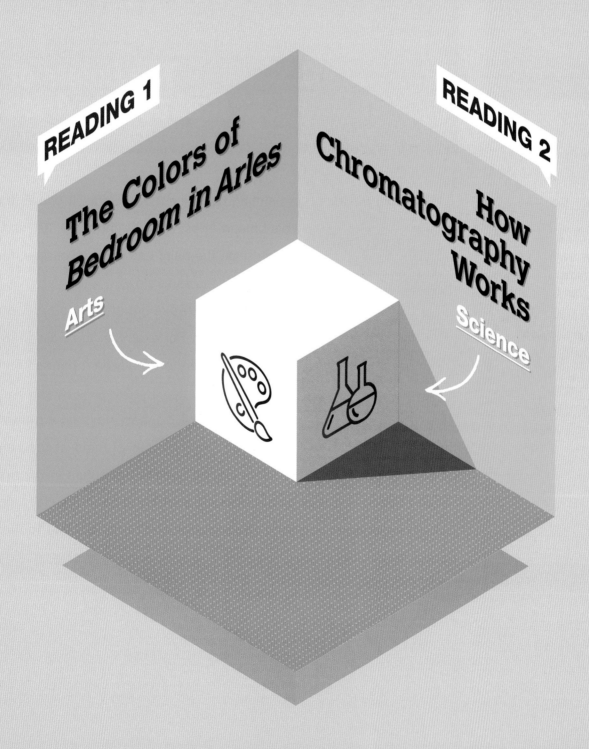

READING 1

The Colors of Bedroom in Arles

Arts

READING 2

How Chromatography Works

Science

The Colors of *Bedroom in Arles*

▲ Vincent van Gogh
(1853 ~ 1890)

V Mini Quiz

Paragraph 1

Q: How many versions
of *Bedroom in Arles*
did Van Gogh make?

A: He made _____
versions of the
painting.

Bedroom in Arles is a painting by Vincent van Gogh. It shows the room he stayed in during his time in Arles. In 1888 and 1889, he made three versions of this painting. Since the paint has faded over time, the colors in these paintings look almost the same now.

Conservators have discovered, however, that the colors were 5 originally quite different from each other. For example, the walls in the paintings all **look blue** now. But they were originally light purple in the first version.

(①) Because of this discovery, the conservators now believe that the original colors reflect Van Gogh's state of mind at the time 10 he painted them. (②) For instance, he used warm colors in the first version because it was painted during a happy time in his life. (③) But the second version from 1889 was painted in colors that **looked darker and colder**. (④)

With further investigation, the conservators hope to _____ 15 _____.

Reading Comprehension

1 What is the passage mainly about?

  a. ways to express emotion through art

  b. why *Bedroom in Arles* has become so famous

  c. how conservators revealed Van Gogh's favorite color

  d. why Van Gogh painted different versions of paintings

2 Write T if the statement about *Bedroom in Arles* is true or F it's false.

  (1) The walls in the painting were originally painted blue. _____

  (2) The colors in the second version are darker than the first one. _____

3 Where would the following sentence best fit?

  > At that time, he had just lost a long-term friendship and had cut off part of his own ear.

  a. ①   b. ②   c. ③   d. ④

4 What is the best choice for the blank?

  a. reveal Van Gogh's reasons for becoming an artist

  b. learn how Van Gogh mixed colors for his paintings

  c. confirm that there are only three versions of *Bedroom in Arles*

  d. gain a clearer understanding of Van Gogh and his emotional state

---

Q **GRAMMAR Inside** LEVEL 1 ☰

감각동사＋형용사

「look/feel/sound/smell/taste＋형용사」는 '~해 보이다/~하게 느껴지다/~하게 들리다/~한 냄새가 나다/~한 맛이 나다'의 의미이다. 이러한 감각동사는 형용사를 보어로 쓰며 그 자리에 부사를 쓰지 않도록 주의한다.

Link to ...
📁 Chapter 05
📁 Unit 01

For example, the walls in the paintings all **look** *blue* now.

The cookies **smell** *delicious*.   I'm **feeling** *sad*.

Check Up 다음 문장의 밑줄 친 부분을 바르게 고치시오.

  1 You look <u>greatly</u> in that shirt.   _____

  2 He feels <u>sleep</u>. He needs to get some sleep.   _____

How Chromatography Works

When you look at sunlight through a prism, you will notice the prism separates it into all of the colors in a rainbow. Likewise, the pigments in a color can also be separated. This technique is known as chromatography, or "color writing."

All the pigments have a different weight. This means that they ⁵ are moved around at different speeds and end up in different places. In chromatography, scientists use liquids, such as water, to carry pigments along a piece of paper. By doing so, they can discover which pigments the original color is composed of.

You can separate the color black by using this technique. All you ¹⁰ need is a filter paper, black markers, and some water. First, apply the black color on the filter paper and dip it into some water. Then the

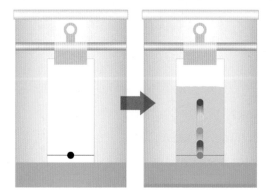

water will start spreading. Watch what happens to that color **until** the water stops ¹⁵ spreading. You will find that the black will separate into other pigments such as *magenta or **cyan. It's that easy!

*magenta 자홍색   **cyan 청록색

� Mini Quiz

Paragraph 2

While you read, write T if it is true, or F if it's false.

1 All the pigments have the same weight.

_____

2 In chromatography, scientists use liquids.

_____

Reading Comprehension

1　**What is the passage mainly about?**
　a. a technique for separating colors
　b. the way artists mix various colors
　c. reasons we cannot trust our own eyes
　d. sunlight's effect on different pigments

2　**What can be answered according to the passage?**
　a. How does a prism separate light?
　b. Why are humans able to see colors?
　c. Which pigment is carried the fastest?
　d. What do we need to perform chromatography?

Writing Practice
3　**According to the passage, what can scientists discover in chromatography?**
　They can discover _____.

Writing Practice
4　**How does chromatography work? Fill in the blanks using the words from the passage.**

Experiment	Result
Apply a color on the filter _____ and dip it into some _____.	The color will _____ into other pigments.

Q　**GRAMMAR Inside** LEVEL 1　≡

시간의 접속사

when(~할 때, ~하면), until(~할 때까지), before(~하기 전에), after(~한 후에)는 〈시간〉을 나타내는 접속사로, 절과 절을 연결한다.

When you look at sunlight through a prism, you will notice ... .

Watch what happens to that color **until** the water stops spreading.

Before you turn off the computer, save all of your work.

I washed my hands **after** I got home.

Link to ...
　📁 Chapter 11
　📁 Unit 02

Check Up 다음 ( ) 안에서 알맞은 것을 고르시오.

　1 (When / Until) he saw her, she smiled at him.
　2 We must stay inside (after / until) the storm is over.

⬡ VOCABULARY INSIDE

READING 1	READING 2
☐ **fade** ⓥ to slowly lose color or brightness	☐ **separate** ⓥ to divide into parts or groups ⓐ separate ⓝ separation
☐ **discover** ⓥ to find out something new ⓝ discovery	☐ **pigment** ⓝ something that gives color to something else
☐ **original** ⓐ existing from the beginning ⓐ𝒹 originally	☐ **liquid** ⓝ a substance that easily flows and changes shape, like water ⓐ liquid synonym fluid
☐ **state** ⓝ the physical or mental condition of someone or something synonym condition	☐ **apply** ⓥ to put or spread something onto a surface ⓝ application
☐ **investigation** ⓝ the process of searching for information about something ⓥ investigate	☐ **spread** ⓥ to cover a larger area ⓝ spread

Check Up

Fill in the blanks with the words above. Change the form if necessary.

1 Weather can affect your _____ of mind.

2 This criminal case is under further _____ .

3 I don't know what _____ it is in the bottle.

4 Jeans tend to _____ in color and become softer.

5 They drew a line in the middle to _____ the group into two.

6 He spilled some water and it began to _____ across the floor.

7 Many people believe that Christopher Columbus _____ America.

8 Many years have passed, but the town still has most of its _____ features.

UNIT
10 | Technology

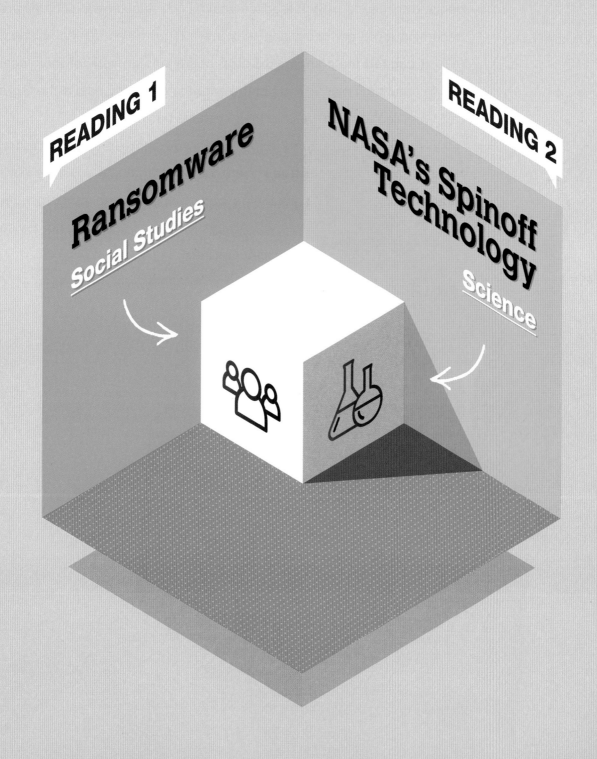

READING 1
Ransomware
Social Studies

READING 2
NASA's Spinoff Technology
Science

Technology

161 words

Social Studies

V Mini Quiz

Paragraph 3

What do security experts say in most ransomware cases? Find and underline the answer.

Ransomware

Like any other day, you start your computer and get ready to work. You click on your latest project, but a warning window pops up. It says you must pay money to open the file! You've been attacked by ransomware.

Ransomware is a form of *malicious software. Cybercriminals 5 use it to lock individual files or even entire systems. (①) Then they demand money to unlock the files again. (②) Ransomware crimes are becoming more common, and they are a big problem for companies. (③) It **caused** the company **to stop** operations at many of their local and international plants. (④) In the end, the company paid a **ransom 10 of $11 million to get access to their systems back.

In most cases, security experts say you shouldn't pay ransoms. Paying hackers **encourages** them **to do** it again. Also, it doesn't guarantee you will get your files back. To deal with ransomware, _____. Always keep your security and device 15 software up to date, and be careful online.

*malicious 악성의   **ransom 몸값

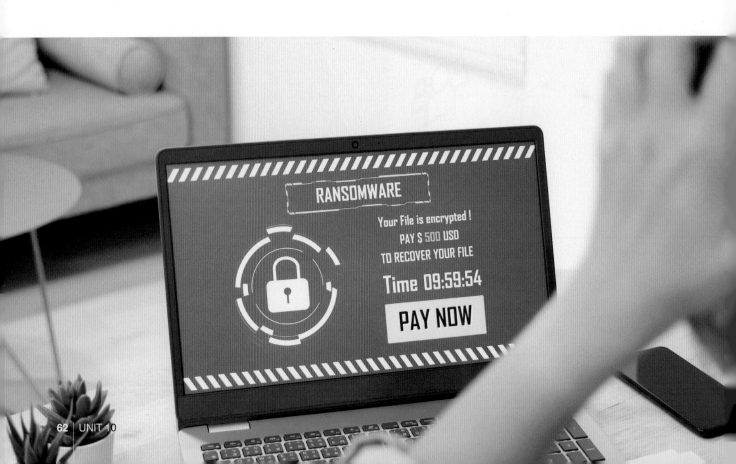

Reading Comprehension

1 **What is the best title for the passage?**

  a. Why Hackers Use Ransomware

  b. Ways to Prevent Malicious Software

  c. American Company Pays Hackers $11 million

  d. Ransomware: What It Does and How to Handle It

Writing Practice

2 **Fill in the blanks using the words from the passage.**

> Q: How do cybercriminals use ransomware?
>
> A : Cybercriminals use it to _____ individual files and demand _____
>   to unlock the files again.

3 **Where would the following sentence best fit?**

> In 2021, a meat supplying company in the US was attacked with ransomware.

  a. ①   **b.** ②   **c.** ③   **d.** ④

4 **What is the best choice for the blank?**

  a. be prepared to pay

  b. contact your local police

  c. prevention is better than cure

  d. start by rebooting your device

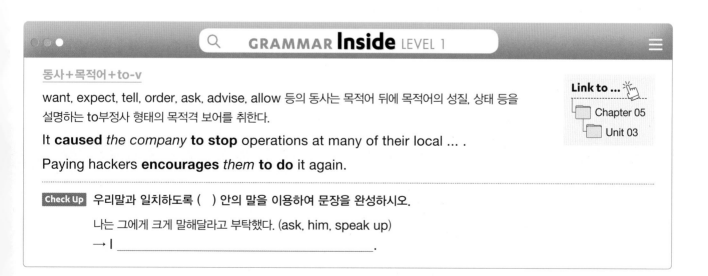

GRAMMAR **Inside** LEVEL 1

동사＋목적어＋to-v

want, expect, tell, order, ask, advise, allow 등의 동사는 목적어 뒤에 목적어의 성질, 상태 등을 설명하는 to부정사 형태의 목적격 보어를 취한다.

It **caused** *the company* **to stop** operations at many of their local ... .

Paying hackers **encourages** *them* **to do** it again.

Link to ...
  Chapter 05
  Unit 03

Check Up 우리말과 일치하도록 ( ) 안의 말을 이용하여 문장을 완성하시오.

  나는 그에게 크게 말해달라고 부탁했다. (ask, him, speak up)

  → I _____ .

NASA's Spinoff Technology

Mini Quiz

Paragraph 2, 3, 4

While you read, find and write three of NASA's spinoffs.

_____

_____

_____

NASA **has achieved** much in space, but their research **has** greatly **impacted** the Earth as well. Importantly, it **has led** to NASA *spinoffs. These products **have improved** the everyday life of people on Earth.

One such example is memory foam. Originally, researchers designed it to protect test pilots during flights. However, people now 5 use it in their sofas, shoes, and beds.

Even your handheld vacuum was inspired by space research! NASA wanted to extract particles from below the surface of the Moon during the Apollo 11 Moon landing mission. So, NASA worked with a manufacturing company. The company later created the cordless 10 vacuum.

(①) NASA also created a water purification system. (②) It can convert sweat, breath, and urine into clean drinking water. (③) In addition, the water from this system is actually cleaner than most of our planet's drinking water. (④) 15 These are just a handful of the practical inventions from NASA. In the future, we will see more incredible NASA spinoffs!

*spinoff 스핀오프(특정한 연구 프로젝트에 참여했던 연구원이 연구 결과를 갖고 창업하는 것)

Reading Comprehension

1 **What is the passage mainly about?**
   a. items astronauts need to survive in space
   b. practical inventions from NASA research
   c. NASA's positive effect on the environment
   d. solutions for making space flights comfortable

Writing Practice

2 **According to the passage, why was memory foam created?**
   Originally, it was designed to _____.

3 **Why did NASA work with a manufacturing company for the Apollo 11 Moon landing mission?**
   a. to protect astronauts as they land on the Moon
   b. to make a device to clean the inside of a rocket
   c. to find a way to extract particles from the Moon
   d. to create special oxygen tanks for space stations

4 **Where would the following sentence best fit?**

   > This process might seem disgusting, but it has saved many astronauts on the
   > International Space Station.

   a. ①   **b.** ②   **c.** ③   **d.** ④

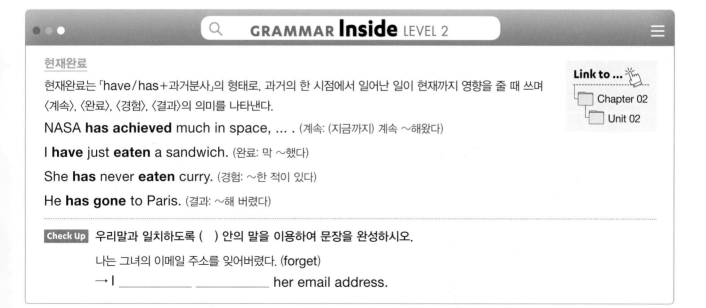

● ● ●   🔍 GRAMMAR **Inside** LEVEL 2   ☰

현재완료
현재완료는 「have/has+과거분사」의 형태로, 과거의 한 시점에서 일어난 일이 현재까지 영향을 줄 때 쓰며
〈계속〉, 〈완료〉, 〈경험〉, 〈결과〉의 의미를 나타낸다.

NASA **has achieved** much in space, ... (계속: (지금까지) 계속 ~해왔다)

I **have** just **eaten** a sandwich. (완료: 막 ~했다)

She **has** never **eaten** curry. (경험: ~한 적이 있다)

He **has gone** to Paris. (결과: ~해 버렸다)

Link to ... 👆
📁 Chapter 02
📁 Unit 02

Check Up 우리말과 일치하도록 (   ) 안의 말을 이용하여 문장을 완성하시오.
         나는 그녀의 이메일 주소를 잊어버렸다. (forget)
         → I _____ _____ her email address.

⬡ VOCABULARY INSIDE

READING 1	READING 2
☐ **lock** ⓥ to fasten or make inaccessible	☐ **impact** ⓥ to affect something strongly ⓝ impact [synonym] affect
☐ **individual** ⓐ considered separately from other people or things in a group [antonym] entire	☐ **vacuum** ⓝ an electrical machine that cleans floors by sucking up dirt
☐ **demand** ⓥ to make a forceful request for something ⓝ demand [synonym] require	☐ **inspire** ⓥ to bring about or motivate ⓝ inspiration
☐ **crime** ⓝ an illegal act that is punishable by the law ⓝ criminal ⓐ criminal	☐ **astronaut** ⓝ a person who travels to space in a spacecraft
☐ **guarantee** ⓥ to promise that something will happen or that you will do something [synonym] ensure	☐ **practical** ⓐ relating to a real situation rather than an idea or theory [antonym] theoretical

Check Up **Fill in the blanks with the words above. Change the form if necessary.**

1 The movie was _____ by a tragic story.

2 He is the first _____ to step on the Moon.

3 This floor is really dirty, so I'll bring the _____.

4 I need a(n) _____ backup plan, not a theoretical one.

5 The company provided _____ lunches to all the employees.

6 This graph shows an increase in violent _____ in recent years.

7 I _____ that I will provide everything you need for this project.

8 He _____ an apology from her for the mistake she made yesterday.

UNIT
11 | Food

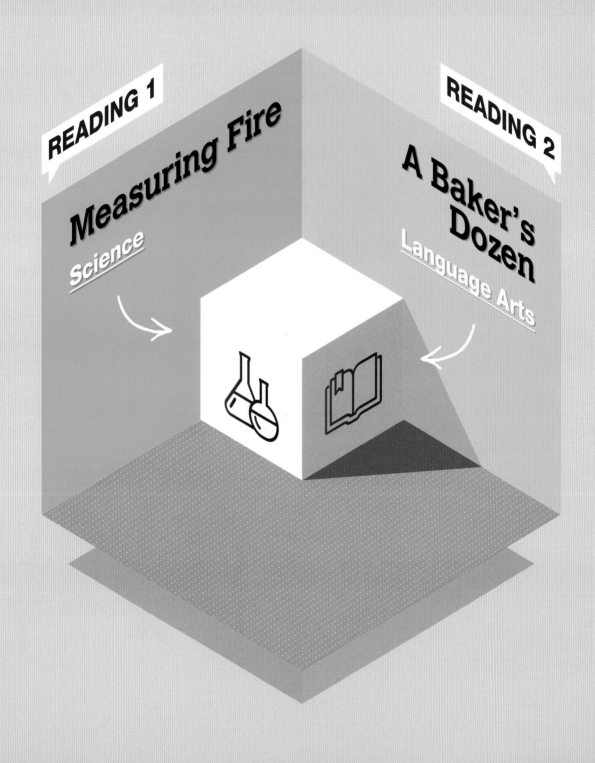

READING 1

Measuring Fire

Science

READING 2

A Baker's Dozen

Language Arts

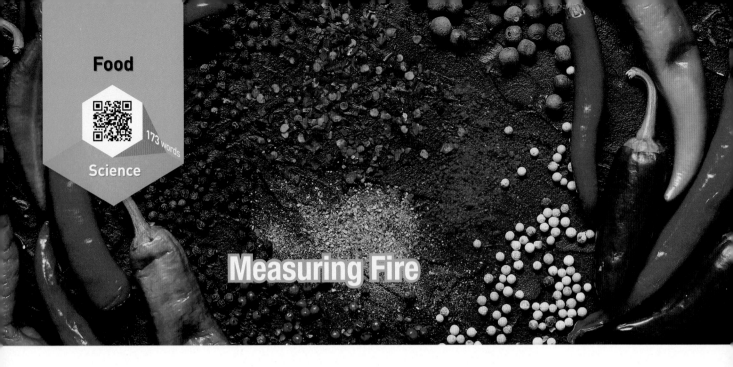

Measuring Fire

V Mini Quiz

Paragraph 3

What is the hottest pepper on Earth? Find and underline the answer.

You just ate an unfamiliar pepper. Your mouth is on fire, and you are sweating! Next time, check the Scoville Heat Unit Scale before eating any strange peppers! American scientist Wilbur Scoville created this scale in 1912. It is used to measure the spiciness of peppers. Each pepper has a special number from zero to over a million units. Peppers 5 with **larger** Scoville numbers are **hotter**!

To test a pepper's spiciness, tasters drink a mix of sugar water and pepper extract. Sugar water is added until the heat _____. This ratio of pepper extract to sugar water is the pepper's Scoville number. For example, 8,000 is **the hottest** jalapeño's Scoville number. 10 This means 8,000 grams of sugar water is needed before the heat from one gram of the jalapeño extract disappears! Luckily for tasters' tongues, machines are now often used to measure how hot peppers are.

In 2013, the Carolina Reaper 15 became **the hottest** pepper on Earth. Its Scoville number is 2.2 million! That is **stronger than** pepper spray. Can you imagine it? 20

Reading Comprehension

1 **What is the best title for the passage?**
a. A Variety of Pepper Recipes
b. A Special Scale to Rate Heat
c. Why Do Peppers Vary in Spiciness?
d. Useful Tips for Reducing the Spiciness of Peppers

2 **What is NOT true about the Scoville Heat Unit Scale?**
a. An American scientist created this system.
b. Its numbers represent the spiciness of peppers.
c. The hotter the pepper, the smaller its Scoville number.
d. Sugar water is used to measure the Scoville number.

3 **What is the best choice for the blank?**
a. is gone
b. appears
c. affects sugar water
d. gets really strong

Writing Practice

4 **Answer the following question based on the passage.**

> Q: Before the heat from one gram of Pepper A's extract disappeared, 500 grams
> of sugar water had to be added. What's Pepper A's Scoville number?
> A: It is _____.

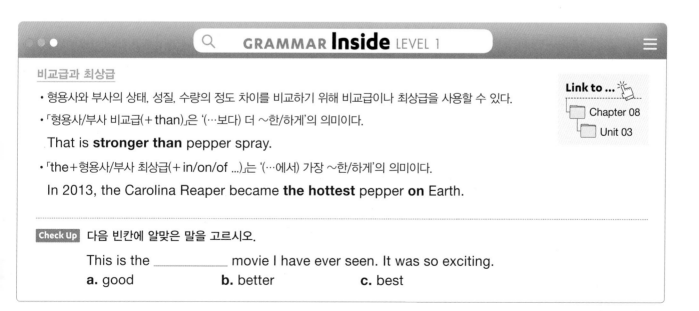

GRAMMAR **Inside** LEVEL 1

비교급과 최상급
• 형용사와 부사의 상태, 성질, 수량의 정도 차이를 비교하기 위해 비교급이나 최상급을 사용할 수 있다.
• 「형용사/부사 비교급(+ than)」은 '(…보다) 더 ~한/하게'의 의미이다.
  That is **stronger than** pepper spray.
• 「the+형용사/부사 최상급(+ in/on/of …)」는 '(…에서) 가장 ~한/하게'의 의미이다.
  In 2013, the Carolina Reaper became **the hottest** pepper **on** Earth.

Link to ...
Chapter 08
Unit 03

Check Up 다음 빈칸에 알맞은 말을 고르시오.

This is the _____ movie I have ever seen. It was so exciting.
a. good   b. better   c. best

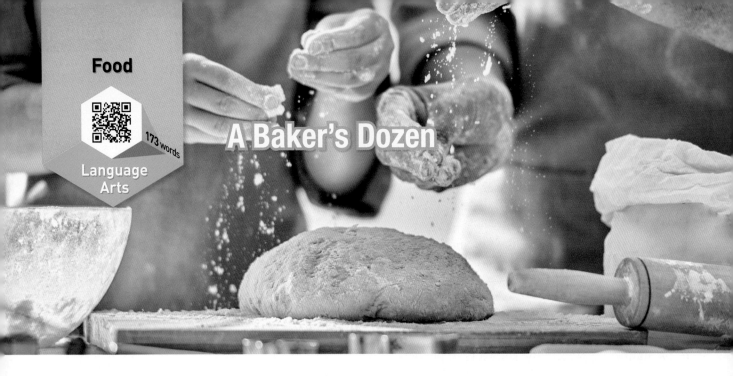

A Baker's Dozen

Food

173 words

Language Arts

v Mini Quiz

Paragraph 3

What does "a baker's dozen" usually mean? Find and underline the answer.

Imagine that you go to a bakery to buy a dozen cookies. You come back with a baker's dozen. How many cookies do you have? The answer is not 12. It's 13. And, **even better**, the extra cookie is free!

Where did the phrase "a baker's dozen" come from? Many people think it originated from ancient laws against selling bread that weighed 5 too little. In many countries, if a baker was caught cheating his customers by selling lighter-than-normal loaves, he could be severely punished. _____(A)_____, bakers in England gave their customers extra bread. When customers asked for a dozen loaves, they received 13 instead. And eventually people began to use 10 the term "a baker's dozen" to refer to the custom.

Although this phrase was first used over 400 years ago, it is still well known today. Usually "a baker's dozen" means 13 baked items, but sometimes people use it to mean 13 of anything. ____(B)____, you could take a baker's dozen of your friends with you next time you 15 go to the bakery.

Reading Comprehension

1 **What is the passage mainly about?**
   a. the origin of "a baker's dozen"
   b. various phrases related to numbers
   c. a strict ancient law against cheating
   d. the hidden meaning of the number 13

2 **What is the best choice for blank (A)?**
   a. To avoid cheating anyone accidentally
   b. To promote their new items to customers
   c. To sell the entire amount that they prepared
   d. To persuade their customers to keep visiting their bakery

Writing Practice

3 **What does the underlined the custom refer to?**
   When customers asked bakers for a dozen loaves, _____.

4 **What is the best choice for blank (B)?**
   a. However   **b.** As a result
   c. For example   **d.** On the other hand

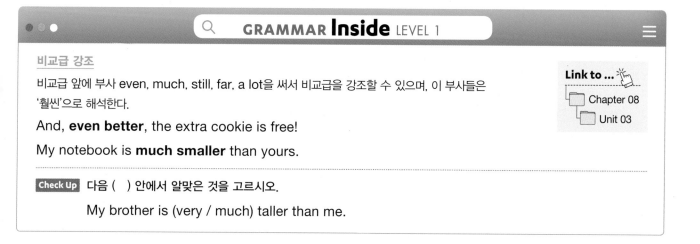

GRAMMAR **Inside** LEVEL 1

비교급 강조

비교급 앞에 부사 even, much, still, far, a lot을 써서 비교급을 강조할 수 있으며, 이 부사들은 '훨씬'으로 해석한다.

And, **even better**, the extra cookie is free!

My notebook is **much smaller** than yours.

Link to ...
Chapter 08
Unit 03

Check Up 다음 ( ) 안에서 알맞은 것을 고르시오.

My brother is (very / much) taller than me.

VOCABULARY INSIDE

READING 1	READING 2
☐ **measure** ⓥ to determine the exact amount or size of something ⓝ measurement	☐ **originate** ⓥ to come from a particular time or place, or start from a particular situation
☐ **unfamiliar** ⓐ not recognized or known [synonym] strange	☐ **ancient** ⓐ belonging to a time that happened long ago [synonym] old [antonym] new
☐ **scale** ⓝ a set of numbers that is used to measure or compare things	☐ **weigh** ⓥ to have a particular weight ⓝ weight
☐ **ratio** ⓝ a relationship between two amounts that shows how much larger one is than the other [synonym] proportion	☐ **cheat** ⓥ to behave dishonestly in order to gain an advantage
☐ **disappear** ⓥ to go out of sight ⓝ disappearance	☐ **custom** ⓝ a habit or tradition of a particular group of people [synonym] tradition, practice

Check Up

Fill in the blanks with the words above. Change the form if necessary.

1 We saw a(n) _____ book in the museum.

2 It is Korean _____ to bow to older people.

3 Mix flour and sugar in the _____ of five to one.

4 She tried to _____ on the test, but they caught her.

5 This food is _____ to me. Do you know what it is?

6 A thermometer is used to _____ how hot something is.

7 Did jazz and blues _____ from traditional African music?

8 A farmer in my town sells watermelons that _____ more than 7 kg.

UNIT
12 | Places

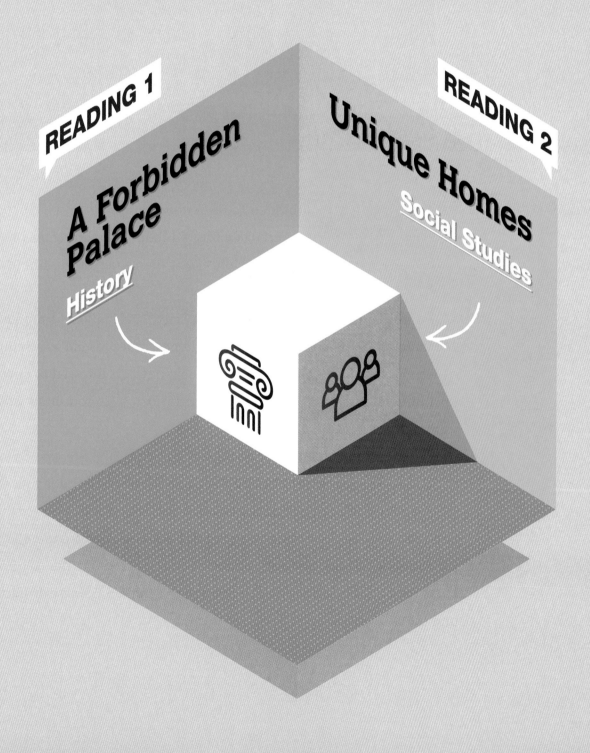

READING 1

A Forbidden Palace

History

READING 2

Unique Homes

Social Studies

A Forbidden Palace

Mini Quiz

Paragraph 3

Why are all the roofs of the Forbidden City yellow? Find and underline the answer.

We have all **been forbidden to do** certain things. But can a city be forbidden? Yes, it can! The Forbidden City was built in Beijing from 1406 to 1420. This Chinese imperial palace was the center of the Chinese government for about 500 years.

You might wonder why it **is called a** "city." This palace is not just 5 one building. There are almost 1,000 buildings, so it is as big as a small city. And it **is called** "forbidden" because no one **was allowed to enter** it without permission from the emperor. In fact, a 26-foot-high wall surrounded it!

But everything changed when the last emperor, Puyi, stepped down 10 in 1912. (①) The Forbidden City became a World Heritage Site in 1987, and it is now known as the Palace Museum. (②) It is one of the best places to see the beauty of traditional Chinese architecture. (③) For example, all the roofs are yellow because yellow was the color of the emperor! (④) Furthermore, it holds over 1 million Chinese artifacts 15 and works of art!

Reading Comprehension

1 **What is the best title for the passage?**

   a. Puyi, the Last Emperor of China

   b. Beijing: The Political Center of China

   c. The Beauty of Traditional Chinese Architecture

   d. The Forbidden City: Part of China's Cultural Heritage

2 **What is NOT true about the Forbidden City?**

   a. It took longer than ten years to build it.

   b. It consists of one giant building.

   c. It was surrounded by a 26-foot-high wall.

   d. It became a World Heritage Site.

Writing Practice

3 **According to the passage, why does the Forbidden City have "forbidden" in its name?**

   This is because no one was _____.

4 **Where would the following sentence best fit?**

After that, its role as a political center ended, but its great historical value continued.

   a. ①   **b.** ②   **c.** ③   **d.** ④

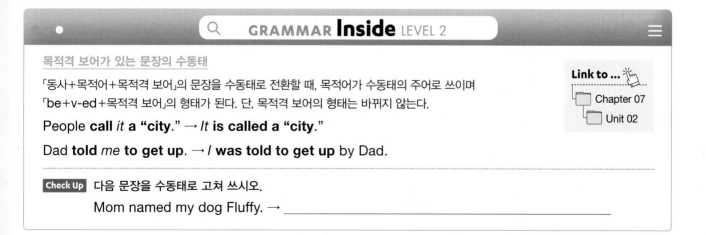

🔍 **GRAMMAR Inside** LEVEL 2

목적격 보어가 있는 문장의 수동태

「동사+목적어+목적격 보어」의 문장을 수동태로 전환할 때, 목적어가 수동태의 주어로 쓰이며 「be+v-ed+목적격 보어」의 형태가 된다. 단, 목적격 보어의 형태는 바뀌지 않는다.

People **call** *it* **a "city."** → *It* **is called a "city."**

Dad **told** *me* **to get up.** → *I* **was told to get up** by Dad.

Link to ... 👆
📁 Chapter 07
　📄 Unit 02

Check Up 다음 문장을 수동태로 고쳐 쓰시오.

   Mom named my dog Fluffy. → _____

Unique Homes

✔ Mini Quiz

Paragraph 2

For whom were yurts the main type of home? Find and underline the answer.

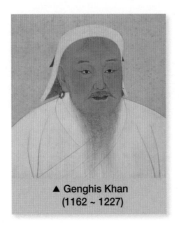

▲ Genghis Khan
(1162 ~ 1227)

You are the ruler of a vast kingdom. You go outside to look at your land. But instead of a huge castle, you leave your tent! That's what Genghis Khan, emperor of the Mongol Empire, did. He lived in a yurt, a kind of tent. Traditionally known as a *ger*, it is a round, portable home. Its frame is made of bendable wood to withstand strong winds. The outside is wrapped in *felt to keep the inside warm. Five to fifteen people can live in a yurt. 5

10

For thousands of years, this was the main type of home for **nomadic people from Central Asia, such as Mongolians. They would move three to four times every year. Their yurts **could be taken** down, **moved**, and **put** back together easily. It also took only thirty minutes to three hours to build them. 15

Yurts **can** also **be found** outside of Mongolia. As Genghis Khan's empire expanded outside of Central Asia, so did yurt culture. Yurts were used in Turkey until the 1970s. Even now, you can see them in the countryside of Hungary.

*felt 펠트(모직이나 털을 압축해서 만든 천)   **nomadic 유목의

Reading Comprehension

1 **What is the passage mainly about?**
   a. nomadic cultures around the world
   b. the history of Genghis Khan's empire
   c. an interesting camping trend in Mongolia
   d. a kind of portable tent used by nomadic people

2 **How does the writer introduce the topic?**
   a. by making a funny joke
   b. by asking a difficult question
   c. by giving an imaginary situation
   d. by talking about a personal experience

3 **What is NOT mentioned about yurts?**
   a. who first invented them
   b. how many people can stay inside one
   c. how long it takes to set them up
   d. where they can be found outside of Mongolia

Writing Practice

4 **According to the passage, why is the frame of a yurt made of bendable wood?**
   It is made of bendable wood _____.

🔍 **GRAMMAR Inside** LEVEL 2   ≡

조동사의 수동태

조동사 can/could, will/would, must, should 등은 「조동사+be v-ed」의 형태로 수동태와 함께 쓰일 수 있다.

Link to ...
Chapter 07
Unit 02

They **could take** their yurts down, ... (~할 수 있었다)

→ Their yurts **could be taken** down, ... (by them). (~될 수 있었다)

All the students **must follow** the school rules. (~해야 한다)

→ The school rules **must be followed** by all the students. (~되어야 한다)

Check Up 다음 문장을 수동태로 바꾸어 쓰시오.

They will ship your order tomorrow. → _____

VOCABULARY INSIDE

READING 1	READING 2
☐ forbid ⓥ to not allow someone to do something [synonym] ban	☐ vast ⓐ extremely large in size, amount, or range [antonym] tiny
☐ government ⓝ the group of people who rule over a country	☐ castle ⓝ a large and strong building that was originally built to protect against attacks
☐ wonder ⓥ to be curious about something	☐ portable ⓐ able to be carried or moved around with ease [antonym] fixed
☐ permission ⓝ the act of allowing someone to do something ⓥ permit	☐ withstand ⓥ to remain unharmed or unaffected by something
☐ architecture ⓝ the design or style of a building ⓐ architectural	☐ expand ⓥ to become or make larger in size, range, or amount ⓝ expansion [antonym] contract

Check Up

Fill in the blanks with the words above. Change the form if necessary.

1 Oceans are _____ resources for humans.

2 I can't take my father's car without _____ .

3 He has the inner power to _____ all difficulties.

4 This cathedral is famous for its beautiful _____ .

5 I _____ why her novel is so popular around the world.

6 _____ emergency lights are installed in every hotel room.

7 If you really want to go out, I won't _____ you from doing it.

8 If you want to read English better, you should _____ your vocabulary.

UNIT
13 | Activities

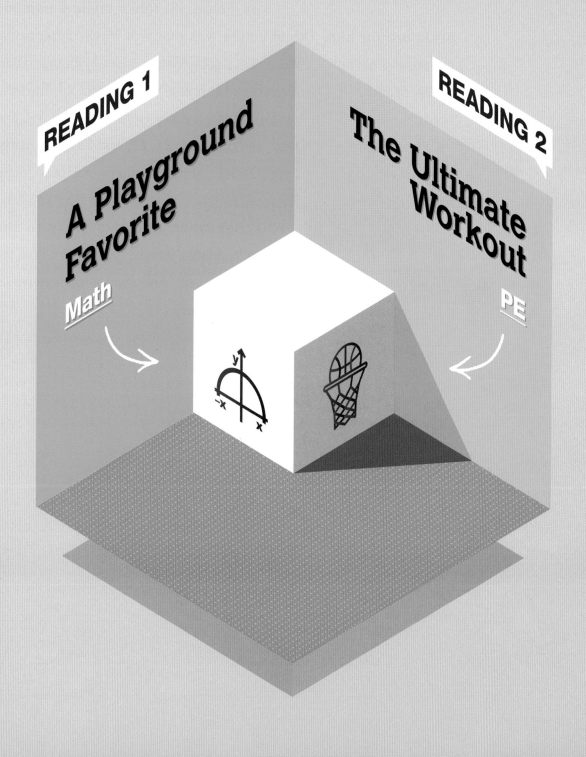

READING 1

A Playground Favorite

Math

READING 2

The Ultimate Workout

PE

A Playground Favorite

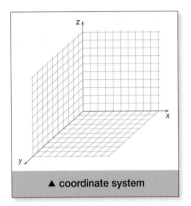

▲ coordinate system

Jungle gyms are simple structures that can be found on most school playgrounds. They are popular because they don't need much space, are entertaining for kids, and can even help teach math! 5

The first official jungle gym was invented by Sebastian Hinton. When ① he was a child, his father **made a bamboo structure for him**. The structure was made of three-dimensional cubes, and his father used it like a coordinate system in mathematics. 10 ② He called one set of *horizontal poles $X1$, $X2$, and $X3$, and the horizontal poles at right angles to the X poles were called $Y1$, $Y2$, and $Y3$. Finally, ③ he called the **vertical poles $Z1$, $Z2$, and $Z3$. As a game, ④ he would yell out "$X1$, $Y3$, $Z2$! Go!", and Sebastian would race to get to the correct spot. 15

(ⓐ) One day in 1920, Sebastian **told this story to the ***superintendent** of schools in Winnetka, Illinois. (ⓑ) That's how the first official "jungle gym" was created. (ⓒ) And soon after, they would be built on playgrounds around the country. (ⓓ)

*horizontal 수평의   **vertical 수직의   ***superintendent 교육감

Reading Comprehension

1 **What is the passage mainly about?**
  a. how to make jungle gyms
  b. how jungle gyms were invented
  c. playgrounds of schools in Illinois
  d. the inventions of Sebastian Hinton

2 **What is NOT true about the structure Sebastian Hinton played on as a child?**
  a. It was made by his father.
  b. It was made of iron pipes.
  c. It was three-dimensional.
  d. It was used to play games.

3 **Among ①~④, which refers to a different person?**
  a. ①   b. ②   c. ③   d. ④

4 **Where would the following sentence best fit?**

The superintendent was interested in the idea, so they worked on it together.

  a. ⓐ   b. ⓑ   c. ⓒ   d. ⓓ

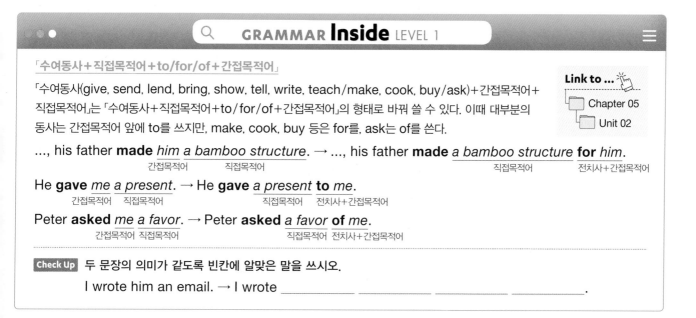

🔍 **GRAMMAR Inside** LEVEL 1

「수여동사＋직접목적어＋to/for/of＋간접목적어」

「수여동사(give, send, lend, bring, show, tell, write, teach/make, cook, buy/ask)＋간접목적어＋직접목적어」는 「수여동사＋직접목적어＋to/for/of＋간접목적어」의 형태로 바꿔 쓸 수 있다. 이때 대부분의 동사는 간접목적어 앞에 to를 쓰지만, make, cook, buy 등은 for를, ask는 of를 쓴다.

Link to ... 👆
📁 Chapter 05
📁 Unit 02

..., his father **made** *him a bamboo structure*. → ..., his father **made** *a bamboo structure* **for** *him*.
　　　　　　　　간접목적어　　　직접목적어　　　　　　　　　　　　　　　직접목적어　　　전치사＋간접목적어

He **gave** *me a present*. → He **gave** *a present* **to** *me*.
　　　간접목적어　직접목적어　　　　　　직접목적어　전치사＋간접목적어

Peter **asked** *me a favor*. → Peter **asked** *a favor* **of** *me*.
　　　　간접목적어 직접목적어　　　　　　직접목적어 전치사＋간접목적어

Check Up 두 문장의 의미가 같도록 빈칸에 알맞은 말을 쓰시오.
　　I wrote him an email. → I wrote ＿＿＿＿ ＿＿＿＿ ＿＿＿＿ ＿＿＿＿.

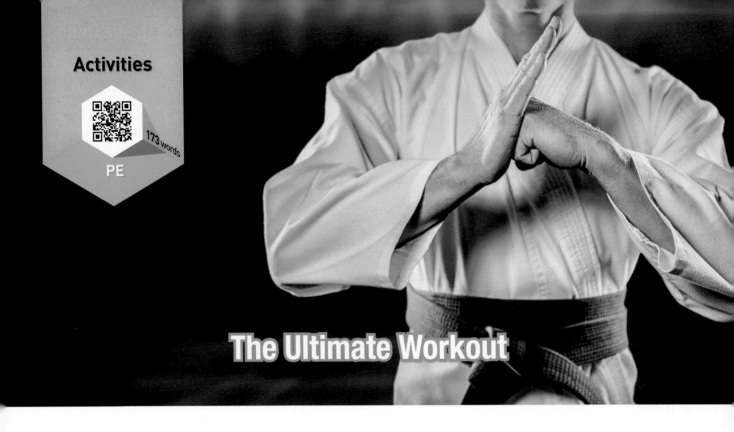

The Ultimate Workout

ⓥ Mini Quiz

Find and underline the main idea sentences of the 2nd, 3rd, and 4th paragraph.

Do you want to work out your mind, body, and spirit at the same time? How about trying out martial arts? For thousands of years, people have been using martial arts to exercise and defend themselves. But there are other reasons to learn martial arts.

First, if you **consistently** train **hard**, you'll get in shape **quickly**.   5
By doing high-intensity workouts in martial arts such as judo or taekwondo, you can lose calories and burn excess fat. In addition, you can gain muscle as you train.

Secondly, martial arts help you reduce your stress levels. They can help you let out your anger in kicks and punches. **Moreover**, 10
meditation-focused martial arts like tai chi and karate will help you calm yourself down.

Lastly, practicing martial arts will improve your memory. To combine movements **naturally** and **effectively**, you have to recall every action. The brain's *neural **synapses and pathways grow stronger with 15
each repeated movement, and this leads to a better memory.

Clearly, martial arts are fantastic workouts. So why not give one a try?

*neural 신경의

**synapse 시냅스(뉴런과 다른 세포 사이에서 신경 물질을 전달하는 접합 부위)

Reading Comprehension

1   What is the best title for the passage?
   a. The Best Martial Art to Learn
   b. How to Transform Your Body
   c. A Workout for Reducing Stress
   d. Why You Should Learn Martial Arts

2   Circle the correct word in each parenthesis.

> As you do high-intensity workouts in martial arts, you'll (burn / gain) calories and fat and you'll (lose / gain) muscle.

Writing Practice

3   Find the word from the passage which has the given meaning.

> to bring something back into one's mind

_____

Writing Practice

4   According to the passage, what happens to your brain with each repeated movement in martial arts?

The brain's neural synapses and pathways _____.

Q   **GRAMMAR Inside** LEVEL 1   ≡

부사의 역할

• 부사는 주로 동사, 형용사, 다른 부사, 그리고 문장 전체를 꾸며준다.
   ..., if you **consistently** *train* **hard**, you'll *get in shape* **quickly**.

• fast(빠르게), early(일찍), late(늦게), high(높게), hard(열심히)와 같은 부사는 형용사와 그 형태가 같다.

• 〈부사+ly〉은 다른 뜻을 가지기도 한다.
   hard → hard**ly**(거의 ~하지 않는)   high → high**ly**(매우)   late → late**ly**(최근에)   near → near**ly**(거의)

Link to ...
☐ Chapter 08
☐ Unit 02

Check Up 밑줄 친 부사가 꾸며주는 말에 동그라미 하시오.

   1 He speaks loudly.   **2** Honestly, I don't remember you.

VOCABULARY INSIDE

READING 1	READING 2
☐ **structure** ⓝ something that is built such as a building	☐ **workout** ⓝ physical exercise you do to improve your fitness
☐ **entertaining** ⓐ giving amusement ⓥ entertain ⓝ entertainment	☐ **spirit** ⓝ a special force within a person that is thought to give them power and energy
☐ **official** ⓐ used to describe that has been announced publicly ⓐⓓ officially	☐ **defend** ⓥ to protect or keep danger away from someone or something ⓝ defense [antonym] attack
☐ **spot** ⓝ a particular place	☐ **combine** ⓥ to join two or more things together into one thing ⓝ combination
☐ **race** ⓥ to move at a very fast speed	☐ **memory** ⓝ the ability to remember things, experiences etc. ⓥ memorize

Check Up   **Fill in the blanks with the words above. Change the form if necessary.**

1 This _____ was built with bricks.

2 Let's _____ to the beach, shall we?

3 She sweated a lot during her _____.

4 This beach is my favorite vacation _____.

5 Vaccines can _____ your body from viruses.

6 I think this TV series is both _____ and useful.

7 Let's _____ the butter and the sugar in the bowl.

8 My grandmother doesn't remember me. Her _____ is failing.

UNIT
14 | Senses

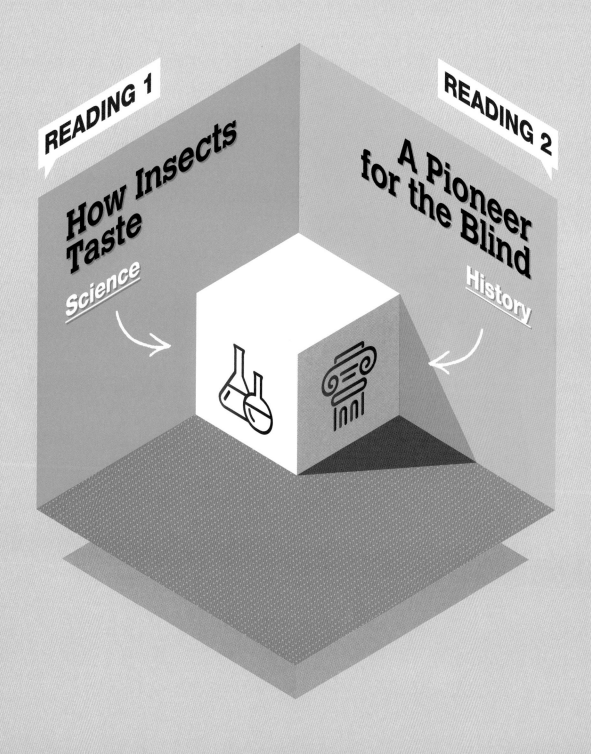

READING 1

How Insects Taste

Science

READING 2

A Pioneer for the Blind

History

How Insects Taste

Almost all animals can taste. As the sense helps with eating and finding food, it is essential for survival.

Taste works differently for humans and insects. There are insects with more sensitive *taste buds than humans. Honey bees are able to detect low concentrations of a sugar from plants. _____(A)_____, 5 they can figure out whether a sweetener is artificial. The bees need to make honey to survive. So they ignore any sweeteners that cannot be processed into honey.

(①) Humans and insects also use different body parts for tasting. (②) Humans taste with the thousands of taste buds on their tongue. 10 (③) Although insects do use their mouths for tasting, they can also use their antennae or legs. (④) For these insects, walking on good food is enough to trigger their appetite. _____(B)_____, food good **enough to stand** on is good **enough to eat**!

*taste bud 미뢰(맛을 느끼는 미세포가 모여 있는 구조)

Mini Quiz

While you read, check T if it is true, or F if it's false.

1 Humans have the most sensitive taste buds of all creatures.
   □ T □ F
2 Insects don't use their mouths for tasting.
   □ T □ F

Reading Comprehension

1 **What is the passage mainly about?**
   a. comparing taste in humans and insects
   b. how animals use their senses to survive
   c. how bees make honey with their taste buds
   d. why insects are better at tasting than humans

2 **What is the best pair for blanks (A) and (B)?**

	(A)		(B)			(A)		(B)
a.	However	–	Otherwise		b.	However	–	In other words
c.	In addition	–	Otherwise		d.	In addition	–	In other words

Writing Practice

3 **According to the passage, why do honey bees ignore any sweeteners that cannot be processed into honey?**
   It is because they need to _____.

4 **Where would the following sentence best fit?**

> For example, butterflies and flies first taste something with their feet before using their tube-shaped mouth to eat it.

   a. ①   b. ②   c. ③   d. ④

```
● ● ●          🔍  GRAMMAR Inside LEVEL 2                          ≡
```

〈정도〉를 나타내는 to부정사의 관용 표현

to부정사가 부사적 용법으로 〈정도〉를 의미하여, 형용사 또는 부사를 수식할 수 있다.

Link to ... 👆
  Chapter 04
  Unit 04

• 「형용사/부사+enough+to-v」: ~할 만큼 충분히 …한/하게
  ..., food *good* **enough to stand** on is *good* **enough to eat**!
  He was *foolish* **enough to spend** all the money.
• 「too+형용사/부사+to-v」: 너무 ~해서 …할 수 없는, …하기에 너무 ~한/하게
  You are **too** *young* **to live** alone.

Check Up 우리말과 일치하도록 ( ) 안에 주어진 말을 바르게 배열하시오.

   Jenny는 혼자 해외에 갈 만큼 충분히 용감하다. (go / brave / to / enough)

   → Jenny is _____ abroad by herself.

Senses

History

164 words

A Pioneer for the Blind

Mini Quiz

Paragraph 3

Q: Was Braille's 6-dot writing system popular when he was alive?

A: No. It remained _____ until his _____ in 1852.

Reading is possible for the blind thanks to *braille. It was developed by Louis Braille. He was born with perfect vision in France in 1809. But when he was three, he hurt his eye and infection made him blind.

Still, he was a bright student and won a scholarship to the National Institute for Blind Youth at age ten. (①) By using the system, soldiers 5 could communicate at night without speaking. (②) When the soldier spoke at Braille's school in 1822, Braille thought the system could be used for the blind. (③) So he decided **to improve** it. (④)

Braille completed and published a 6-dot writing system in 1837. To read it, a single fingertip is moved from left to right across raised dots. 10 It was easy to use, but wide acceptance was slow in coming. The system remained unpopular until his death in 1852. It was in 1917 that the US settled on a Braille standard, and in 1932, other English-speaking countries also started **to use** it.

*braille 브라유 점자

Reading Comprehension

1 What is the passage mainly about?

a. how blind people learn to read

b. the ways soldiers communicated at night

c. Braille's new writing system for the blind

d. Braille's time at the National Institute for Blind Youth

2 What is NOT true about Louis Braille according to the passage?

a. He was born in France in 1809.

b. He had no vision from birth.

c. He developed a 6-dot writing system for the blind.

d. He completed his braille system in 1837.

3 Where would the following sentence best fit?

That year, a French soldier created a raised 12-dot writing system.

a. ①   **b.** ②   **c.** ③   **d.** ④

Writing Practice

4 According to the passage, when did the US settle on a Braille standard?

It was in _____ that the US settled on a Braille standard.

Q   GRAMMAR **Inside** LEVEL 1   ☰

to부정사의 명사적 용법

• 명사적 용법의 to부정사는 문장 안에서 주어, 목적어, 보어 역할을 한다.

  [**To watch** soccer games] is exciting. (주어, 잘 쓰이지 않음)

  ..., other English-speaking countries also started [**to use** it]. (목적어)

  My plan is [**to finish** the essay by this Friday]. (보어)

• 동사 want, need, decide, hope, expect, plan, promise, like, start 등은 목적어로 to부정사를 취한다.

  So, he *decided* **to improve** it.   I *hope* **to see** you again soon.

Link to ...
Chapter 09
Unit 01

Check Up 다음 ( ) 안에서 알맞은 것을 고르시오.

    1 Kelly promised (helping / to help) me.

    2 Sean decided (selling / to sell) his bike to Amber.

VOCABULARY INSIDE

READING 1	READING 2
☐ **sense** Ⓝ one of the five natural abilities to see, hear, smell, taste, and feel	☐ **vision** Ⓝ the ability to see
☐ **survival** Ⓝ the continuation of the existence or life of a person or animal Ⓝ survive	☐ **improve** Ⓥ to increase the quality of something Ⓝ improvement
☐ **detect** Ⓥ to notice or discover the existence of something Ⓝ detection	☐ **complete** Ⓥ to finish doing something Ⓝ completion　Ⓐⓓ completely
☐ **ignore** Ⓥ to refuse to pay attention to something Ⓝ ignorance　[synonym] disregard	☐ **acceptance** Ⓝ agreement with an idea or opinion Ⓥ accept　Ⓐ acceptable　[antonym] rejection
☐ **trigger** Ⓥ to cause something to happen Ⓝ trigger	☐ **standard** Ⓝ an idea or thing considered to be a model or norm

Check Up

Fill in the blanks with the words above. Change the form if necessary.

1 Air and water are necessary for _____.

2 She lost her _____ of hearing at age seven.

3 Some foods can _____ an allergic reaction.

4 His idea quickly gained wide _____ in his company.

5 He bought new glasses because his _____ got worse.

6 You shouldn't _____ her advice, because it makes sense.

7 His mother was happy that he _____ his homework before dinner.

8 The system has become an industry _____, and now everyone uses it.

UNIT
15 | Psychology

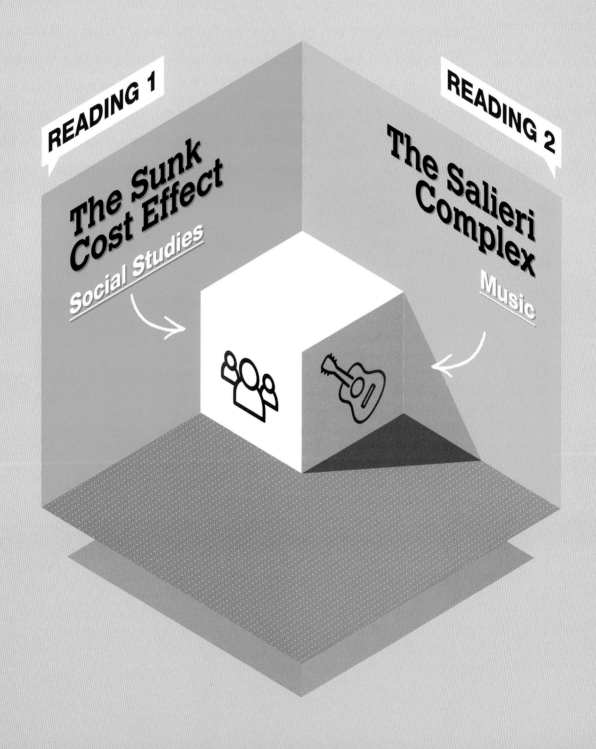

READING 1
The Sunk Cost Effect
Social Studies

READING 2
The Salieri Complex
Music

The Sunk Cost Effect

V Mini Quiz

How does the writer introduce the topic?

a. by defining an economic term
b. by quoting a famous economist
c. by giving an example from daily life

Imagine you are watching a movie in a theater. Unfortunately, the movie is terrible. But you keep sitting there because you paid for the ticket. You are experiencing the sunk cost effect.

To understand the effect, you must understand the term "sunk cost." A sunk cost is time, money, or effort that a person has spent and 5 can't get back — like the money for the ticket. Now, imagine a man purchases a restaurant, and it doesn't bring any profit. (①) He should accept his failure and give up. (②) But he doesn't want to think that he wasted the money he spent — the "sunk cost." (③) So he keeps spending money on the restaurant. (④) This is the sunk cost effect. 10

It can happen to anyone. **It** is hard **to admit** when you are unsuccessful at something because you don't want your efforts to be wasted. But **it** is much wiser **to accept** your losses and **move** on to something better.

Reading Comprehension

1 **What is the passage mainly about?**
   a. why it is hard to accept failure
   b. how to make smart investments
   c. how people usually waste their time and money
   d. why people continue to do something that causes a loss

Writing Practice

2 **According to the passage, what is a sunk cost?**
   It is time, money, or effort that _____.

3 **Where would the following sentence best fit?**

> In the end, it is a waste of even more money, just like enduring a bad movie is a waste of your time.

   a. ①   b. ②   c. ③   d. ④

4 **What should we do when we have a problem due to the sunk cost effect?**
   a. We should find the causes of the problem.
   b. We should accept our losses and move on.
   c. We should face the problem and try to fix it.
   d. We should consult experts about the problem.

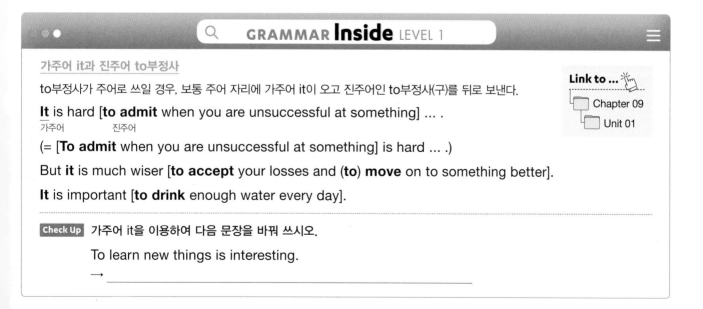

GRAMMAR **Inside** LEVEL 1

가주어 it과 진주어 to부정사
to부정사가 주어로 쓰일 경우, 보통 주어 자리에 가주어 it이 오고 진주어인 to부정사(구)를 뒤로 보낸다.

It is hard [**to admit** when you are unsuccessful at something] ... .
가주어   진주어

(= [**To admit** when you are unsuccessful at something] is hard ... .)

But **it** is much wiser [**to accept** your losses and (**to**) **move** on to something better].

It is important [**to drink** enough water every day].

Check Up 가주어 it을 이용하여 다음 문장을 바꿔 쓰시오.
   To learn new things is interesting.
   → _____

Link to ...
Chapter 09
Unit 01

The Salieri Complex

Paragraph 1

What is the Salieri Complex? Find and underline the answer.

▲ Antonio Salieri
(1750 ~ 1825)

The Salieri Complex refers to the envy of ordinary people toward talented ones. This complex originated from stories about Antonio Salieri, an Italian musician that was said to be 5 extremely jealous of his contemporary Amadeus Mozart. ____(A)____, many historians now believe these stories to be inaccurate.

In 1750, Salieri was born in the city of Legnago in Italy. He 10 traveled to Vienna from Venice for a children's church choir. He eventually became a court composer there **in** 1774. **During** his career, he created forty operas and various other compositions.

Although Salieri was probably not as talented as Mozart, he was still considered a top composer in Austria. His knowledge of 15 music was comprehensive. Then, where did the tales of jealousy originate? They may have begun with the release of the film *Amadeus* **in** 1985. In the film, Salieri is portrayed as being highly jealous of Mozart. ____(B)____, 20 the film is fictional. It's more likely he respected Mozart. History even shows that Salieri mourned Mozart's passing. Clearly, not all rumors are necessarily true.

▲ Amadeus Mozart
(1756 ~ 1791)

25

Reading Comprehension

1 **What is the passage mainly about?**
   a. how Antonio Salieri became envious of Mozart
   b. the life and career of Italian composer Antonio Salieri
   c. the truth about Antonio Salieri and the Salieri Complex
   d. why many musicians suffered from the Salieri Complex

2 **Write T if the statement about Antonio Salieri is true or F if it's false.**
   (1) He was born in Vienna. _____
   (2) He actually had more talent than Mozart. _____
   (3) He was considered one of the top composers in Austria. _____

3 **What is the best choice for blanks (A) and (B)?**
   a. However   b. Moreover
   c. As a result   d. For instance

Writing Practice
4 **According to the passage, where did the tales of Salieri's jealousy originate from?**
   They may have begun _____.

Q GRAMMAR Inside LEVEL 1 ≡

시간을 나타내는 전치사
• in + 오전, 오후, 저녁, 월, 계절, 연도   • at + 밤, 구체적인 시각   • on + 날짜, 요일, 특정한 날
• for + 구체적인 시간의 길이   • during + 특정한 때·기간을 나타내는 명사

Link to ...
☐ Chapter 10
  ☐ Unit 02

He eventually became a court composer there **in** *1774*.

He usually eats dinner **at** *7:00 p.m.*

We will throw a party for her **on** *March 24*.

I lived in New York **for** *three years*.

During *his career*, he created forty operas and various other compositions.

Check Up 다음 ( ) 안에서 알맞은 것을 고르시오.

   1 Alex traveled to Spain (for / during) the holidays.
   2 I got a lot of presents from my friends (in / on) my birthday.

⬡ VOCABULARY INSIDE

READING 1	READING 2
☐ **purchase** ⓥ to obtain something, usually with money ⓝ purchase ⸨synonym⸩ buy ⸨antonym⸩ sell	☐ **envy** ⓝ the painful awareness that you desire something that somebody else has ⓥ envy ⓐ envious ⸨synonym⸩ jealousy
☐ **profit** ⓝ money that has been gained ⓥ profit ⓐ profitable ⸨antonym⸩ loss	☐ **ordinary** ⓐ not different, special, or unexpected ⸨synonym⸩ usual, normal
☐ **failure** ⓝ lack of achieving something or succeeding at something ⓥ fail ⸨synonym⸩ success	☐ **comprehensive** ⓐ covering a wide range of information ⸨antonym⸩ limited
☐ **admit** ⓥ to agree that something is true, especially when you don't want to ⓝ admission ⸨antonym⸩ deny	☐ **portray** ⓥ to play the part of another person in a film or on stage
☐ **endure** ⓥ to deal with an unpleasant experience without giving up ⓝ endurance ⓐ endurable	☐ **fictional** ⓐ created by the imagination ⓝ fiction

Check Up

Fill in the blanks with the words above. Change the form if necessary.

1 I felt _____ at the thought of his success.

2 She did her best, but her efforts ended in _____ .

3 I couldn't _____ the pain, so I took some medicine.

4 She is a novelist, so she always writes _____ stories.

5 The actor intended to _____ his character as being cruel.

6 This unpopular business is not bringing in much _____ at all.

7 A(n) _____ study on the issue was done by the research team.

8 Nowadays, people can _____ many things using their smartphones.

UNIT 16 | Light

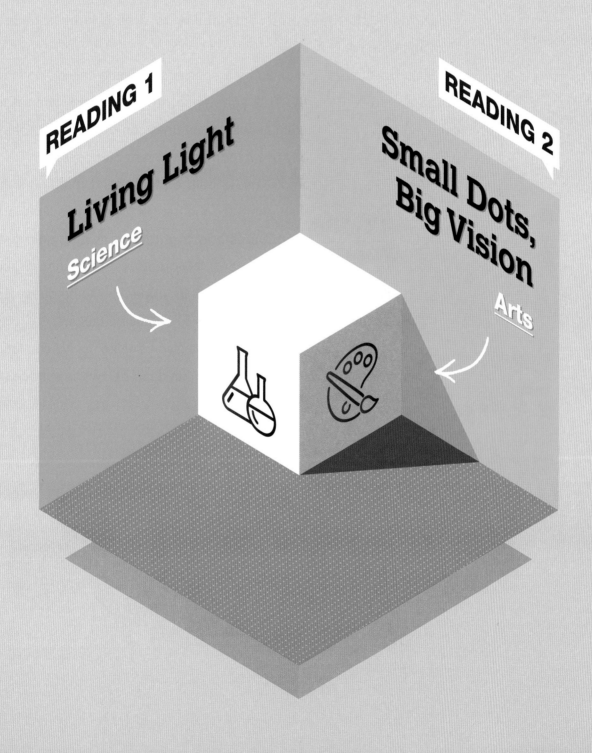

READING 1
Living Light
Science

READING 2
Small Dots, Big Vision
Arts

Living Light

Mini Quiz

Paragraph 1

Q: What is bioluminescence?

A: It is the ability to

_____ _____ .

① Imagine an ocean filled with millions of tiny lights. ② It may sound like a fantasy, but it is reality! ③ Deep in our oceans, many sea creatures make their own light. ④ There are still a lot of unknown creatures in the deep sea. This ability to create light is called "bioluminescence."

Bioluminescence is caused by a special substance called *luciferin inside a creature's body. This substance produces light when it is exposed to oxygen. Bioluminescent creatures can control when they produce the light, and they use it for many different purposes.

Anglerfish, for example, use a bulb on their head that lights up to attract prey. Smaller fish don't see the danger behind this light and swim toward it. **Attracting mates and **frightening** away bigger fish are other uses of bioluminescence. ***Ostracods, small shrimp-like creatures, attract mates by **lighting** up their upper lip. Some deep-sea worms also shoot bioluminescent bullets to confuse attackers.

The bioluminescence of sea creatures also benefits us: we can look upon our oceans and see the beautiful lights deep below the surface.

*luciferin 루시페린(생물체 발광에 관여하는 물질)   **anglerfish 아귀
***ostracod 오스트라코드(갑각 동물의 일종)

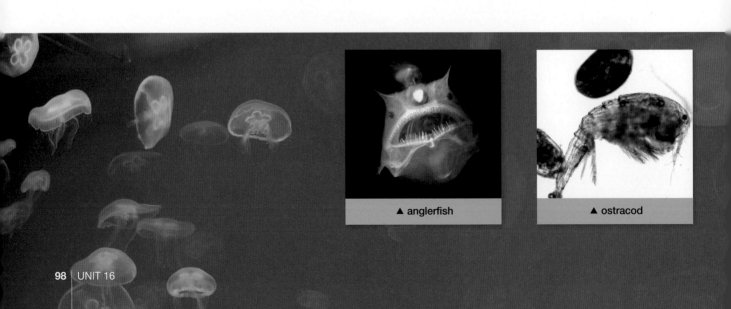

▲ anglerfish

▲ ostracod

Reading Comprehension

1 **What is the passage mainly about?**
   a. how different animals attract their prey or mates
   b. the ability of some sea creatures to produce light
   c. how smaller fish protect themselves from attackers
   d. what chemical reactions happen inside of sea creatures

2 **Which sentence is NOT needed in the passage?**
   a. ①   **b.** ②   **c.** ③   **d.** ④

3 **Write T if the statement is true or F if it's false.**
   (1) Luciferin produces light when it is exposed to oxygen.   _____
   (2) Sea creatures with luciferin cannot control when they produce the light.   _____

Writing Practice

4 **Complete the chart with words from the passage.**

Bioluminescent Sea Creatures		
Name	Method	Purpose
anglerfish	light up a bulb on their head	to attract (1) _____
ostracods	light up their (2) _____ _____	to attract mates
deep-sea worms	shoot bioluminescent bullets	to confuse (3) _____

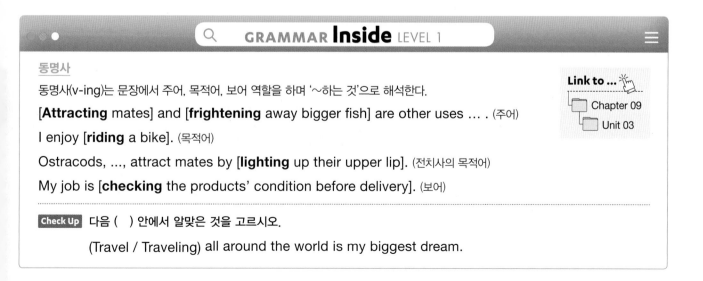

Q GRAMMAR **Inside** LEVEL 1

동명사

동명사(v-ing)는 문장에서 주어, 목적어, 보어 역할을 하며 '~하는 것'으로 해석한다.

[**Attracting** mates] and [**frightening** away bigger fish] are other uses … . (주어)

I enjoy [**riding** a bike]. (목적어)

Ostracods, …, attract mates by [**lighting** up their upper lip]. (전치사의 목적어)

My job is [**checking** the products' condition before delivery]. (보어)

Link to …

Chapter 09
Unit 03

Check Up 다음 ( ) 안에서 알맞은 것을 고르시오.

   (Travel / Traveling) all around the world is my biggest dream.

Light

180 words

Arts

Small Dots, Big Vision

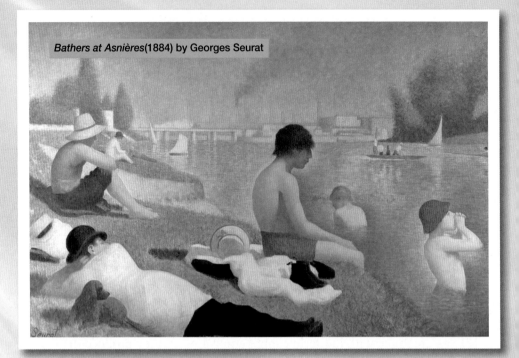

Bathers at Asnières(1884) by Georges Seurat

ⓥ Mini Quiz

[Paragraph 1]
What did the pointillism technique involve? Find and underline the answer.

Georges Seurat was a nineteenth-century painter. He was famous for his creation of Pointillism. The technique involved using tiny dots and various contrasting colors to portray the movement of light.

This style was _____. He was inspired by 5 certain renowned chemists and physicists of his time. He was particularly interested in how the human brain and eyes process these colors. This is why he used tiny dots. He didn't mix colors or use continuous lines to express light. However, when people view his work at a distance, most will probably only see the painting as 10 a whole and not the small marks he made on the canvas.

One of his famous paintings is called *Bathers at Asnières*. The painting consists of thousands of tiny dots that show the contrast of light and shadow. It portrays some young men **relaxing on a grassy bank by a river on a summer day**. It also depicts trees, 15 boats, buildings, and factories with smoke **rising above them**. It is a shining example of the perfect mix of light, simplicity of form, contrast, and composition.

Reading Comprehension

1 **What is the best title for the passage?**
   a. Small Paintings with More Detail
   b. The Painting Style of Georges Seurat
   c. Georges Seurat: A Painter of Emotion
   d. How Did Science Influence Modern Artwork?

2 **What is the best choice for the blank?**
   a. considered to be outdated
   b. characterized by political beliefs
   c. related to portrait painting
   d. largely based on scientific theories

3 **Write T if the statement about Georges Seurat is true or F if it's false.**
   (1) He portrayed light using connected lines.   _____
   (2) He created a theory on how the brain processes colors.   _____

4 **What is NOT mentioned about *Bathers at Asnières*?**
   a. It shows the contrast of light and shadow.
   b. It portrays a scene from the summer.
   c. It has factories with smoke above them.
   d. Behind one man, a dog is barking at the river.

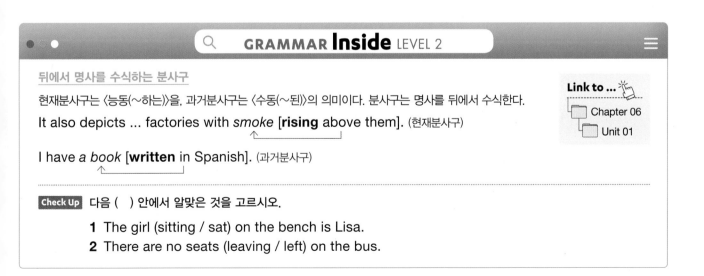

GRAMMAR **Inside** LEVEL 2

뒤에서 명사를 수식하는 분사구
현재분사구는 〈능동(~하는)〉을, 과거분사구는 〈수동(~된)〉의 의미이다. 분사구는 명사를 뒤에서 수식한다.

It also depicts ... factories with *smoke* [**rising** above them]. (현재분사구)

I have a *book* [**written** in Spanish]. (과거분사구)

Link to ...
Chapter 06
Unit 01

Check Up 다음 ( ) 안에서 알맞은 것을 고르시오.
   1 The girl (sitting / sat) on the bench is Lisa.
   2 There are no seats (leaving / left) on the bus.

VOCABULARY INSIDE

READING 1	READING 2
☐ **substance** ⓝ a kind of solid, liquid, or gas that has particular qualities	☐ **contrasting** ⓐ different from each other in style, color, or attitude ⓝ contrast ⓥ contrast
☐ **expose** ⓥ to uncover something or remove the protection from it	☐ **renowned** ⓐ well known and respected for something synonym famous
☐ **purpose** ⓝ the reason for doing or using something	☐ **relax** ⓥ to become calm and at ease ⓝ relaxation
☐ **attract** ⓥ to cause a person or animal to be interested in something or to want to be involved in it ⓝ attraction	☐ **depict** ⓥ to describe something or someone using words or images synonym portray, describe
☐ **confuse** ⓥ to cause a person or animal to misunderstand or be uncertain about something ⓝ confusion	☐ **rise** ⓥ to move in an upward direction antonym fall

Check Up

Fill in the blanks with the words above. Change the form if necessary.

1 _____! Everything will be okay.

2 A helicopter is _____ into the air.

3 Try not to _____ your skin to strong sunlight.

4 The old bicycle was covered in a sticky _____.

5 This hotel is _____ for having amazing spa facilities.

6 This picture shows _____ colors of red, green, and yellow.

7 This kind of explanation can _____ readers. It should be simpler.

8 The _____ of this meeting is to find solutions for the problems we are facing.

WORD LIST

UNIT 01 Shapes

O△X	a variety of	다양한
O△X	according to	~에 따르면
O△X	amount	몡 양
O△X	be born	태어나다
O△X	burst	몡 폭발, 파열
O△X	cell	몡 세포; 감방; (큰 구조의 작은) 칸
O△X	childhood	몡 어린 시절
O△X	communicate	몽 의사소통하다; 전(달)하다
O△X	compared to	~와 비교하면
O△X	cover	몽 덮다; 둘러싸다
O△X	create	몽 만들다, 창조하다
O△X	efficiently	뷔 효율적으로
O△X	emotion	몡 감정
O△X	encourage	몽 권장[장려]하다
O△X	example	몡 예시
O△X	fit	몽 (꼭) 맞다
O△X	full of	~로 가득 찬
O△X	gap	몡 틈, 간격
O△X	gradually	뷔 서서히, 점차
O△X	hexagon	몡 육각형
O△X	honeycomb	몡 벌집
O△X	impressive	뎡 인상적인, 인상 깊은
O△X	influential	뎡 영향력 있는
O△X	musical	뎡 음악의
O△X	produce	몽 만들어내다, 생산하다
O△X	represent	몽 나타내다
O△X	secret	몡 비밀
O△X	shape	몡 모양, 형태
O△X	silence	몡 침묵
O△X	space	몡 공간, 자리
O△X	square	몡 정사각형
O△X	store	몽 저장[보관]하다
O△X	term	몡 용어, 말
O△X	view	몽 보다
O△X	wax	몡 밀랍, 왁스

UNIT 02 Origins

O△X	admit	몽 인정하다
O△X	apologize	몽 사과하다
O△X	appear	몽 ~인 것 같다; 나타나다
O△X	argue	몽 다투다
O△X	basic	뎡 기초[기본]적인
O△X	beyond	젼 ~의 너머[저편]에
O△X	creativity	몡 창의력, 독창력
O△X	defeat	몽 패배시키다; 몡 패배
O△X	device	몡 기구, 장치
O△X	enter	몽 들어오다, 들어가다
O△X	explain	몽 설명하다
O△X	expression	몡 표현 (어구)
O△X	following	뎡 다음에 나오는
O△X	greatly	뷔 대단히, 크게
O△X	happen	몽 일어나다, 발생하다
O△X	imagine	몽 상상하다
O△X	improve	몽 개선하다, 향상시키다
O△X	invention	몡 발명
O△X	language	몡 언어
O△X	magnify	몽 확대하다
O△X	match	몡 경기, 시합
O△X	observation	몡 관찰, 관측
O△X	opponent	몡 (게임 등의) 상대
O△X	opposite	뎡 맞은 편[쪽]의, 건너편의
O△X	prior to	~ 이전에, ~에 앞서
O△X	realize	몽 깨닫다, 알아차리다
O△X	rest	몽 휴식을 취하다
O△X	rope	몡 로프, 밧줄
O△X	sentence	몡 문장
O△X	several	뎡 몇몇(의)
O△X	telescope	몡 망원경
O△X	totally	뷔 완전히, 전적으로
O△X	unknown	뎡 알려지지 않은, 미지의
O△X	up to	~까지
O△X	version	몡 형태, 판

WORD LIST

UNIT 03 | Sports

⬜ attend	동 참석하다
⬜ ban	동 금지하다
⬜ clearly	부 명확하게
⬜ competition	명 경쟁; 대회
⬜ consume	동 소비하다; 먹다
⬜ convenient	형 편리한, 간편한
⬜ cruel	형 잔인한, 잔혹한
⬜ early	형 초창기의
⬜ equipment	명 기구, 장비
⬜ event	명 사건; 행사
⬜ exhausted	형 녹초가 된, 기진맥진한
⬜ fashionable	형 유행하는
⬜ fitness	명 신체 단련, 건강
⬜ force	동 강요하다, ~하게 만들다
⬜ gym	명 체육관
⬜ mill	명 방아, 방앗간
⬜ originally	부 원래, 본래
⬜ power	동 동력을 공급하다, 작동시키다
⬜ prison	명 감옥
⬜ punishment	명 (처)벌
⬜ reason	명 이유
⬜ remain	동 여전히[계속] ~이다
⬜ rotation	명 회전
⬜ rule	명 규칙
⬜ serve	동 제공하다
⬜ stain	명 자국, 얼룩
⬜ steps	명 계단
⬜ strict	형 엄격한, 엄한
⬜ stunning	형 (깜짝) 놀랄 만한
⬜ sweat	명 땀
⬜ take part in	~에 참여[참가]하다
⬜ take place	개최되다, 일어나다
⬜ tradition	명 전통
⬜ treadmill	명 트레드밀, 러닝머신
⬜ wheel	명 바퀴

UNIT 04 | Jobs

⬜ adjust	동 조절[조정]하다
⬜ advantage	명 강점, 이점, 유리한 점
⬜ analyze	동 분석하다
⬜ artwork	명 미술품
⬜ athlete	명 (운동) 선수
⬜ beat	동 이기다, 물리치다
⬜ checkup	명 검진
⬜ communication	명 의사소통
⬜ complex	형 복잡한
⬜ condition	명 상태
⬜ conservator	명 [미술] 복원전문가
⬜ damage	명 손상, 피해
⬜ data	명 자료, 데이터
⬜ expert	명 전문가
⬜ hitter	명 타자
⬜ humidity	명 습도
⬜ identify	동 (신원을) 확인하다; 찾다, 발견하다
⬜ material	명 직물, 천; 재료
⬜ notice	동 알아차리다
⬜ opposition	명 상대[반대]측
⬜ patient	명 환자
⬜ pitcher	명 투수
⬜ practice	명 연습, 실습
⬜ repair	동 보수[수리]하다
⬜ restore	동 복원[복구]하다
⬜ reward	명 보상
⬜ ruin	동 엉망으로 만들다
⬜ sculpture	명 조각(품)
⬜ skill	명 기량, 기술
⬜ specialty	명 전공
⬜ strength	명 힘; 강점, 장점
⬜ tactic	명 전술
⬜ treatment	명 치료, 처치
⬜ weaken	동 약화시키다
⬜ weakness	명 약함; 약점

☐O ☐△ ☐X O = I know this word and its meaning.
△ = I know either the word spelling or its meaning.
X = I've never seen this word before.
• Study the words that you've checked △ or X.

UNIT 05 | Solutions

☐O☐△☐X	according to	~에 따르면
☐O☐△☐X	anger	명 분노
☐O☐△☐X	be born	태어나다
☐O☐△☐X	brain	명 (두)뇌
☐O☐△☐X	complicated	형 복잡한
☐O☐△☐X	conduct	동 실시하다
☐O☐△☐X	constantly	부 끊임없이
☐O☐△☐X	cost	명 비용
☐O☐△☐X	disease	명 (질)병
☐O☐△☐X	effectiveness	명 효과성
☐O☐△☐X	electricity	명 전력, 전기
☐O☐△☐X	embrace	명 포옹
☐O☐△☐X	fat	명 (체)지방
☐O☐△☐X	function	명 기능
☐O☐△☐X	intense	형 격한
☐O☐△☐X	key	명 비결
☐O☐△☐X	latest	형 최신의
☐O☐△☐X	lead to	~로 이어지다
☐O☐△☐X	major	형 중대한, 주요한
☐O☐△☐X	melt	동 녹다; 녹이다
☐O☐△☐X	method	명 방법
☐O☐△☐X	outsider	명 제삼자; 외부인
☐O☐△☐X	passion	명 열정
☐O☐△☐X	perspective	명 관점
☐O☐△☐X	premature	형 조산의, 정상보다 이른
☐O☐△☐X	regulate	동 규제하다; 조절하다
☐O☐△☐X	relief	명 해소, 완화
☐O☐△☐X	requirement	명 필수 요건
☐O☐△☐X	separate	동 분리하다
☐O☐△☐X	solution	명 해결책, 해법
☐O☐△☐X	staff	명 직원
☐O☐△☐X	task	명 과제
☐O☐△☐X	technique	명 기법
☐O☐△☐X	tiny	형 아주 작은
☐O☐△☐X	unavoidable	형 피할 수 없는

UNIT 06 | Future

☐O☐△☐X	appearance	명 외모, (겉)모습
☐O☐△☐X	architect	명 건축가
☐O☐△☐X	atmosphere	명 대기(권)
☐O☐△☐X	climate	명 기후
☐O☐△☐X	continue	동 지속되다, 계속되다
☐O☐△☐X	deal with	~을 다루다[처리하다]
☐O☐△☐X	develop	동 발달[성장]시키다
☐O☐△☐X	dig	동 파(내)다
☐O☐△☐X	efficiently	부 효율[능률]적으로
☐O☐△☐X	entire	형 전체의
☐O☐△☐X	forbid	동 금지하다
☐O☐△☐X	forehead	명 이마
☐O☐△☐X	gradually	부 점진적으로, 서서히
☐O☐△☐X	groundbreaking	형 획기적인
☐O☐△☐X	heritage	명 유산
☐O☐△☐X	hidden	형 숨겨진, 숨은
☐O☐△☐X	historical	형 역사적인
☐O☐△☐X	human	명 인간, 사람
☐O☐△☐X	imagine	동 상상하다
☐O☐△☐X	influence	명 영향(력)
☐O☐△☐X	issue	명 쟁점; 문제(점)
☐O☐△☐X	look at	~을 (자세히) 살피다[검토하다]
☐O☐△☐X	massive	형 거대한
☐O☐△☐X	population	명 인구
☐O☐△☐X	preserve	동 보존[보호]하다
☐O☐△☐X	release	동 풀어 주다; 방출[발산]하다
☐O☐△☐X	researcher	명 연구원
☐O☐△☐X	rise	동 오르다
☐O☐△☐X	skyscraper	명 고층 건물
☐O☐△☐X	specific	형 특정한, 구체적인
☐O☐△☐X	square	명 정사각형; 광장
☐O☐△☐X	structure	명 건축물, 구조물
☐O☐△☐X	technology	명 (과학) 기술
☐O☐△☐X	temperature	명 온도, 기온
☐O☐△☐X	underground	부 지하에

UNIT 07 | Environment

⊙△✗	additionally	🅱 게다가
⊙△✗	amount	🅜 양
⊙△✗	bead	🅜 구슬
⊙△✗	build	🅢 짓다; 축적되다
⊙△✗	chemical	🅜 화학 물질
⊙△✗	common	🅗 흔한
⊙△✗	cosmetics	🅜 화장품
⊙△✗	creature	🅜 생물
⊙△✗	damaging	🅗 해로운
⊙△✗	drain	🅜 배수관
⊙△✗	fatal	🅗 치명적인
⊙△✗	footwear	🅜 신발
⊙△✗	for instance	예를 들어
⊙△✗	form	🅜 형태
⊙△✗	habitat	🅜 서식지
⊙△✗	harmful	🅗 유해한, 해로운
⊙△✗	impact	🅜 영향
⊙△✗	including	🅟 ~을 포함하여
⊙△✗	initial	🅗 초기[최초]의
⊙△✗	innovation	🅜 혁신
⊙△✗	jersey	🅜 (운동 경기용) 셔츠
⊙△✗	marine	🅗 해양[바다]의
⊙△✗	oil	🅜 기름; 석유
⊙△✗	on and on	계속해서, 쉬지 않고
⊙△✗	partially	🅱 부분적으로
⊙△✗	physical	🅗 물리적인
⊙△✗	pollute	🅢 오염시키다
⊙△✗	process	🅢 가공하다; 🅜 과정
⊙△✗	produce	🅢 생산하다
⊙△✗	product	🅜 제품, 상품
⊙△✗	reduce	🅢 줄이다
⊙△✗	rely on	~에 의존[의지]하다
⊙△✗	require	🅢 필요로 하다
⊙△✗	toothpaste	🅜 치약
⊙△✗	toxic	🅗 (유)독성의

UNIT 08 | Health

⊙△✗	affect	🅢 영향을 미치다
⊙△✗	allow	🅢 허락하다, 가능하게 하다
⊙△✗	attack	🅢 공격하다
⊙△✗	because of	~ 때문에
⊙△✗	cell	🅜 세포
⊙△✗	contain	🅢 함유[포함]하다
⊙△✗	cough	🅜 기침
⊙△✗	defense	🅜 방어(물)
⊙△✗	device	🅜 장치, 기구
⊙△✗	direction	🅜 방향
⊙△✗	electronic	🅗 전자의
⊙△✗	feed	🅢 먹여주다
⊙△✗	fever	🅜 열
⊙△✗	immune system	면역 체계
⊙△✗	independent	🅗 독립적인
⊙△✗	infection	🅜 감염
⊙△✗	inject	🅢 주사[주입]하다
⊙△✗	instead of	~ 대신에
⊙△✗	invade	🅢 침입하다
⊙△✗	meal	🅜 식사, 끼니
⊙△✗	medical	🅗 의학의
⊙△✗	nervous system	신경계
⊙△✗	opportunity	🅜 기회
⊙△✗	opposite	🅗 반대의, 다른 편의
⊙△✗	part	🅜 부분, 일부
⊙△✗	protect	🅢 보호하다
⊙△✗	record	🅢 기록하다
⊙△✗	shake	🅢 흔들다; 떨다, 떨리다
⊙△✗	suffer	🅢 앓다, 고통받다
⊙△✗	survive	🅢 살아남다; (고난 등을) 견디다
⊙△✗	symptom	🅜 증상, 징후
⊙△✗	the same A as B	B와 같은 A
⊙△✗	threat	🅜 위협
⊙△✗	uncontrollably	🅱 통제할 수 없이
⊙△✗	work	🅢 일하다; 효과가 있다

UNIT 09 | Colors

O△X	almost	男 거의
O△X	along	전 ~을 따라
O△X	apply	동 묻히다, 바르다
O△X	carry	동 옮기다, 나르다
O△X	composed of	~로 구성된
O△X	dip	동 담그다
O△X	discover	동 발견하다
O△X	during	전 ~ 동안
O△X	each other	서로
O△X	end up	결국 ~하게 되다
O△X	fade	동 바래다, 희미해지다
O△X	further	형 더 먼; 추가의
O△X	investigation	명 조사, 수사
O△X	known as	~로 알려진
O△X	likewise	男 마찬가지로
O△X	liquid	명 액체
O△X	mind	명 심리, 마음
O△X	notice	동 알아차리다
O△X	originally	男 원래
O△X	over time	시간이 지나면서
O△X	pigment	명 색소
O△X	quite	男 상당히, 꽤
O△X	rainbow	명 무지개
O△X	reflect	동 반영하다
O△X	separate	동 나누다, 분리하다; 분리되다
O△X	speed	명 속도
O△X	state	명 상태
O△X	stay	동 머무르다
O△X	such as	~와 같은
O△X	technique	명 기법
O△X	through	전 ~을 통해
O△X	version	명 버전, ~판
O△X	wall	명 벽
O△X	weight	명 무게
O△X	work	동 일하다, 작용하다

UNIT 10 | Technology

O△X	a handful of	소수의, 한 움큼의
O△X	as well	~도
O△X	contact	동 연락하다
O△X	convert	동 바꾸다
O△X	cordless	형 무선의
O△X	crime	명 범죄
O△X	cybercriminal	명 사이버 범죄자
O△X	deal with	~을 처리하다
O△X	demand	동 요구하다
O△X	disgusting	형 역겨운
O△X	encourage	동 부추기다
O△X	expert	명 전문가
O△X	extract	동 추출하다
O△X	flight	명 비행
O△X	get access to	~에 접속[접근]하다
O△X	guarantee	동 보장하다
O△X	handheld	형 소형인, 손에 쥐고 쓸 수 있는
O△X	impact	명 영향; 동 영향을 끼치다
O△X	improve	동 개선하다
O△X	individual	형 개별의
O△X	inspire	동 영감을 주다
O△X	international	형 국제적인
O△X	land on	~에 착륙하다
O△X	lead to	~로 이어지다
O△X	lock	동 잠그다
O△X	operation	명 운영
O△X	particle	명 입자
O△X	purification	명 정화
O△X	research	명 연구
O△X	security	명 보안
O△X	supply	동 공급하다
O△X	unlock	동 열다
O△X	up to date	최신의
O△X	vacuum	명 진공청소기
O△X	warning	명 경고

UNIT 11 Food

⃞⃞⃞ a variety of	다양한
⃞⃞⃞ add	통 더하다, 첨가하다
⃞⃞⃞ ask for	(물건 등)을 요청하다
⃞⃞⃞ baker	명 제빵사
⃞⃞⃞ cheat	통 속이다, 사기 치다
⃞⃞⃞ come from	~에서 나오다[비롯되다]
⃞⃞⃞ customer	명 고객
⃞⃞⃞ disappear	통 사라지다
⃞⃞⃞ extract	명 추출물
⃞⃞⃞ heat	명 열; 매움, 매운맛
⃞⃞⃞ hot	형 더운; 매운
⃞⃞⃞ law	명 법
⃞⃞⃞ light	형 밝은; 가벼운
⃞⃞⃞ measure	통 측정하다, 재다
⃞⃞⃞ normal	형 보통의; 표준의
⃞⃞⃞ on fire	(몸의 일부가) 불타는 듯한
⃞⃞⃞ originate	통 유래하다
⃞⃞⃞ pepper	명 후추; 고추
⃞⃞⃞ persuade	통 설득하다
⃞⃞⃞ promote	통 홍보하다
⃞⃞⃞ punish	통 처벌하다
⃞⃞⃞ rate	통 등급을 매기다
⃞⃞⃞ ratio	명 비율
⃞⃞⃞ receive	통 받다
⃞⃞⃞ refer to	~을 지칭하다
⃞⃞⃞ related to	~와 관련된
⃞⃞⃞ represent	통 나타내다
⃞⃞⃞ scale	명 규모; 척도
⃞⃞⃞ spiciness	명 매운 정도[맛]
⃞⃞⃞ strange	형 이상한; 낯선
⃞⃞⃞ sweat	통 땀을 흘리다
⃞⃞⃞ tongue	명 혀
⃞⃞⃞ unfamiliar	형 낯선, 익숙지 않은
⃞⃞⃞ vary	통 다양하다
⃞⃞⃞ weigh	통 무게가 ~이다

UNIT 12 Places

⃞⃞⃞ architecture	명 건축 양식
⃞⃞⃞ artifact	명 공예품; 유물
⃞⃞⃞ bendable	형 구부릴 수 있는
⃞⃞⃞ center	명 중심
⃞⃞⃞ consist of	~로 구성되다
⃞⃞⃞ continue	통 계속되다
⃞⃞⃞ countryside	명 시골 지역
⃞⃞⃞ emperor	명 황제
⃞⃞⃞ empire	명 제국
⃞⃞⃞ enter	통 들어가다
⃞⃞⃞ expand	통 확장[확대]되다; 확장하다
⃞⃞⃞ forbidden	형 금지된
⃞⃞⃞ frame	명 틀, 액자; 뼈대
⃞⃞⃞ furthermore	부 뿐만 아니라, 더욱이
⃞⃞⃞ government	명 정부, 정권
⃞⃞⃞ historical	형 역사(상)의
⃞⃞⃞ imperial	형 제국의; 황제의
⃞⃞⃞ known as	~로 알려진
⃞⃞⃞ last	형 마지막의
⃞⃞⃞ made of	~로 만들어진
⃞⃞⃞ palace	명 성, 궁전
⃞⃞⃞ permission	명 허가, 허락
⃞⃞⃞ political	형 정치적인
⃞⃞⃞ portable	형 이동이 가능한
⃞⃞⃞ put ~ back together	~을 재조립하다
⃞⃞⃞ roof	명 지붕
⃞⃞⃞ set up	~을 설치하다
⃞⃞⃞ step down	실각하다, 물러나다
⃞⃞⃞ surround	통 에워싸다, 둘러싸다
⃞⃞⃞ take down	(해체하여) 치우다, 분해하다
⃞⃞⃞ traditional	형 전통의
⃞⃞⃞ vast	형 광대한, 거대한
⃞⃞⃞ withstand	통 견디다, 이겨 내다
⃞⃞⃞ wonder	통 궁금하다
⃞⃞⃞ work of art	명 예술품, 미술품

UNIT 13 Activities

action	명 행동	
anger	명 분노	
at the same time	동시에	
calm down	진정하다	
combine	동 결합하다	
consistently	부 지속해서	
correct	형 정확한	
cube	명 정육면체	
defend	동 방어하다	
entertaining	형 즐겁게 하는	
excess	형 과도한, 초과한	
gain	동 얻다	
get in shape	좋은 몸 상태를 유지하다	
give ~ a try	~을 한번 (시도)해보다	
intensity	명 강도, 세기	
interested in	~에 관심이 있는	
lead to	~로 이어지다	
let out	풀어내다, 내보내다	
meditation	명 명상	
memory	명 기억력	
official	형 공식적인	
pathway	명 경로	
pole	명 막대기; 축	
popular	형 인기 있는	
race	동 쏜살같이[급히] 가다	
recall	동 기억해 내다, 상기하다	
right angle	직각	
simple	형 단순한	
spirit	명 정신	
spot	명 지점, 장소	
structure	명 구조물, 건축물	
three-dimensional	3차원의, 입체적인	
transform	동 탈바꿈하다	
workout	명 운동	
yell out	외치다, 소리치다	

UNIT 14 Senses

acceptance	명 수용, 받아들임	
appetite	명 식욕	
artificial	형 인공적인	
blind	형 눈이 먼	
bright	형 밝은; 똑똑한	
compare	동 비교하다	
complete	동 완성하다	
concentration	명 집중; 농도	
death	명 사망, 죽음	
detect	동 감지[발견]하다	
dot	명 점	
essential	형 필수적인	
figure out	알아내다	
fingertip	명 손가락 끝	
improve	동 개선하다	
infection	명 감염	
insect	명 곤충	
pioneer	명 선구자	
plant	명 식물	
process	동 가공[처리]하다	
publish	동 발표[공표]하다	
raised	형 솟아오른; 양각의	
sense	명 감각	
sensitive	형 민감한	
settle on	~로 정하다	
soldier	명 군인	
standard	명 표준	
sugar	명 설탕; 당분	
survival	명 생존	
taste	동 맛보다; 명 미각	
thousands of	수천의	
tongue	명 혀	
trigger	동 유발[촉발]하다	
vision	명 시력	
writing	명 쓰기; 표기	

◆ WORD LIST

UNIT 15 Psychology

O△X	admit	동 인정하다
O△X	career	명 경력, 이력
O△X	choir	명 합창단
O△X	composition	명 작곡; 작품
O△X	comprehensive	형 광범위한
O△X	consult	동 상담하다
O△X	contemporary	형 동시대의
O△X	effort	명 노력, 수고
O△X	endure	동 견디다, 인내하다
O△X	envious of	~을 부러워하는
O△X	envy	명 질투, 선망
O△X	fictional	형 허구[소설]의
O△X	give up	포기하다
O△X	imagine	동 상상하다
O△X	in the end	결국
O△X	inaccurate	형 부정확한
O△X	investment	명 투자
O△X	jealous of	~을 질투하는
O△X	loss	명 분실; 손실, 손해
O△X	mourn	동 애도하다, 슬퍼하다
O△X	move on to	~로 넘어가다
O△X	ordinary	형 평범한, 보통의
O△X	originate	동 비롯되다, 유래하다
O△X	passing	명 죽음
O△X	portray	동 묘사하다; 연기하다
O△X	profit	명 이익, 수익
O△X	purchase	동 매입[구매]하다
O△X	refer to	~을 가리키다[나타내다]
O△X	release	명 개봉, 출시
O△X	respect	동 존경하다
O△X	spend	동 (돈·시간·노력 등을) 소비하다
O△X	talented	형 (타고난) 재능이 있는
O△X	terrible	형 끔찍한; 형편없는
O△X	unsuccessful	형 성공하지 못한
O△X	wise	형 현명한

UNIT 16 Light

O△X	as a whole	전체로서
O△X	at a distance	멀리서, 떨어져서
O△X	attract	동 유인하다, 마음을 끌다
O△X	bank	명 둑, 제방
O△X	based on	~에 기초한[근거하여]
O△X	benefit	동 유익하다
O△X	characterize	동 특징 짓다
O△X	confuse	동 혼란시키다
O△X	contrasting	형 대비되는, 대조적인
O△X	danger	명 위험
O△X	depict	동 표현[묘사]하다
O△X	dot	명 점
O△X	expose	동 노출시키다
O△X	express	동 표현하다
O△X	filled with	~로 가득 찬
O△X	frighten away	~을 겁주어 쫓아내다
O△X	grassy	형 풀로 덮인
O△X	involve	동 포함[수반]하다
O△X	light	명 빛
O△X	look upon	~을 구경하다[보다]
O△X	millions of	수백만의; 무수히 많은
O△X	mix	동 섞다; 혼합
O△X	movement	명 움직임
O△X	ocean	명 바다, 대양
O△X	of one's time	당대의
O△X	portray	동 묘사[표현]하다
O△X	process	동 처리하다
O△X	relax	동 휴식을 취하다
O△X	renowned	형 저명[유명]한, 명성 있는
O△X	rise	동 오르다, 올라가다
O△X	substance	명 물질
O△X	technique	명 기법
O△X	theory	명 이론
O△X	unknown	형 알려지지 않은
O△X	vision	명 시력; 시야

지은이

NE능률 영어교육연구소

NE능률 영어교육연구소는 혁신적이며 효율적인 영어 교재를 개발하고
영어 학습의 질을 한 단계 높이고자 노력하는 NE능률의 연구조직입니다.

READING Inside ⟨Level 1⟩

펴 낸 이   주민홍
펴 낸 곳   서울특별시 마포구 월드컵북로 396(상암동) 누리꿈스퀘어 비즈니스타워 10층
          ㈜ NE능률 (우편번호 03925)
펴 낸 날   2022년 9월 15일 개정판 제1쇄 발행
          2024년 6월 15일 제6쇄
전   화   02 2014 7114
팩   스   02 3142 0356
홈페이지   www.neungyule.com
등록번호   제1-68호
I S B N   979-11-253-4031-7 53740
정   가   15,500원

NE능률

고객센터

교재 내용 문의 : contact.nebooks.co.kr (별도의 가입 절차 없이 작성 가능)
제품 구매, 교환, 불량, 반품 문의 : 02-2014-7114
☎ 전화문의는 본사 업무시간 중에만 가능합니다.

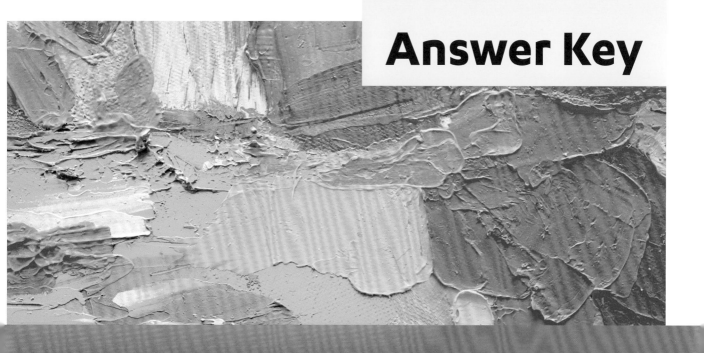

Answer Key

READING Inside

LEVEL 1

A 4-level curriculum
integration reading course

NE_ Neungyule

READING Inside

LEVEL 1

UNIT 01 | Shapes

READING 1 The Secret of Honeycombs

Mini Quiz
1 T 2 F

▶ **Reading Comprehension**
1 d 2 c 3 hexagon, least 4 a

▶ **Grammar Inside Level 1**
Check Up must

해석 벌은 놀라운 꿀 제조자이다. 하지만 그들은 인상적인 벌집 건축가이기도 하다. 벌집을 짓기 위해, 벌들은 그들의 몸에서 만들어내는 특별한 밀랍으로 서서히 벌집 칸들을 만든다. 그 밀랍은 만들어내기 어려워서, 그들은 그것을 효율적으로 사용해야 한다.

그러므로, 벌집 칸은 서로 완벽하게 딱 들어맞아야 한다. 원형은 서로 딱 들어맞지 않기 때문에 벌집 칸으로 좋은 모양이 아니다. 그것들 사이에 틈이 남게 되므로, 밀랍이 낭비된다. 공간을 남기지 않고 서로 딱 들어맞는 모양은 삼각형, 정사각형, 그리고 육각형이다. 벌은 육각형을 선택하는데, 왜일까?

여섯 개의 면이 있는 모양인 육각형은 꿀을 저장하는 데 가장 효율적인 것이다. 육각형은 다른 육각형들과 완벽하게 서로 딱 들어맞고, 그것은 아주 견고하다. 하지만 가장 중요한 것은, 그것이 가장 적은 양의 밀랍을 가지고 가장 많은 양의 꿀을 저장한다는 점이다. 그것은 다른 모양들과 비교하면, 육각형이 같은 면적을 둘러싸기 위해 최소한의 둘레를 사용하기 때문이다. 벌은 꿀을 만드는 데만 능숙한 게 아닌 듯하다. 그들은 수학에도 뛰어나다!

어휘 secret 몡 비밀 honeycomb 몡 벌집 impressive 혱 인상적인, 인상 깊은 builder 몡 건축가 (build 동 짓다) gradually 뷔 서서히, 점차 cell 몡 세포; 감방; *(큰 구조의 작은) 칸 special 혱 특별[특수]한 wax 몡 밀랍, 왁스 produce 동 만들어내다, 생산하다 efficiently 뷔 효율적으로 (efficient 혱 효율적인) fit 동 (꼭) 맞다 circle 몡 원, 원형 shape 몡 모양, 형태 gap 몡 틈, 간격 leave 동 떠나다; *남기다 waste 동 낭비하다 space 몡 공간, 자리 triangle 몡 삼각형 square 몡 정사각형 hexagon 몡 육각형 choose 동 선택하다, 고르다 store 동 저장[보관]하다 amount 몡 양 compared to ~와 비교하면 cover 동 덮다; *둘러싸다 area 몡 지역; *면적 good at ~을 잘하는 mathematics 몡 수학 (mathematical 혱 수학의) [문제] beneficial 혱 이로운 purpose 몡 목적 a variety of 다양한

구문 **2행** **To build a honeycomb**, bees gradually make cells from a special wax [that they produce from their bodies].
→ to build a honeycomb은 '벌집을 짓기 위해'라는 뜻으로, 〈목적〉을 나타내는 부사적 용법의 to부정사구이다.
→ [ ]는 선행사 a special wax를 수식하는 목적격 관계대명사절이다.

3행 The wax is hard **to produce**, so they must use it efficiently.
→ to produce는 형용사 hard를 수식하는 부사적 용법의 to부정사이다.

7행 The shapes [that fit together *without leaving* spaces] are the triangle, ...
→ [ ]는 선행사 the shapes를 수식하는 주격 관계대명사절이다.
→ 「without + v-ing」는 '~하는 것 없이', '~하지 않고'의 의미이다.

15행 **It seems that bees are** not only good at *making honey*.

→ 「it seems that + 주어 + 동사」는 '~은 …인 것 같다'의 의미이다.

→ making honey는 전치사 at의 목적어로 쓰인 동명사구이다.

READING 2 Composition Ⅷ

[V] Mini Quiz
Kandinsky wanted people who viewed his paintings to feel like they were listening to music.

▶ **Reading Comprehension**
1 d 2 d 3 c 4 loud bursts of sound

▶ **Grammar Inside Level 2**
[Check Up] 1 who 2 which

해석 Wassily Kandinsky는 1866년에 모스크바에서 태어났다. 그의 유아기에, 그의 부모님은 그에게 음악을 듣도록 권장했고, 그는 음악을 사랑하게 되었다. 이 사랑은 그의 예술에 큰 영향을 끼쳤다. 그는 심지어 그의 작품들의 이름을 '인상', '즉흥', '구성'과 같은 음악 용어들을 따서 지었다.

Kandinsky는 모양과 색이 음악의 다양한 소리와 감정을 전달할 수 있다고 믿었다. 한 가지 예가 「구성 Ⅷ」이다. 그는 그것을 1923년에 그렸다. 그것은 삼각형 그리고 원과 같은 모양들로 가득 찬 그림이다. 그리고 이 모양들은 모두 함께 작용하여 캔버스에 다양한 기하학적 형태를 만든다. 그는 검은색, 노란색, 분홍색과 같은 특정한 색으로 이러한 형태를 칠했다. Kandinsky에 따르면, 검은색은 침묵을 나타내고 노란색은 트럼펫이나 호른에 의해 만들어진 것과 같은 큰 폭발음을 나타낸다.

Kandinsky는 그의 그림을 보는 사람들이 음악을 듣고 있는 것처럼 느끼기를 원했다. 그는 이것으로 그들이 강한 감정을 느끼게 되길 바랐다. 당신은 「구성 Ⅷ」을 보면 어떤 음악이 들리는가? 그것은 당신이 어떻게 느끼게 하는가?

어휘 be born 태어나다 childhood [명] 어린 시절 encourage [동] 권장[장려]하다 influential [형] 영향력 있는 (influence [명] 영향(력); [동] 영향을 미치다) musical [형] 음악의 term [명] 용어, 말 communicate [동] 의사소통하다; *전(달)하다 emotion [명] 감정 example [명] 예시 full of ~로 가득 찬 create [동] 만들다, 창조하다 a variety of 다양한 form [명] 형태 according to ~에 따르면 represent [동] 나타내다 silence [명] 침묵 loud [형] (소리가) 큰 burst [명] 폭발, 파열 view [동] 보다 feel like ~처럼 느끼다 [문제] achievement [명] 업적 specific [형] 특정한

구문 [2행] ..., his parents **encouraged him to listen** to music, and he grew *to love it*.

→ 「encourage + 목적어 + to-v」는 '~가 …하도록 권장하다'라는 의미이다. 동사 encourage는 목적격 보어로 to부정사(to listen)를 취한다.

→ to love it은 〈결과〉를 나타내는 부사적 용법의 to부정사구이다.

[5행] He even **named** his works **after** music terms ... .

→ name A after B는 'A의 이름을 B를 따서 짓다'라는 의미이다.

[11행] ... all work together **to create** a variety of geometric forms on the canvas.

→ to create 이하는 〈결과〉를 나타내는 부사적 용법의 to부정사구이다.

[13행] ... yellow represents loud bursts of sound, such as **those** *made by* trumpets or horns.

→ 지시대명사 those는 앞의 명사구 loud bursts of sound를 가리킨다.

→ made by 이하는 지시대명사 those를 수식하는 과거분사구이다.

16행 Kandinsky **wanted people** [**who viewed his paintings**] **to feel** like they **were listening** ... .
→ 「want + 목적어 + to-v」는 '~가 …하기를 원하다'라는 의미이다. 동사 want는 목적격 보어로 to부정사(to feel)를 취한다.
→ [ ]는 선행사 people을 수식하는 주격 관계대명사절이다.
→ 「feel like + 주어 + 동사」는 '~가 …하는 것처럼 느끼다'의 의미이다.
→ 「was/were + v-ing」는 과거진행형으로 '~하고 있었다'라는 의미이다.

19행 How does it **make** you **feel**?
→ 「사역동사 make + 목적어 + 동사원형」은 '~가 …하게 하다'의 의미이다. 사역동사 make는 목적격 보어로 동사원형(feel)을 취한다.

● **VOCABULARY INSIDE**

Check Up　**1** efficient　**2** communicate　**3** emotion　**4** wasted　**5** store　**6** burst
　　　　　7 encourage　**8** gap

UNIT 02 | Origins

pp. 13-18

READING 1　The Language of Boxing

▶ **Reading Comprehension**
　1 b　**2** boxing, popular, England　**3** c　**4** b

▶ **Grammar Inside Level 2**
　Check Up c

해석　Q: 저는 다음에 나오는 문장들을 읽었는데 그것들을 이해할 수 없었어요.
　　　"나는 반 친구와 다퉜는데, 아무도 '나의 코너에 있지' 않았어. 완전히 '로프로 몰렸기' 때문에 나는 '수건을 던지고' 먼저 사과했어." 그것들을 설명해 주실 수 있나요?
　　A: 사실 그 표현들은 권투에서 온 것입니다. 백 년도 더 전의 영국에서는, 권투가 매우 인기가 있어서 몇몇 권투 용어가 영어에 들어오게 됐죠.
　　　1. 'In my corner'
　　　권투 경기의 라운드 사이에, 권투 선수들은 링의 맞은편 코너에서 휴식을 취하고 그동안 코치들이 그들을 북돋아 줍니다. 그래서 'in my corner'는 누군가가 나의 편에 있다는 것을 의미합니다.
　　　2. 'Throw in the towel'
　　　전통적으로, 권투 선수의 코치들은 링 안으로 수건을 던짐으로써 패배를 인정했고, 그래서 'throw in the towel'은 항복한다는 뜻입니다.
　　　3. 'On the ropes'

권투 링 가장자리 둘레에는 네 개의 로프가 있습니다. 권투 선수가 상대편에 의해 로프로 몰리면, 그 선수는 거의 패배한 것이죠. 따라서 'on the ropes'는 곤경에 처했다는 의미입니다.

이제 그 문장들이 이해되나요?

어휘 language 몡 언어 following 혱 다음에 나오는 sentence 몡 문장 argue 동 다투다 in one's corner ~의 편에 있는 throw in the towel 패배를 인정하다, 항복하다 apologize 동 사과하다 totally 뷔 완전히, 전적으로 on the ropes 궁지에 몰린 rope 몡 로프, 밧줄 explain 동 설명하다 expression 몡 표현 (어구) century 몡 100년, 세기 several 혱 몇몇(의) term 몡 용어, 말 enter 동 들어오다, 들어가다 round 몡 한 차례; *(권투·레슬링의) 라운드[회] match 몡 경기, 시합 rest 동 휴식을 취하다 opposite 혱 맞은 편[쪽]의, 건너편의 coach 몡 코치 encourage 동 (용기를) 북돋우다, 격려하다 on one's side ~의 편에 있는 traditionally 뷔 전통적으로 admit 동 인정하다 give up 항복[포기]하다 edge 몡 가장자리, 모서리 opponent 몡 (게임 등의) 상대 nearly 뷔 거의 defeat 동 패배시키다; 몡 패배 [문제] debt 몡 빚, 부채 trouble 몡 곤경, 곤란

구문

9행 ..., boxers rest in opposite corners of the ring **while** their coaches encourage them.
→ while은 〈시간〉을 나타내는 접속사로, '~하는 동안[사이]'라는 의미이다.

10행 So "in my corner" means [that someone is on my side].
→ [ ]는 동사 means의 목적어 역할을 하는 명사절이다.

13행 Traditionally, boxers' coaches admitted defeat **by throwing** a towel into the ring, ...
→ 「by + v-ing」는 '~함으로써'의 의미로, 〈수단〉 및 〈방법〉을 나타낸다.

16행 When a boxer **is driven** onto the ropes by the opponent, he or she **is** nearly **defeated**.
→ is driven과 is defeated는 모두 「be + v-ed」 형태의 수동태이다.

18행 So "on the ropes" means **to be** in trouble.
→ 동사 means의 목적어로 to be 이하의 to부정사구가 쓰였다.

READING 2 Looking at the Sky

Ⓥ Mini Quiz
The first telescope was built in 1608.

▶ **Reading Comprehension**
1 b 2 a 3 (1) F (2) T 4 b

▶ **Grammar Inside Level 2**
Check Up 1 wash 2 finish

해석   1600년대 이전에, 사람들은 밤하늘을 바라보았지만, 이것은 그들이 무슨 일이 일어나고 있는지 상상만 하게 했다. 구름 너머에 알려지지 않은 세상이 있었다. 하지만 이는 망원경의 발명으로 모두 바뀌었다.

최초의 망원경은 1608년에 만들어졌다. 사람들은 대개 이탈리아 과학자인 Galileo Galilei가 그것을 발명했다고 생각한다. 하지만 사실은, 독일인 안경 제작자인 Hans Lippershey였다. 하지만 그의 망원경은 아주 기초적이어서, 그것은 사물을 겨우 세 배 더 크게 보이도록 할 수 있었다.

Galileo는 Lippershey의 기구에 대해 듣고 자신만의 형태를 만들기로 결심했다. Galileo는 Lippershey의 디자인을 크게 개선했다. 그의 망원경은 Lippershey의 것보다 훨씬 더 견고했다. 안에 더 많은 렌즈가 있어서, 그의

망원경은 그가 사물을 서른 배까지 확대할 수 있게 했다. 그리고 그는 별을 연구하기 위해 망원경을 사용한 최초의 인물이었다. 그의 관찰을 통해, 그는 태양이 우리 태양계의 중심이라는 것을 깨닫게 되었다.

　　망원경의 발명은 우리가 우주를 더 잘 이해하는 데 도움을 주었다. Lippershey와 Galileo의 창의력과 노력은 과학이 크게 약진하도록 했다.

어휘　**prior to** ~ 이전에, ~에 앞서　**imagine** 통 상상하다　**happen** 통 일어나다, 발생하다　**beyond** 전 ~의 너머[저편]에　**unknown** 형 알려지지 않은, 미지의　**invention** 명 발명 (**invent** 통 발명하다)　**telescope** 명 망원경　**build** 통 짓다; *만들어내다　**eyeglass** 명 (외알) 안경　**basic** 형 기초[기본]적인　**appear** 통 ~인 것 같다; *나타나다　**times** 명 ~배　**device** 명 기구, 장치　**version** 명 형태, 판　**greatly** 부 대단히, 크게　**improve** 통 개선하다, 향상시키다　**magnify** 통 확대하다　**up to** ~까지　**through** 전 ~을 통해　**observation** 명 관찰, 관측 (**observe** 통 관찰[관측]하다)　**realize** 통 깨닫다, 알아차리다　**solar system** 태양계　**creativity** 명 창의력, 독창력　**effort** 명 수고; *노력　**take a leap forward** 약진[발전]하다　[문제] **space** 명 공간; *우주　**confirm** 통 확인[확증]하다　**previous** 형 이전의　**theory** 명 이론　**religious** 형 종교적인　**perspective** 명 견해, 관점

구문

1행　..., but this only let them imagine **what was happening**.
→ what 이하는 동사 imagine의 목적어 역할을 하는 의문사절이다.

2행　**Beyond the clouds** was **an unknown world**.
→ 〈방향〉 및 〈위치〉를 나타내는 전치사구 beyond the clouds가 문장의 맨 앞에 위치한 형태이다. 이 문장의 주어는 명사구 an unknown world이다.

5행　People usually think [Galileo Galilei, the Italian scientist, invented it].
→ [ ]는 동사 think의 목적어 역할을 하는 명사절로, 앞에 접속사 that이 생략되어 있다.

9행　Galileo [heard about Lippershey's device] **and** [*decided to make* his own version].
→ 접속사 and로 heard ... device와 decided 이하가 대등하게 연결되었다.
→ 동사 decide는 목적어로 to부정사(to make)를 취한다.

10행　His telescope was **much stronger** than Lippershey's.
→ 부사 much는 '훨씬'이란 의미로, 비교급 stronger를 강조한다.

11행　**With** more lenses in it, his telescope *allowed him to magnify* things up to thirty times.
→ 전치사 with는 〈동시상황〉을 나타내며, '~가 …해서[한 채로]'의 의미이다.
→ 「allow + 목적어 + to-v」는 '~가 …하는 것을 허락하다[가능하게 하다]'라는 의미이다. 동사 allow는 목적격 보어로 to부정사(to magnify)를 취한다.

12행　And he was the first person **to use** a telescope *to study* the stars.
→ to use 이하는 '~을 사용한'이라는 의미로, 명사구 the first person을 수식하는 형용사적 용법의 to부정사구이다.
→ to study 이하는 '~을 연구하기 위해'의 의미로, 〈목적〉을 나타내는 부사적 용법의 to부정사구이다.

16행　The invention of the telescope **helped us understand** space better.
→ 「help + 목적어 + 동사원형」은 '~가 …하는 것을 도와주다'라는 의미이다. 동사 help는 목적격 보어로 동사원형(understand)을 취한다.

UNIT 03 | Sports

pp. 19-24

READING 1   Wimbledon Traditions

◐ Mini Quiz

• the 2nd paragraph: First, the players must wear all white.
• the 3rd paragraph: Second, fans will consume a stunning 28,000 kilograms of strawberries and 7,000 liters of cream.

▶ **Reading Comprehension**

1 c   **2** d   **3** c   **4** in the summer, the season of the competition

▶ **Grammar Inside Level 1**

Check Up as tall as Ann

해석   이번 6월과 7월의 13일 동안, 수천 명의 테니스 팬들은 거의 테니스 그 자체만큼이나 오래된 행사인 윔블던에 참석할 것이다. 이 토너먼트는 1877년에 시작되었다. 그것은 개최되는 런던의 지역 이름을 따서 명명되었다. 팬들은 올해 대회를 즐기는 동안, 두 가지 재미있는 전통 또한 경험할 것이다.

첫째로, 선수들은 전부 흰옷을 입어야 한다. 오늘날 이것은 엄격한 복장 규정 규칙이지만, 원래 흰옷은 선수들이 팬들에게 더 잘 보이기 위한 방법이었다. 흰옷은 어두운 옷만큼 땀자국이 명확하게 보이지 않아서, 초창기의 윔블던 선수들은 땀에 젖어 보이는 것을 막기 위해 흰옷을 입었다.

둘째로, 팬들은 놀라울 정도인 28,000킬로그램의 딸기와 7,000리터의 크림을 먹게 될 것이다. 딸기와 크림은 윔블던에서 최초의 토너먼트 이후로 제공되어왔다. 그 당시, 그것은 유행하는 후식이었다. 영국 딸기는 대회 시즌인 여름에 자라기 때문에, 딸기와 크림은 여전히 윔블던에 완벽한 간식이다.

올여름 윔블던을 볼 계획이라면, 한번 이 전통에 참여해보면서 가장 좋아하는 선수를 응원하라!

어휘   tradition 몡 전통   thousands of 수천의   attend 동 참석하다   event 몡 사건; *행사   tournament 몡 토너먼트, 시합   begin 동 시작되다   area 몡 지역   take place 개최되다, 일어나다   competition 몡 경쟁; *대회   experience 동 경험하다   interesting 혱 재미있는, 흥미로운   strict 혱 엄격한, 엄한   dress code 복장 규정   rule 몡 규칙   originally 円 원래, 본래   clothing 몡 옷   sweat 몡 땀 (sweaty 혱 땀에 젖은, 땀투성이의)   stain 몡 자국, 얼룩   clearly 円 명확하게   dark 혱 어두운   early 혱 초창기의   consume 동 소비하다; *먹다   stunning 혱 (깜짝) 놀랄 만한   serve 동 제공하다   since 전 ~ 이후; 접 ~이기 때문에   fashionable 혱 유행하는   dessert 몡 후식   season 몡 계절; *(1년 중 특정 활동이 행해지는) 시즌   remain 동 여전히[계속] ~이다   perfect 혱 완벽한, 완전한   snack 몡 간식   plan 동 계획하다   take part in ~에 참여[참가]하다   cheer for ~을 응원하다   [문제] origin 몡 기원   hold 동 잡다; *개최하다   participate 동 참가[참여]하다   attract 동 (주의·흥미를) 끌다

attention [명] 주의 avoid [동] 막다, 방지하다

구문

[1행] **For** thirteen days this June and July, thousands of tennis fans will attend an event [almost as old as tennis **itself**]: Wimbledon.
→ '~ 동안'을 의미하는 전치사 for 뒤에는 thirteen days처럼 <시간의 길이>를 나타내는 말이 온다.
→ [ ] 앞에 「주격 관계대명사 + be동사」인 that[which] is가 생략되어 있다.
→ 재귀대명사 itself는 명사 tennis를 강조하기 위해 사용되었으며, '그 자체'라는 의미이다.

[3행] It **is named after** the area of London [where it takes place].
→ 「be + named after」는 '~의 이름을 따서 명명되다'를 의미한다.
→ [ ]는 선행사 the area of London을 수식하는 관계부사절이다. 관계부사 where는 「전치사 + 관계대명사」인 in which로 바꿔 쓸 수 있다.

[6행] ..., white clothes were a way **for players** *to look* better for their fans.
→ for player는 to부정사구 to look 이하의 의미상 주어이다.
→ to look 이하는 명사 a way를 수식하는 형용사적 용법의 to부정사구이다.

[8행] ..., so early Wimbledon players wore white **to *avoid*** *looking* sweaty
→ to avoid 이하는 '~을 막기 위해'라는 의미로, <목적>을 나타내는 부사적 용법의 to부정사구이다.
→ 동사 avoid는 동명사(looking)를 목적어로 취한다.

[12행] **Strawberries and cream *has*** *been served* at Wimbledon **since** the first tournament.
→ 주어부에서 strawberries와 cream이 접속사 and로 연결되어 있으나, '크림에 찍어 먹는 딸기'의 의미, 즉 하나의 음식 개념으로 인식되므로, 단수동사 has가 쓰였다.
→ has been served는 현재완료 수동태로 '(계속) ~되어왔다'의 의미이다.
→ since는 '~ 이후'의 의미인 전치사로, 보통 완료 시제와 함께 쓰인다.

[17행] **If** you *plan to watch* Wimbledon this summer, **try taking** part in these traditions, ...
→ if는 '(만약) ~라면'의 의미로, <조건>을 나타내는 접속사이다.
→ 동사 plan은 to부정사(to watch)를 목적어로 취한다.
→ 「try + v-ing」는 '한번 ~해보다'의 의미이다.

READING 2 From the Prison to the Gym

Mini Quiz
being too cruel

Reading Comprehension
1 b 2 punish prisoners 3 wheel, rotation, power 4 c

Grammar Inside Level 2
[Check Up] 1 are used 2 is elected

해석

체육관에서 트레드밀 위를 달리는 것은 힘든 일이다. 고작 15분이 마치 몇 시간처럼 느껴질 수 있다. 몇몇 사람들에게는, 그것이 벌처럼 느껴진다. 사실, 벌이 최초의 트레드밀 발명의 이유였다.

19세기 영국에서 트레드밀은 죄수들을 벌하기 위해 발명되었다. 그들은 거대한, 움직이는 바퀴의 계단을 걷도록

강요받았다. 바퀴의 회전은 방아에 동력을 공급하는 데 사용되었다. 그리고 그것이 '트레드밀'이라는 이름의 기원이다. 죄수들은 트레드밀 위에서 하루에 대략 여섯 시간을 보냈다. 그것은 매일 등산을 하는 것과 같다! 아니나 다를까, 많은 죄수들은 트레드밀 위를 걷는 것으로 녹초가 되었다.

　　(C) 트레드밀은 감옥에서 19세기 후반까지 사용되었다. (A) 1898년에, 그것은 너무 잔인하다는 이유로 금지되었다. (B) 하지만 트레드밀은 1950년대에 운동 기구로 놀라운 복귀를 했다. 신체 단련을 좋아하는 사람들에게 새로운 트레드밀은 운동하기에 쉽고 편리한 방법이었고, 오늘날에도 그것은 여전히 인기가 있다.

어휘　prison 몡 감옥 (prisoner 몡 죄수, 재소자)　gym 몡 체육관　treadmill 몡 트레드밀, 러닝머신　punishment 몡 (처)벌 (punish 동 처벌하다, 벌주다)　reason 몡 이유　invention 몡 발명 (invent 동 발명하다)　century 몡 세기　force 동 강요하다, ~하게 만들다　steps 몡 계단　wheel 몡 바퀴　rotation 몡 회전　power 동 동력을 공급하다, 작동시키다　mill 몡 방아, 방앗간　origin 몡 기원　spend 동 (돈을) 쓰다; *(시간을) 보내다　climb 동 오르다, 올라가다　unsurprisingly 뷔 아니나 다를까, 놀랄 것도 없이　exhausted 혱 녹초가 된, 기진맥진한　ban 동 금지하다　cruel 혱 잔인한, 잔혹한　make a comeback 복귀하다　equipment 몡 기구, 장비　fitness 몡 신체 단련, 건강　convenient 혱 편리한, 간편한　exercise 동 운동하다　remain 동 여전히[계속] ~이다　popular 혱 인기 있는, 유명한　[문제] painful 혱 고통스러운

구문

　1행　[Running on a treadmill at the gym] is hard work.
　　→ [ ]는 주어 역할을 하는 동명사구이다.

　4행　In 19th-century England, the treadmill was invented **to punish** prisoners.
　　→ to punish 이하는 '~을 벌하기 위해서'라는 뜻으로, 〈목적〉을 나타내는 부사적 용법의 to부정사구이다.

　5행　They **were forced to tread** on the steps of a large, moving wheel.
　　→ 「be + forced + to-v」은 '~하도록 강요받다'라는 의미이다.

　11행　In 1898, they **were banned** *for* [being too cruel].
　　→ were banned는 「be + v-ed」 형태의 수동태이다.
　　→ 전치사 for는 〈이유〉나 〈원인〉을 나타내며, '~ 때문에'의 의미이다.
　　→ [ ]는 전치사 for의 목적어 역할을 하는 동명사구이다.

　14행　... an easy and convenient way **to exercise**, and it *remains popular* today.
　　→ to exercise는 명사구 an easy and convenient way를 수식하는 형용사적 용법의 to부정사이다.
　　→ 「remain + 형용사」는 '여전히[계속] ~이다'라는 의미이다. 이때 형용사 popular는 주격 보어의 역할을 한다.

● **VOCABULARY INSIDE**

Check Up　**1** competition　**2** exhausted　**3** attend　**4** punishment　**5** convenient　**6** strict　**7** sweat　**8** banned

UNIT 04 | Jobs

pp. 25–30

READING 1 Analyze and Win

Mini Quiz
a game plan, to win

▶ **Reading Comprehension**
1 a 2 b 3 create[make] tactics to beat the opposition 4 c

▶ **Grammar Inside Level 1**
[Check Up] Peter sent me a message

해석 스포츠에서는, 작은 강점들이 커다란 보상을 가져올 수 있습니다. 스포츠 전력 분석가들은 스포츠팀이 그들이 이기도록 해주는 경기 전략을 세우는 것을 도와줍니다. 그런데 어떻게 하는 것일까요? 스포츠 전력 분석가인 James Parker에게 물어봅시다.

Q: 스포츠 전력 분석가들은 무엇을 하나요?

A: 저희는 팀과 선수들을 살펴보고, 그들의 강점과 약점을 찾습니다. 저희는 경기와 연습에 가고 경기 영상을 봄으로써 자료를 수집합니다. 그런 다음 저희는 코칭스태프에게 저희의 분석을 제공하죠. 그들은 상대편을 이기는 전술을 짜기 위해 그 자료를 사용합니다.

Q: 저에게 예를 들어줄 수 있나요?

A: 그러죠. 야구를 생각해 봅시다. 경기를 보고 나서, 저희는 한 타자가 왼손잡이 투수에 대해 타격률이 더 높다는 것을 알아차릴 수도 있습니다. 저희는 전술을 바꿀 수 있도록 코칭스태프에게 이 정보를 말해줍니다.

Q: 스포츠 전력 분석가가 되기 위해서 어떤 종류의 기량들이 필요한가요?

A: 우선, 스포츠에 아주 흥미가 있어야 합니다. 데이터베이스를 만들기 위해 뛰어난 수학, 연구, 그리고 분석 능력도 필요하죠. 마지막으로, 코칭 스태프에게 복잡한 자료를 설명하기 위해 훌륭한 의사소통 기량이 중요합니다.

어휘 analyze [동] 분석하다 (analyst [명] 분석가 analysis [명] 분석 analytical [형] 분석적인) advantage [명] 강점, 이점, 유리한 점 reward [명] 보상 plan [명] 계획; *(스포츠의) 전략, 작전 athlete [명] (운동) 선수 identify [동] (신원을) 확인하다; *찾다, 발견하다 strength [명] 힘; *강점, 장점 weakness [명] 약함; *약점 practice [명] 연습, 실습 data [명] 자료, 데이터 tactic [명] 전술 beat [동] 이기다, 물리치다 opposition [명] 상대[반대]측 example [명] 예, 사례 notice [동] 알아차리다 hitter [명] 타자 left-handed [형] 왼손잡이의 pitcher [명] 투수 interested in ~에 흥미가[관심이] 있는 excellent [형] 훌륭한, 탁월한 skill [명] 기량, 기술 communication [명] 의사소통 explain [동] 설명하다 complex [형] 복잡한 [문제] duty [명] 직무 train [동] 훈련시키다

구문 [1행] ... **help sports teams make** a game plan [that **allows them to win**].

→ 「help + 목적어 + 동사원형」은 '~가 …하는 것을 돕다'의 의미이다. 동사 help는 목적격 보어로 동사원형(make)을 취한다.

→ [ ]는 선행사 a game plan을 수식하는 주격 관계대명사절이다.

→ 「allow + 목적어 + to-v」는 '~가 …하는 것을 가능하게 하다[허락하다]'의 의미이다. 동사 allow는 목적격 보어로 to부정사(to win)를 취한다.

[6행] We collect data **by [going** to games and practices], *and* [**watching** videos ...].

→ 「by + v-ing」는 '~함으로써'라는 뜻으로, 〈수단〉 및 〈방법〉을 나타낸다.

→ 등위접속사 and로 going ... practices와 watching 이하가 대등하게 연결되었다.

10행 Could you **give me an example**?
→ 「give + 간접목적어 + 직접목적어」는 '~에게 …을 주다'의 의미이다.

11행 After **watching games**, we might notice [that a hitter has ... pitchers].
→ watching games는 전치사 after의 목적어 역할을 하는 동명사구이다.
→ [ ]는 동사 might notice의 목적어 역할을 하는 명사절이다.

13행 We **tell the coaching staff this information** *so that they can change* their tactics.
→ 「tell + 간접목적어 + 직접목적어」는 '~에게 …을 말해[알려]주다'의 의미이다.
→ 「so that + 주어 + can[could] + 동사원형」은 '~가 …할 수 있도록'이라는 의미이다.

16행 You also need excellent math, research, and analytical skills **to create** databases.
→ to create 이하는 '~을 만들기 위해'의 뜻으로, 〈목적〉을 나타내는 부사적 용법의 to부정사구이다.

READING 2 Art Conservators

Ⓥ Mini Quiz
A conservator is an expert at keeping artwork in good condition and repairing any damage.

▶ **Reading Comprehension**
1 b   2 c   3 (carefully) removing the damaged varnish and recoating it   4 c

▶ **Grammar Inside Level 1**
Check Up to buy some milk

해석   사람들은 검진이나 치료를 받기 위해 병원에 간다. 그런데 당신은 예술 작품도 치료가 필요하다는 것을 알고 있었는가? 복원전문가들은 꼭 의사가 환자를 돌보는 것처럼 예술품을 돌본다.
복원전문가는 예술품을 좋은 상태로 유지하고 손상을 보수하는 데 전문가이다. 예를 들어, 1990년에 누군가가 Rembrandt의 「야경꾼」에 산을 뿌렸다. 경비 요원들이 산을 약화시키기 위해 재빨리 물을 더했지만, 그럼에도 불구하고 광택제는 엉망이 되었다. 복원전문가들은 주의 깊게 손상된 광택제를 제거하고 덧칠하여 그 그림을 복원했다.
바로 의사들이 그러한 것처럼, 복원전문가들도 서로 다른 전공이 있다. 그들은 유화, 사진, 또는 조각과 같은 서로 다른 유형의 예술과 재료에 대해 전문가이다. 그들은 또한 각 재료들을 전시하는 가장 안전한 방법들을 안다. 예를 들어, 복원전문가들은 목재 조각품에 최상의 환경을 제공하기 위해 습도를 조절할 수 있다.
복원전문가들 덕분에, 더 많은 해 동안 Leonardo da Vinci, Raphael, 그리고 다른 위대한 예술가들의 작품을 즐기게 될 것이다. 그들의 시간과 노력이 우리의 소중한 문화사를 지키도록 도와준다.

어휘   conservator 명 [미술] 복원전문가   checkup 명 검진   treatment 명 치료, 처치   take care of ~을 돌보다   artwork 명 미술품   patient 명 환자   expert 명 전문가   condition 명 상태   repair 동 보수[수리]하다   damage 명 손상, 피해 (damaged 형 손상된)   throw 동 던지다   acid 명 산(酸)   guard 명 경비 요원   weaken 동 약화시키다   still 부 여전히; *그런데도, 그럼에도 불구하고   ruin 동 엉망으로 만들다   restore 동 복원[복구]하다   remove 동 제거하다   recoat 동 덧칠[겉칠]하다   specialty 명 전공   material 명 직물, 천; *재료   such as ~와 같은   photography 명 사진(술)   sculpture 명 조각(품)   adjust 동 조절[조정]하다   humidity 명 습도   provide 동 제공하다   environment 명 (주변의) 환경   valuable 형 소중한, 귀중한   cultural 형 문화의   [문제]   thanks to ~ 덕분에   display 동 전시하다, 내보이다

구문

4행 ... an expert **at** [keeping artwork in good condition] *and* [repairing any damage].
→ keeping ... condition과 repairing 이하는 전치사 at의 목적어 역할을 하는 동명사구이다.
→ 등위접속사 and로 동명사구 keeping ... condition과 repairing 이하가 대등하게 연결되었다.

6행 **Although** the guards quickly added water *to weaken the acid*, ...
→ although는 '비록 ~이지만'의 의미로, 〈양보〉를 나타내는 종속접속사이다.
→ to weaken the acid는 '산을 약화시키기 위해'라는 의미로, 〈목적〉을 나타내는 부사적 용법의 to부정사구이다.

10행 Conservators have different specialties, just as doctors **do**.
→ 대동사 do는 앞에 나온 have different specialties를 대신한다.

12행 They also know **the safest** ways *to display* each material.
→ safest는 형용사 safe의 최상급이고, 최상급 앞에는 보통 the를 쓴다.
→ to display 이하는 명사구 the safest ways를 수식하는 형용사적 용법의 to부정사구이다.

12행 For example, conservators can adjust the humidity **to provide** the best environment ... .
→ to provide 이하는 '~을 제공하기 위해'의 의미로, 〈목적〉을 나타내는 부사적 용법의 to부정사구이다.

15행 ..., and other great artists **will be enjoyed** for many more years.
→ 「will be + v-ed」는 '~될 것이다'의 의미로, 미래시제의 수동태이다.

19행 Their time and effort **helps protect** our valuable cultural history.
→ 동사 help는 목적어로 동사원형(protect)을 취할 수 있으며, 「help + 동사원형」은 '~하는 것을 돕다'의 의미이다.

● **VOCABULARY INSIDE**

Check Up　**1** expert　**2** restore　**3** valuable　**4** reward　**5** communication　**6** adjust
　　　　　　7 analyze　**8** tactic

UNIT 05 | Solutions

pp. 31-36

READING 1　The "Fly on the Wall" Method

Ⓥ **Mini Quiz**
you can separate your emotions from your experiences

▶ **Reading Comprehension**
1 b　**2** (1) F (2) T　**3** b　**4** prevent you from making calm, clear decisions

▶ **Grammar Inside Level 1**
Check Up to worry

해석　우리는 스트레스가 많은 사회에 살고 있어서, 스트레스는 피할 수 없는 것처럼 보인다. 그 결과, 스트레스 해소법은 우리의 일상생활에서 필수 요건이 되었다. 우리는 끊임없이 최신의 기법들을 찾고 그것들이 효과 있기를 바란다.

하지만, 스트레스 해소가 복잡할 필요는 없다. 사실, 오하이오 대학교에서 실시된 한 연구에 따르면, 스트레스를 해소하는 것은 꽤 간단하다. 당신은 그저 벽 위의 파리가 되어야 한다. 이상하게 들릴 수도 있지만, 그 연구 결과는 '벽에 붙은 파리' 기법의 효과성을 입증했다. 실험에서, 이 방법을 사용한 참가자들은 스트레스를 받는 상황에서 그들의 분노를 줄일 수 있었다. 게다가, 주어진 과제에서 그들의 성과는 30퍼센트가 향상했다.

비결은 자신의 상황을 객관적으로 보는 것이다. 벽에 붙은 파리의 관점처럼, 제삼자의 관점에서 그것을 바라봄으로써, 당신은 당신의 경험에서 감정을 분리할 수 있다. 격한 감정은 차분하고 명확한 결정을 내리는 것을 방해하기 때문에 이것은 중요하다. 하지만 외부의 관점을 갖는 것은 당신이 이러한 감정들을 통제하고, 더 나은 결정을 내리며, 스트레스를 줄일 수 있게 해준다.

어휘　fly 몡 파리　method 몡 방법　society 몡 사회　unavoidable 혱 피할 수 없는　relief 몡 해소, 완화 (relieve 동 해소하다, 줄이다)　requirement 몡 필수 요건　constantly 믠 끊임없이　look for ~을 찾다　latest 혱 최신의　technique 몡 기법　complicated 혱 복잡한　according to ~에 따르면　conduct 동 실시하다　prove 동 입증[증명]하다　effectiveness 몡 효과성　experiment 몡 실험　participant 몡 참가자　reduce 동 줄이다　anger 몡 분노　stressful 혱 스트레스가 많은　situation 몡 상황　furthermore 믠 게다가　performance 몡 성과, 실적　task 몡 과제　improve 동 향상되다　key 몡 비결　outsider 몡 제삼자; 외부인 (outside 혱 외부의)　point of view 관점　separate 동 분리하다　emotion 몡 감정　experience 몡 경험　intense 혱 격한　prevent 동 방해하다, 막다　decision 몡 결정　perspective 몡 관점　control 동 통제하다　lower 동 낮추다　[문제] face 동 직면하다　objectively 믠 객관적으로　handle 동 처리하다

구문

[3행] We constantly look for the latest techniques and hope [they work].
→ [ ]는 동사 hope의 목적어 역할을 하는 명사절로, 앞에 접속사 that이 생략되어 있다.

[5행] In fact, according to a study [conducted at Ohio University], *relieving stress is* ... .
→ [ ]는 명사 a study를 수식하는 과거분사구이다.
→ relieving stress는 주어 역할을 하는 동명사구이다.

[9행] In the experiment, participants [who used this method] were able to reduce ... .
→ [ ]는 선행사 participants를 수식하는 주격 관계대명사절이다.

[12행] **By looking** at it from an outsider's point of view, like *that* of a fly on the wall, you can **separate** your emotions **from** your experiences.
→ 「by + v-ing」는 '~함으로써'의 의미로, 〈수단〉 및 〈방법〉을 나타낸다.
→ 지시대명사 that은 앞의 a point of view를 가리킨다.
→ separate A from B는 'B에서 A를 분리하다'의 의미이다.

[14행] ... intense emotions **prevent** you **from making** calm, clear decisions.
→ 「prevent + 목적어 + from + v-ing」는 '~가 …하지 못하게 방해하다[막다]'의 의미이다.

[16행] But [having an outside perspective] *allows you **to control*** these emotions, ***make*** better decisions, *and **lower*** stress.
→ [ ]는 주어 역할을 하는 동명사구이다.
→ 「allow + 목적어 + to-v」는 '~가 …하게 하다'라는 의미로, 동사 allow는 목적격 보어로 to부정사(to control)를 취한다.
→ 등위접속사 and가 동사 allow의 목적격 보어인 to control, (to) make, (to) lower를 대등하게 연결한다.

READING 2   A Warm Embrace

ⓥ **Mini Quiz**
1 F   2 F

▶ **Reading Comprehension**
1 c   2 b   3 The price of incubators and their electricity costs are too high   4 b

▶ **Grammar Inside Level 1**
Check Up difficult

해석   아기들이 너무 일찍 태어나면, 그들은 자신을 따뜻하게 유지해주는 체지방이 거의 없다. 그들은 너무 작아서 자신의 체온을 조절할 수 없고, 이는 심장병이나 좋지 않은 두뇌 기능과 같은 중대한 건강 문제로 이어질 수 있다. 하지만, 그러한 문제들은 조산아들을 따뜻하게 유지함으로써 막을 수 있다.

그것이 인큐베이터의 역할이다. 안타깝게도, 대부분의 개발도상국에게 인큐베이터의 가격과 그것들의 전력비는 너무 비싸다. 보건 의료에 열정이 있는 한 젊은 경영학 석사 학생인 Jane Chen은 이 문제를 해결하고 싶었다. 그녀는 병원 직원들과 부모들은 전기를 사용하지 않는 저렴한 비용의 해결책이 필요하다는 것을 알고 있었다. Chen에게는 영리하면서도 간단한 아이디어가 있었는데, 바로 Embrace Warmer였다.

Embrace Warmer는 조산아를 따뜻하게 유지해주는 아주 작은 침낭이다. 안에는 왁스 주머니가 들어있다. 그 왁스는 인간의 체온인 섭씨 37도에서 녹는다. 사용자들은 간단하게 뜨거운 물로 그 왁스를 녹여 그것을 Embrace Warmer 내부에 다시 넣으면 된다. 그러면 Embrace Warmer는 한 번에 아기를 4시간에서 6시간까지 따뜻하게 유지할 수 있다. 이제 이 간단한 발명품이 수많은 조산아들을 따뜻하게 유지해주고 있다.

어휘   warm 형 따뜻한 (warmer 명 따뜻하게 하는 물건)   embrace 명 포옹   be born 태어나다   fat 명 (체)지방   regulate 동 규제하다; *조절하다   body temperature 체온   lead to ~로 이어지다   major 형 중대한, 주요한   disease 명 (질)병   poor 형 가난한; *좋지 않은   brain 명 (두)뇌   function 명 기능   premature 형 조산의, 정상보다 이른   incubator 명 인큐베이터   electricity 명 전력, 전기   cost 명 비용   developing country 개발도상국   passion 명 열정   healthcare 명 보건 의료 (서비스)   staff 명 직원   solution 명 해결책, 해법   simple 형 간단한, 단순한   tiny 형 아주 작은   sleeping bag 침낭   melt 동 녹다; 녹이다   degree 명 [온도 단위] 도   Celsius 형 섭씨의   user 명 사용자   place 동 놓다, 두다   inside 전 ~의 내부에; 부 안(쪽)에, 내부로   at a time 한 번에   thousands of 수천의; *수많은   [문제] pouch 명 주머니

구문   **1행** When babies are born too early, they have little body fat **to keep** them warm.
→ to keep 이하는 '~을 유지할'이란 의미로, 명사구 body fat을 수식하는 형용사적 용법의 to부정사구이다.

2행 They are **too small to regulate** their body temperature, ...
→ 「too + 형용사 + to-v」는 '너무 ~해서 …할 수 없는'의 의미이다.

4행 However, such problems **can be prevented** *by keeping* premature babies warm.
→ 조동사 can이 있는 수동태는 「can be + v-ed」로 나타내며, '~될 수 있다'의 의미이다.
→ 「by + v-ing」는 '~함으로써'의 의미로, 〈수단〉 및 〈방법〉을 나타낸다.

6행 That's [what incubators are for].
→ [ ]는 선행사를 포함한 관계대명사 what이 이끄는 관계대명사절로, 문장의 주격 보어 역할을 한다.

8행 Jane Chen, a young MBA student [with a passion for healthcare], *wanted to solve* ... .
→ [ ]는 명사구 a young MBA student를 수식하는 전치사구로, 전치사 with는 '~가 있는, ~을 가진'의 의미로

쓰였다.

→ 동사 want는 to부정사(to solve)를 목적어로 취한다.

9행 She knew [that ... parents needed a low-cost solution *that didn't use electricity*].

→ [ ]는 동사 knew의 목적어 역할을 하는 명사절이다.

→ that didn't use electricity는 선행사 a low-cost solution을 수식하는 주격 관계대명사절이다.

12행 The Embrace Warmer is a tiny sleeping bag [that keeps premature babies warm].

→ [ ]는 선행사 a tiny sleeping bag을 수식하는 주격 관계대명사절이다.

14행 Users [simply melt the wax with hot water] **and** [place it back inside ...].

→ 등위접속사 and로 simply melt ... water와 place 이하가 대등하게 연결되었다.

● VOCABULARY INSIDE

Check Up 1 prevent 2 disease 3 electricity 4 unavoidable 5 requirement 6 relief 7 complicated 8 regulate

UNIT 06 | Future

READING 1 Imagining the Future

Ⓥ Mini Quiz
  1 F 2 T

▶ **Reading Comprehension**
  1 a 2 c 3 release heat more efficiently 4 b

▶ **Grammar Inside Level 1**
  Check Up b

해석   십만 년 후 인간은 어떤 모습일까? 연구원들은 인체, 지구의 기후, 그리고 과학 기술을 살펴보았다. 그러고 나서 그들은 미래 인간의 외모에 대해 예측을 했다.

첫째로, 어떤 연구원들은 미래에는 인간의 몸 형태와 크기가 변할 것이라고 예견한다. 14세기 이후, 인간은 점진적으로 더 큰 뇌와 머리를 발달해오고 있다. 만약 이것이 지속된다면, 미래 인간들은 오늘날의 인간들보다 더 넓은 이마를 가지게 될지도 모른다. 지구의 기후 또한 더 따뜻해지고 있다. 만약 지구의 온도가 계속 오른다면, 사람들은 결국 열을 더 효율적으로 방출할 수 있는 키가 더 크고 더 날씬한 신체를 가지게 될지도 모른다.

둘째로, 미래 인간들은 더 어두운 피부와 더 큰 눈을 가질 수도 있다. 사람들은 그들이 다른 행성에서 살 수 있도록 해주는 기술을 만들지도 모른다. 만약 그런 일이 발생한다면, 더 어두운 피부가 지구 대기권 밖의 자외선으로부터 그들을 보호하는 것을 도울 수 있을 것이다. 또한, 더 커다란 눈은 태양으로부터 더 멀리 떨어진 행성에서 그들이 볼 수 있도록 도와줄 것이다.

Reading Inside Level 1 | **15**

다른 영향들이 사람들을 변화시킬 수도 있다. 아마 부모들은 자신들의 아이들을 위한 건강한 신체 또는 심지어 특정 얼굴을 디자인할 수도 있을 것이다. 시간만이 이 예측들이 맞을지 틀릴지를 증명해줄 것이다.

어휘 imagine [동] 상상하다 human [명] 인간, 사람 researcher [명] 연구원 look at ~을 (자세히) 살피다[검토하다] climate [명] 기후 technology [명] (과학) 기술 make a prediction 예측하다 (predict [동] 예측[예견]하다) appearance [명] 외모, (겉)모습 shape [명] 형태, 모양 since [전] ~이후[부터] gradually [부] 점진적으로, 서서히 develop [동] 발달[성장]시키다 brain [명] 뇌 continue [동] 지속되다, 계속되다 forehead [명] 이마 global [형] 지구의 temperature [명] 온도, 기온 rise [동] 오르다 eventually [부] 결국 release [동] 풀어 주다; *방출[발산]하다 heat [명] 열 efficiently [부] 효율[능률]적으로 skin [명] 피부 happen [동] 발생하다, 일어나다 UV radiation 자외선 atmosphere [명] 대기(권) planet [명] 행성 influence [명] 영향(력) design [동] 디자인[설계]하다 specific [형] 특정한, 구체적인 prove [동] 증명[입증]하다

구문

[4행] ... predict [that the shape and size of people's bodies will change in the future].

→ [ ]는 동사 predict의 목적어 역할을 하는 명사절이다.

[5행] Since the 14th century, humans **have been** gradually **developing** larger brains ... .

→ 「have/has been + v-ing」는 '~해오고 있다'라는 의미의 현재완료 진행형이다.

[6행] If this continues, future people may have **larger** foreheads **than** people today.

→ larger는 형용사 large의 비교급으로, 「형용사 비교급 + than」은 '…보다 더 ~한'이라는 의미이다.

[8행] If global temperatures **keep rising**, people may eventually have taller, thinner bodies [that can release heat more efficiently].

→ 「keep + v-ing」는 '계속해서 ~하다'의 의미로, 동사 keep은 목적어로 동명사(rising)를 취한다.

→ [ ]는 선행사 taller, thinner bodies를 수식하는 주격 관계대명사절이다.

[11행] ..., future humans **could** have darker skin and bigger eyes.

→ 조동사 could는 〈가능성〉을 나타내는 조동사로, '~일지도 모른다'의 의미이다. 조동사 could는 can보다 발생할 〈가능성〉이 더 낮은 일을 나타낼 때 쓰인다.

[12행] People might create technology [that will *allow them to live* on other planets].

→ [ ]는 선행사 technology를 수식하는 주격 관계대명사절이다.

→ 「allow + 목적어 + to-v」는 '~가 …하도록 해주다'의 의미로, 동사 allow는 목적격 보어로 to부정사(to live)를 취한다.

[12행] ..., darker skin could **help *protect*** them *from* UV radiation ... .

→ 동사 help는 동사원형(protect)을 목적어로 취할 수 있다.

→ protect A from B는 'B로부터 A를 보호하다'의 의미이다.

[13행] Also, larger eyes would **help them see** on planets [farther from the Sun].

→ 「help + 목적어 + 동사원형」은 '~가 …하는 것을 돕다'의 의미로, 동사 help는 목적격 보어로 동사원형(see)을 취한다.

→ [ ]는 명사 planets를 수식하는 형용사구로, 앞에 「주격 관계대명사 + be동사」인 that[which] are가 생략된 것으로 볼 수 있다.

[17행] Only time will **prove these predictions right or wrong**.

→ 「prove + 목적어 + 형용사」는 '~가 …하다고 증명[입증]하다'의 의미이며, 동사 prove는 목적격 보어로 형용사(right or wrong)를 취한다.

ⓥ Mini Quiz
upside-down, architects

▶ **Reading Comprehension**
1 b　2 (1) Mexico has a fast-growing population but little space. (2) Tall buildings are forbidden in order to preserve the city's cultural heritage.　3 d　4 a

▶ **Grammar Inside Level 1**
Check Up　time

해석
　　저리 비켜라, 고층 건물들아! 'Earthscraper'가 여기 있다! 이 뒤집힌 피라미드 형태는 멕시코 시티 건축가들의 획기적인 아이디어이다. 현재, 멕시코는 빠르게 인구가 늘고 있지만 공간은 작다. 또한, 도시의 문화유산을 보존하기 위해 높은 건물은 금지되어 있다. 이러한 문제점들을 다루는 한 방법으로써, 건축가들은 멕시코 시티의 주 광장인 소칼로 아래를 파낼 것을 제안했다.

　　지하에 숨겨질 것이므로, 65층짜리 Earthscraper는 도시의 역사적인 모습과 공공 공간을 유지할 것이다. 그리고 그 광장은 여전히 콘서트, 거리 행진과 같은 행사를 그 건축물의 거대한 유리 지붕 위에서 개최할 수 있을 것이다. 더욱이, 자연광이 유리를 통해 들어와서 건물 전체를, 심지어 가장 아래층까지도 밝혀줄 것이다! Earthscraper는 사무실, 상가, 그리고 거주를 위한 공간을 제공할 뿐만 아니라 박물관도 포함할 것이다. 게다가, 매 10번째 층은 정원 층이 될 것이다. 거기에 있는 식물들은 천연 공기 정화 장치로 작용할 것이다.

　　Earthscraper는 아직 계획 단계에 있지만, 그것은 미래의 중요한 건물 유형이 될 수 있다.

어휘
hidden ⓗ 숨겨진, 숨은 (hide ⓥ 감추다, 숨기다)　move over 자리를 양보하다　skyscraper ⓝ 고층 건물　upside-down ⓗ (위아래가) 뒤집힌　groundbreaking ⓗ 획기적인　architect ⓝ 건축가　currently ⓐ 현재, 지금　fast-growing ⓗ 빠르게 성장하는　population ⓝ 인구　space ⓝ 공간　forbid ⓥ 금지하다　preserve ⓥ 보존[보호]하다　cultural ⓗ 문화의　heritage ⓝ 유산　deal with ~을 다루다[처리하다]　issue ⓝ 쟁점; *문제(점)　suggest ⓥ 제안[제의]하다　dig ⓥ 파(내)다　square ⓝ 정사각형; *광장　underground ⓐ 지하에　maintain ⓥ 유지하다, 지키다　historical ⓗ 역사적인　look ⓝ 보기, 눈길; *모습　public ⓗ 공공의, 대중을 위한　hold ⓥ 잡고 있다; *개최하다, 열다　parade ⓝ 거리 행진, 퍼레이드　structure ⓝ 건축물, 구조물　massive ⓗ 거대한　brighten ⓥ 밝아지다; *밝히다　entire ⓗ 전체의　include ⓥ 포함하다　provide ⓥ 제공[공급]하다　in addition 게다가　filter ⓝ 정화 장치　planning ⓝ 계획　stage ⓝ 단계, 시기

구문
6행 Also, tall buildings **are forbidden** *in order to preserve* the city's cultural heritage.
→ are forbidden은 「be + v-ed」의 수동태이다.
→ 「in order + to-v」는 '~하기 위해'라는 의미이다.

8행 ..., architects **suggested digging** under Zócalo, ...
→ 동사 suggest는 목적어로 동명사(digging)를 취한다.

11행 Because it **will be hidden** underground, the 65-floor Earthscraper will maintain ... .
→ 「will be + v-ed」는 '~될 것이다'의 의미로, 미래시제의 수동태이다.

12행 And the square **will** still **be able to hold** events, ...
→ 「will be able + to-v」는 미래의 〈가능성〉 및 〈능력〉을 나타내며, '~할 수 있을 것이다'라는 의미이다.

16행 The Earthscraper will include a museum **as well as** provide space for ... .

→ A as well as B는 'B뿐만 아니라 A도'라는 의미로, A와 B의 품사 및 형태는 일치해야 한다.

● VOCABULARY INSIDE

Check Up 1 dig 2 entire 3 maintain 4 preserve 5 atmosphere 6 develop 7 prove 8 predict

UNIT 07 | Environment

pp. 43–48

READING 1 Tiny but Fatal

[V] Mini Quiz
smaller, reduce, marine

▶ Reading Comprehension
1 b 2 d 3 toxic[harmful] chemicals, food chain 4 c

▶ Grammar Inside Level 2
[Check Up] 1 X 2 O

해석 오늘날, 우리는 병, 펜, 그리고 가방을 포함해서, 많은 것들을 만들기 위해 플라스틱에 의존한다. 목록은 계속해서 이어진다. 안타깝게도, 플라스틱은 우리의 해양을 오염시키고 있다. 그리고 지금은 마이크로비즈라고 불리는 새로운 유형의 플라스틱 쓰레기가 상황을 훨씬 더 악화하고 있다.

마이크로비즈는 미세 플라스틱의 한 종류이다. 그것들은 모래보다 훨씬 더 작은 플라스틱 구슬이다. 이러한 마이크로비즈는 샴푸, 얼굴 각질제거제와 치약과 같이, 우리가 매일 사용하는 건강 관리 제품이나 화장품에 사용된다.

이런 제품들은 배수관으로 씻겨 내려가 하수도로 들어가기 때문에, 마이크로비즈가 강과 바다로 들어가게 된다. 마이크로비즈가 유해한 화학 물질을 지니고 있기 때문에 이것은 문제이다. 해양 생물들이 마이크로비즈를 먹으면, 독성 화학 물질이 축적되고 먹이사슬을 따라 전해진다. 이런 화학 물질은 심지어 우리가 먹는 몇몇 해산물에서 발견될지도 모른다.

우리는 해양 서식지에서의 마이크로비즈 양을 줄일 필요가 있다. 우리가 할 수 있는 한 가지 일은 제품을 더 현명하게 구매하는 것이다. 예를 들어, 우리는 유기농 치약을 구매하고 천연 피부 각질제거제로 설탕을 사용할 수 있다. 더 현명한 선택을 통해 우리는 우리의 바다와 우리 자신을 도울 수 있다.

어휘 tiny [형] 아주 작은 fatal [형] 치명적인 rely on ~에 의존[의지]하다 including [전] ~을 포함하여 list [명] 목록, 명단 on and on 계속해서, 쉬지 않고 pollute [동] 오염시키다 trash [명] 쓰레기 situation [명] 상황 microplastic [명] 미세 플라스틱 bead [명] 구슬 sand [명] 모래 product [명] 제품, 상품 cosmetics [명] 화장품 toothpaste [명] 치약 drain [명] 배수관 sewer system 하수도 harmful [형] 유해한, 해로운 chemical [명] 화학 물질 creature [명] 생물 toxic [형] (유)독성의 build [동] 짓다; *축적되다 food chain 먹이사슬 seafood [명] 해산물 reduce [동] 줄이다 amount [명] 양 marine [형] 해양[바다]의 habitat [명] 서식지 wisely [부] 현명하게 [문제] impact [명]

영향 organic ⓗ 유기농의

1행 Nowadays, we rely on plastic **to make** many things, including bottles, pens, and bags.
→ to make 이하는 '~을 만들기 위해'의 의미로, 〈목적〉을 나타내는 부사적 용법의 to부정사구이다.

3행 ... a new type of plastic trash [called microbeads] is *making the situation **even worse***.
→ [ ]는 명사구 a new type of plastic trash를 수식하는 과거분사구이다.
→ 「make + 목적어 + 형용사」는 '~을 …하게 만들다'라는 의미로, 동사 is making의 목적격 보어로 형용사(even worse)가 쓰였다.
→ 부사 even은 형용사 bad의 비교급 worse를 강조하며, '훨씬'의 의미이다.

5행 They are plastic beads [that are *even smaller than sand*].
→ [ ]는 선행사 plastic beads를 수식하는 주격 관계대명사절이다.
→ 「형용사 비교급 + than」은 '~보다 더 …한'의 의미이다.

6행 These microbeads **are used** in health care products and cosmetics [we use every day], ...
→ are used는 「be + v-ed」 형태의 수동태이다.
→ [ ]는 선행사 health care products and cosmetics를 수식하는 목적격 관계대명사절로, 앞에 that [which]이 생략되어 있다.

12행 ..., the toxic chemicals [build up] **and** [are passed up the food chain].
→ build up과 are passed 이하가 등위접속사 and로 병렬 연결되어 있다.

13행 These chemicals **might** even **be found** in some of the seafood we eat.
→ 조동사 might가 있는 수동태는 「might be + v-ed」로 나타내며, '~될지도 모른다'의 의미이다.

16행 One thing we can do is [buy products more wisely].
→ [ ]는 주격 보어이다. 주어부에 do가 포함된 경우 보어로 동사원형을 쓸 수 있다.

READING 2 A New Kind of Sportswear

ⓥ **Mini Quiz**
oil, polyester

▶ **Reading Comprehension**
 1 d 2 b 3 very large amounts of damaging CO_2 4 a, d

▶ **Grammar Inside Level 2**
 Check Up 1 barking 2 broken

많은 사람들이 축구를 사랑한다. 또한 어떤 팬들은 멋진 축구 셔츠를 사는 것을 매우 좋아한다. 하지만, 축구 셔츠가 종종 환경적으로 해로운 직물로 생산된다는 것을 알고 있는가?
   축구 셔츠가 어떻게 만들어지는지 생각해보라. 첫째, 디자이너와 엔지니어 팀은 그들의 초기 아이디어를 물리적 형태로 볼 필요가 있다. 그들은 가장 흔한 합성 직물인 폴리에스터로 셔츠를 만듦으로써 이 일을 한다. 안타깝게도, 폴리에스터는 플라스틱이고, 플라스틱은 석유로 만들어진다. 이는 석유가 셔츠를 위해 폴리에스터로 가공되어야 한다는 것을 의미한다. 하지만 이 과정은 엄청난 양의 에너지가 필요하다. 그리고 그 결과, 매우 많은 양의 해로운 이산화탄소가 대기 중으로 방출된다.

다행히도, 스포츠 브랜드와 축구 구단들은 이러한 환경친화적이지 않은 관행에 맞서 싸우기 시작하고 있다. 예를 들어, 최근 영국의 한 축구 구단은 부분적으로 커피콩으로 만들어진 셔츠를 출시했다. 게다가, 한 유명한 스포츠 의류 회사는 심지어 업사이클 된 해양 플라스틱으로 옷과 신발을 만들기 시작했다. 이러한 혁신들은 폴리에스터를 덜 사용함으로써 셔츠의 환경적 영향을 줄이고 있다.

어휘 **sportswear** 몡 운동복　**jersey** 몡 (운동 경기용) 셔츠　**produce** 동 생산하다　**environmentally** 閉 환경적으로　**harmful** 혱 해로운　**material** 몡 천, 직물　**consider** 동 생각[고려]하다　**initial** 혱 초기[최초]의　**physical** 혱 물리적인　**form** 몡 형태　**common** 혱 흔한　**oil** 몡 기름; *석유　**process** 동 가공하다; 몡 과정　**require** 동 필요로 하다　**damaging** 혱 해로운　**release** 동 방출하다　**atmosphere** 몡 대기　**club** 몡 (각종 스포츠의) 구단　**practice** 몡 연습; *관행, 관례　**for instance** 예를 들어　**partially** 閉 부분적으로　**additionally** 閉 게다가　**footwear** 몡 신발　**upcycle** 동 업사이클하다(기존 제품을 가치가 더 높은 새제품으로 만들다)　**marine** 혱 해양[바다]의　**innovation** 몡 혁신　**reduce** 동 줄이다　**impact** 몡 영향　[문제] **made from** ~로 만들어진

구문

2행 However, did you know [that football jerseys *are* often *produced* ...]?
→ [　]는 동사 know의 목적어 역할을 하는 명사절이다.
→ are produced는 「be + v-ed」 형태의 수동태이다.

7행 This means oil **must *be processed*** *into* polyester for the jerseys.
→ 조동사 must가 있는 수동태는 「must be + v-ed」로 나타내며, '~되어야 한다'의 의미이다.
→ 「be + processed into」는 '~가 …로 가공되다'의 의미로, process ~ into ...의 수동태 형태이다.

9행 ..., very large amounts of damaging CO$_2$ **are released** into the atmosphere.
→ are released는 「be + v-ed」 형태의 수동태이다.

12행 ... recently released a jersey [made partially from coffee beans].
→ [　]는 명사 a jersey를 수식하는 과거분사구이다.

15행 These innovations **are reducing** the environmental impact of jerseys *by using* less polyester.
→ are reducing은 「be + v-ing」 형태의 현재진행형으로, '줄이고 있다'의 의미이다.
→ 「by + v-ing」 형태의 by using은 '~함으로써'의 의미로, 〈수단〉 및 〈방법〉을 나타낸다.

● **VOCABULARY INSIDE**

Check Up　**1** pollute　**2** Harmful　**3** marine　**4** environmentally　**5** habitat　**6** physical　**7** process　**8** innovation

UNIT 08 | Health

pp. 49–54

READING 1 Building the Body's Defenses

Mini Quiz
1796, Edward Jenner

▶ **Reading Comprehension**
1 b 2 (1) T (2) T (3) F 3 the immune system is fighting the virus 4 remove, records, beat

▶ **Grammar Inside Level 1**
[Check Up] that

해석 1796년, 과학자 Edward Jenner는 8살 남자아이에게 우두를 주사했다. Jenner는 약한 우두 바이러스를 견뎌내는 것이 훨씬 더 위험한 바이러스인 천연두로부터 그 남자아이를 보호할 것이라고 정확히 믿었다. 이것이 세계 최초의 백신이었다. 그것은 신체의 면역 체계 때문에 효과가 있었다.

면역 체계는 신체를 보호한다. 바이러스가 공격하면, 우리는 기침이나 열과 같은 증상을 얻는다. 이것은 면역 체계가 바이러스와 싸우고 있다는 것을 의미한다. 면역 체계는 바이러스를 없애려 하고, 그것에 관한 정보를 기록한다. 그래서 같은 바이러스가 다시 공격하면, 면역 체계는 그것을 물리치는 방법을 기억한다.

백신은 약하거나 심지어 죽은 바이러스 세포를 함유하므로, 감염이 질병으로 발전하지는 않는다. 하지만, 신체는 그것이 심각한 위협이라고 생각한다. 이 점이 신체 방어 체계를 만들어서 미래에 온전한 바이러스가 실제로 침입하면 대비가 되는 것이다.

아직도 백신을 만들 수 없는 일부 질병들이 있지만, 과학자들은 우리가 언젠가 모든 위험한 바이러스에 대한 백신을 만들 수 있기를 희망한다!

어휘 build [동] 건축하다; *만들어내다 defense [명] 방어(물) inject [동] 주사[주입]하다 survive [동] 살아남다; *(고난 등을) 견디다 weak [형] 약한 protect [동] 보호하다 dangerous [형] 위험한 vaccine [명] (예방) 백신 work [동] 일하다; *효과가 있다 because of ~ 때문에 immune system 면역 체계 attack [동] 공격하다 symptom [명] 증상, 징후 such as ~와 같은 cough [명] 기침 fever [명] 열 remove [동] 없애다, 제거하다 record [동] 기록하다 beat [동] 물리치다, 이기다 contain [동] 함유[포함]하다 dead [형] 죽은 cell [명] 세포 infection [명] 감염 develop [동] 발전[발달]하다 disease [명] (질)병 serious [형] 심각한 threat [명] 위협 invade [동] 침입하다

구문

[2행] ... that [surviving the weak cowpox virus] would protect ... *much more dangerous* ... .
→ [ ]는 that 이하의 명사절에서 주어 역할을 하는 동명사구이다.
→ 부사 much는 형용사 비교급 more dangerous를 강조하며, '훨씬'의 의미이다.

[9행] So **if** the same virus attacks again, the immune system remembers [how to beat it].
→ if는 '만약 ~한다면'의 의미로, 〈조건〉을 나타내는 접속사이다.
→ [ ]는 '~하는 방법'의 의미인 「how + to-v」의 형태로, 동사 remembers의 목적어 역할을 한다.

[15행] There are still some diseases [that we can't make vaccines for], but scientists hope [that one day we **will be able to make** ...]!
→ 첫 번째 [ ]는 선행사 some diseases를 수식하는 목적격 관계대명사절이다.
→ 두 번째 [ ]는 동사 hope의 목적어 역할을 하는 명사절이다.
→ 「will be + able + to-v」는 미래의 〈가능성〉 및 〈능력〉을 나타내며, '~할 수 있을 것이다'의 의미이다.

READING 2 Liftware: A New Medical Innovation

Mini Quiz
But Liftware allows them to feed themselves.

▶ **Reading Comprehension**
1 d 2 b 3 a 4 opposite, feed

▶ **Grammar Inside Level 1**
[Check Up] c

해석

식사는 우리의 삶에서 중요한 부분이다. 그것은 친구나 가족과 시간을 보낼 기회이다. 안타깝게도, 어떤 사람들은 이런 경험을 온전히 즐길 수 없다. 이는 그들이 파킨슨 병을 앓고 있기 때문이다.

파킨슨병은 신경계에 영향을 미쳐, 사람들이 통제할 수 없이 떨게 만든다. 이것은 그들이 접시에서 입으로 음식을 들어 올리는 것을 극히 힘들게 만든다. 과거에는 손이 떨리는 것을 막기 위해 특수한 장치가 사용되었다. 하지만 그것들은 크게 효과적이지 않았다.

하지만, Liftware라고 불리는 새로운 전자 숟가락은 다르다. 손이 떨리는 것을 막으려 하는 것 대신, Liftware는 숟가락 그 자체를 멈춘다. 이 장치는 디지털카메라와 같은 손 떨림 방지 기술을 사용한다. 사람의 손이 떨면, 손잡이에 있는 아주 작은 모터가 숟가락의 우묵한 부분을 그 반대 방향으로 움직인다. 결과적으로, 떨림이 대략 75퍼센트 감소하게 된다.

파킨슨병을 앓고 있는 사람들은 보통 타인이 먹여줘야 하기 때문에 이것은 중요하다. 하지만 Liftware는 그들이 자기 자신을 먹일 수 있도록 해준다. 이는 그들을 더욱 독립적으로 만들어주고 그들이 다시 식사를 즐길 수 있도록 해준다.

어휘

medical [형] 의학의 innovation [명] 혁신 meal [명] 식사, 끼니 part [명] 부분, 일부 opportunity [명] 기회 spend [동] (돈을) 쓰다; *(시간을) 보내다 fully [부] 완전히, 충분히 experience [명] 경험 suffer [동] 앓다, 고통받다 affect [동] 영향을 미치다 nervous system 신경계 shake [동] 흔들다; *떨다, 떨리다 uncontrollably [부] 통제할 수 없이 past [명] 과거 device [명] 장치, 기구 effective [형] 효과적인 electronic [형] 전자의 instead of ~ 대신에 the same A as B B와 같은 A tiny [형] 아주 작은 handle [명] 손잡이 move [동] 움직이다 bowl [명] 사발; *둥글고 우묵한 부분 opposite [형] 반대의, 다른 편의 direction [명] 방향 reduce [동] 감소하다 feed [동] 먹여주다 allow [동] 허락하다, 가능하게 하다 independent [형] 독립적인 [문제] extremely [부] 극히, 매우 lift [동] 들어 올리다 plate [명] 접시, 그릇

구문

[2행] They are an opportunity **to spend** time with friends or family.
→ to spend 이하는 명사 an opportunity를 수식하는 형용사적 용법의 to부정사구이다.

[5행] **This is because** they suffer from Parkinson's disease.
→ this is because는 '이는 ~하기 때문이다'의 의미로, because 뒤에 〈이유〉 또는 〈원인〉에 해당하는 내용이 온다.

[7행] ..., so it **causes people to shake** uncontrollably.
→ 「cause + 목적어 + to-v」는 '~가 …하게 하다[야기하다]'라는 의미로, 동사 cause는 목적격 보어로 to부정사(to shake)를 취한다.

[8행] This makes **it** extremely difficult **for them to lift** food ... .
→ it은 가목적어, for them은 to lift의 의미상 주어, to lift 이하가 진목적어이다.

8행 In the past, special devices **were used** *to stop* **their hands from shaking**.

→ were used는 「be + v-ed」 형태의 수동태이다.

→ to stop 이하는 '~을 막기 위해'의 뜻으로, 〈목적〉을 나타내는 부사적 용법의 to부정사구이다. .

→ 「stop + 목적어 + from + v-ing」는 '~가 …하는 것을 막다'라는 뜻이다.

11행 A new electronic spoon **called Liftware**, however, is different.

→ called Liftware는 명사구 a new electronic spoon을 수식하는 과거분사구이다.

17행 ... because people with Parkinson's disease often **have to be fed** by others.

→ '~해야 한다'의 의미인 조동사 have to의 수동태는 「have to be + v-ed」로 '~되어야 한다'의 의미이다.

18행 But Liftware **allows them to feed** themselves.

→ 「allow + 목적어 + to-v」는 '~가 …하게 해주다'라는 의미이다. 동사 allow는 목적격 보어로 to부정사(to feed)를 취한다.

19행 This [**makes them more independent**] *and* [allows them to enjoy their meals again].

→ 「make + 목적어 + 형용사」는 '~을 …하게 만들다'의 의미이다. 동사 makes의 목적격 보어로 형용사 more independent가 쓰였다.

→ makes ... independent와 allows 이하는 등위접속사 and로 병렬 연결되어 있다.

● **VOCABULARY INSIDE**

Check Up   1 fever   2 opportunity   3 beat   4 effective   5 feed   6 symptom
7 suffer   8 invade

UNIT 09 | Colors   pp. 55–60

READING 1   The Colors of *Bedroom in Arles*

Ⓥ **Mini Quiz**
three

▶ **Reading Comprehension**
1 d   2 (1) F (2) T   3 d   4 d

▶ **Grammar Inside Level 1**
Check Up 1 great   2 sleepy

해석   「아를의 침실」은 Vincent van Gogh의 그림이다. 그것은 그가 아를에 있는 동안 머물렀던 방을 보여준다. 1888년과 1889년에, 그는 이 그림의 세 가지 버전을 만들었다. 시간이 지나면서 페인트가 바래왔기 때문에, 이 그림들의 색은 현재 거의 똑같아 보인다.

그러나, 복원전문가들은 색깔이 원래 서로 상당히 달랐다는 것을 발견했다. 예를 들어, 그 그림들의 벽들은 지금 모두

파란색으로 보인다. 하지만 첫 번째 버전에서 그것들은 원래 연보라색이었다.

이 발견으로 인해, 이제 복원전문가들은 원래의 색이 Van Gogh가 그것들을 그릴 당시의 심리 상태를 반영한다고 믿는다. 예를 들어, 그는 첫 번째 버전에 따뜻한 색을 사용했는데 왜냐하면 그것은 그의 인생에서 행복한 시기에 그려졌기 때문이다. 하지만 1889년의 두 번째 버전은 더 어둡고 더 차가워 보이는 색으로 칠해졌다. 그 당시, 그는 막 오랜 우정을 잃었고 자기 귀의 일부를 잘랐다.

추가적인 조사를 통해, 복원전문가들은 Van Gogh와 그의 감정 상태에 대한 더 명확한 이해를 얻기를 바란다.

어휘 bedroom 몡 침실 painting 몡 그림 (paint 몡 그림물감; 동 그리다; 칠하다) stay 동 머무르다 during 전 ~ 동안 version 몡 버전, ~판 since 접 ~ 이래로; *~ 때문에 fade 동 바래다, 희미해지다 over time 시간이 지나면서 almost 부 거의 conservator [미술] 복원전문가 discover 동 발견하다 (discovery 몡 발견) originally 부 원래 (original 혱 원래의) quite 부 상당히, 꽤 each other 서로 wall 몡 벽 light 혱 (색 등이) 연한 purple 몡 보라색 reflect 동 반영하다 state 몡 상태 mind 몡 심리, 마음 for instance 예를 들어 further 혱 더 먼; *추가의 investigation 몡 조사, 수사 [문제] express 동 표현하다 emotion 몡 감정 (emotional 혱 감정의) reveal 동 드러내다 long-term 혱 오랜 (기간의), 장기(간)의 confirm 동 확인[확증]하다 gain 동 얻다 clear 혱 명확한

구문

1행 It shows the room [he stayed in] during his time in Arles.
→ [ ]는 선행사 the room을 수식하는 목적격 관계대명사절로, 앞에 목적격 관계대명사 that[which]이 생략되었다.

3행 Since the paint **has faded** over time, the colors in these paintings ... .
→ has faded는 「have/has + v-ed」 형태의 현재완료로, 〈계속〉을 의미한다.

9행 ..., the conservators now believe [that the original colors reflect Van Gogh's state of mind at the time *he painted them*].
→ [ ]는 동사 believe의 목적어 역할을 하는 명사절이다.
→ he painted them은 선행사 the time을 수식하는 관계부사절로, 앞에 관계부사 when이 생략되었다.

13행 But the second version from 1889 **was painted** in colors [that looked darker ...].
→ was painted는 「be + v-ed」 형태의 수동태이다.
→ [ ]는 선행사 colors를 수식하는 주격 관계대명사절이다.

15행 ..., the conservators **hope to gain** a clearer understanding of Van Gogh ... .
→ 동사 hope는 목적어로 to부정사(to gain)를 취한다.

READING 2 How Chromatography Works

Mini Quiz
1 F 2 T

▶ **Reading Comprehension**
1 a 2 d 3 which pigments the original color is composed of 4 paper, water / separate

▶ **Grammar Inside Level 1**
Check Up 1 When 2 until

당신이 프리즘을 통해 햇빛을 볼 때, 당신은 프리즘이 그것을 무지개의 모든 색깔로 나누는 것을 알아차릴 것이다. 마찬가지로, 색깔의 색소도 분리될 수 있다. 이 기법은 크로마토그래피, 또는 '컬러 라이팅'으로 알려져 있다.

모든 색소는 무게가 다르다. 이것은 그들이 다른 속도로 이동되고 결국 다른 곳에 도달하게 된다는 것을 의미한다. 크로마토그래피에서, 과학자들은 종이 한 장을 따라 색소를 옮길 물과 같은 액체를 사용한다. 그렇게 함으로써, 그들은 원래의 색깔이 어떤 색소로 구성되어 있는지를 발견할 수 있다.

이 기법을 사용하여 당신은 검은색을 분리할 수 있다. 당신이 필요한 모든 것은 여과지, 검은 매직펜, 그리고 약간의 물이다. 먼저, 여과지에 검은색을 묻히고 물에 살짝 적신다. 그러고 나면 물은 퍼지기 시작할 것이다. 물이 퍼지는 것을 멈출 때까지 그 색에 어떤 일이 일어나는지 보아라. 당신은 검은색이 자홍색이나 청록색과 같은 다른 색소로 분리된다는 것을 알게 될 것이다. 아주 쉽다!

chromatography 뎡 크로마토그래피, 색층분석법   work 됨 일하다; *작용하다   sunlight 뎡 햇빛   through 졘 ~을 통해   prism 뎡 프리즘   notice 됨 알아차리다   separate 됨 나누다, 분리하다; 분리되다   rainbow 뎡 무지개   likewise 붐 마찬가지로   pigment 뎡 색소   technique 뎡 기법   known as ~로 알려진   weight 뎡 무게   speed 뎡 속도   end up 결국 ~하게 되다   liquid 뎡 액체   such as ~와 같은   carry 됨 옮기다, 나르다   along 졘 ~을 따라   composed of ~로 구성된   filter paper 여과지   marker 뎡 매직펜, 마커   apply 됨 묻히다, 바르다   dip 됨 담그다   spread 됨 퍼지다

1행 ..., you will notice [the prism *separates* it *into* all of the colors in a rainbow].
→ [ ]는 동사 will notice의 목적어 역할을 하는 명사절로, 앞에 접속사 that이 생략되었다.
→ separate A into B는 'A를 B로 분리하다'의 의미이다.

5행 This means [that they *are moved* around at different speeds and end up in ...].
→ [ ]는 동사 means의 목적어 역할을 하는 명사절이다.
→ are moved는 「be + v-ed」 형태의 수동태이다.

7행 ..., scientists use liquids, such as water, **to carry** pigments along a piece of paper.
→ to carry 이하는 명사구 liquids, such as water를 수식하는 형용사적 용법의 to부정사구이다.

8행 **By doing** so, they can discover [which pigments the original color is composed of].
→ 「by + v-ing」는 '~함으로써'의 의미로 〈수단〉 및 〈방법〉을 나타낸다.
→ [ ]는 동사 can discover의 목적어로 쓰인 간접의문문 형태의 명사절이다.

10행 All [you need] is a filter paper, black markers, and some water.
→ [ ]는 선행사 all을 수식하는 목적격 관계대명사절로, 앞에 목적격 관계대명사 that이 생략되었다.

14행 Watch [what happens to that color] until the water *stops spreading*.
→ [ ]는 동사 watch의 목적어로 쓰인 간접의문문 형태의 명사절이다.
→ 동사 stop은 목적어로 동명사(spreading)를 취한다.

16행 You will find [that the black will separate into other pigments *such as magenta or cyan*].
→ [ ]는 동사 will find의 목적어 역할을 하는 명사절이다.
→ 전치사구 such as magenta or cyan은 명사구 other pigments를 수식한다.

19행 It's **that** easy!
→ 부사 that은 '그렇게', '그 정도'라는 의미이며, 형용사 easy를 수식한다.

UNIT 10 | **Technology**

pp. 61–66

READING 1 **Ransomware**

▽ Mini Quiz
In most cases, security experts say you shouldn't pay ransoms.

▶ Reading Comprehension
1 d **2** lock, money[ransom] **3** c **4** c

▶ Grammar Inside Level 1
Check Up asked him to speak up

해석 여느 다른 날과 마찬가지로, 당신은 컴퓨터를 시작하고 일할 준비를 한다. 당신이 최신 프로젝트를 클릭하지만, 경고 창이 나타난다. 그것은 파일을 열기 위해서 당신은 돈을 지불해야 한다고 말한다! 당신은 랜섬웨어에 의해 공격받은 것이다.

랜섬웨어는 악성 소프트웨어의 한 종류이다. 사이버 범죄자들은 개별 파일이나 심지어 전체 시스템을 잠그기 위해 그것을 사용한다. 그런 다음 파일들을 다시 열기 위해 돈을 요구한다. 랜섬웨어 범죄는 더 흔해지고 있으며, 그것들은 기업들에게 큰 문제이다. 2021년에, 미국의 한 육류 공급 회사가 랜섬웨어에 공격받았다. 그것은 그 회사가 많은 현지 및 국제 공장에서 운영을 중단하도록 했다. 결국, 그 회사는 그들의 시스템에 다시 접속하기 위해 1,100만 달러의 몸값을 지불했다.

대부분의 경우, 보안 전문가들은 몸값을 지불하지 말아야 한다고 말한다. 해커들에게 돈을 지불하는 것은 그들이 그것을 다시 하도록 부추긴다. 또한 그것은 당신이 파일을 되돌려 받는다는 것을 보장하지 않는다. 랜섬웨어를 처리하려면, 예방이 치료보다 낫다. 보안 및 장치 소프트웨어를 항상 최신 상태로 유지하고, 온라인에서는 조심하라.

어휘 ransomware 몡 랜섬웨어 warning 몡 경고 pop up 불쑥 나타나다 pay 됭 지불하다 attack 됭 공격하다 form 몡 형태; *종류 cybercriminal 몡 사이버 범죄자 lock 됭 잠그다 individual 옝 개별의 entire 옝 전체의 demand 됭 요구하다 unlock 됭 열다 crime 몡 범죄 common 옝 흔한 operation 몡 운영 local 옝 현지의 international 옝 국제적인 plant 몡 식물; *공장 in the end 결국 million 몡 100만 get access to ~에 접속[접근]하다 security 몡 보안 expert 몡 전문가 hacker 몡 해커 encourage 됭 부추기다 guarantee 됭 보장하다 get ~ back ~을 되찾다 deal with ~을 처리하다 device 몡 장치 up to date 최신의 [문제] supply 됭 공급하다 contact 됭 연락하다 reboot 됭 재시동하다

구문 1행 Like any other day, you start your computer and **get ready to work**.
→ 「get ready + to-v」는 '~할 준비를 하다'의 의미이다.

[2행] It says [you must pay money *to open* the file]!
→ [ ]는 동사 says의 목적어 역할을 하는 명사절로, 앞에 접속사 that이 생략되었다.
→ to open 이하는 '~을 열기 위해'의 의미로, 〈목적〉을 나타내는 부사적 용법의 to부정사구이다.

[3행] You'**ve been attacked** by ransomware.
→ 「have/has been + v-ed」는 현재완료 수동태로, 해당 현재완료는 동작의 〈완료〉를 의미한다.

[5행] Cybercriminals use it **to lock** individual files or even entire systems.
→ to lock 이하는 '~을 잠그기 위해'의 의미로, 〈목적〉을 나타내는 부사적 용법의 to부정사구이다.

[7행] Ransomware crimes **are becoming** more common, ...
→ 「be + v-ing」는 현재진행형으로, '~하는 중이다', '~하고 있다'라는 의미이다.

[13행] [Paying hackers] encourages them to do it again.
→ [ ]는 문장의 주어 역할을 하는 동명사구이다.

READING 2 NASA's Spinoff Technology

Mini Quiz
memory foam, a handheld[cordless] vacuum, and a water purification system

▶ **Reading Comprehension**
1 b 2 protect test pilots during flights 3 c 4 c

▶ **Grammar Inside Level 2**
[Check Up] have forgotten

해석 NASA는 우주에서 많은 것을 성취했지만, 그들의 연구는 지구에도 큰 영향을 미쳤다. 중요한 것은, 그것이 NASA의 스핀오프로 이어졌다는 것이다. 이 제품들은 지구상의 사람들의 일상생활을 개선해왔다.

그러한 하나의 예시가 메모리폼이다. 원래, 연구원들은 비행 중의 시험 조종사를 보호하기 위해 그것을 만들었다. 하지만, 사람들은 이제 소파, 신발, 그리고 침대에 그것을 사용한다.

심지어 당신의 소형 진공청소기도 우주 연구에 의해 영감을 받았다! NASA는 아폴로 11호의 달 착륙 임무 동안 달의 표면 아래로부터 입자를 추출하고 싶었다. 그래서 NASA는 한 제조 회사와 함께 연구했다. 그 회사는 나중에 무선 청소기를 만들어냈다.

NASA는 또한 정수 시스템을 만들었다. 그것은 땀, 호흡, 그리고 소변을 깨끗한 식수로 바꿀 수 있다. 이 과정이 역겨워 보일 수도 있지만, 그것은 국제 우주 정거장의 많은 우주 비행사들을 구해왔다. 게다가, 이 시스템에서 나오는 물은 사실 지구의 대부분의 식수보다 깨끗하다.

이것들은 NASA가 만든 실용적인 발명품 중 소수에 불과하다. 미래에, 우리는 더 놀라운 NASA의 스핀오프를 보게 될 것이다!

어휘 achieve [동] 성취[달성]하다 space [명] 우주 research [명] 연구 (researcher [명] 연구원) impact [명] 영향; [동] *영향을 끼치다 as well ~도 lead to ~로 이어지다 improve [동] 개선하다 everyday [형] 일상의 memory foam 메모리폼 originally [부] 원래 design [동] 만들다 protect [동] 보호하다 flight [명] 비행 handheld [형] 소형인, 손에 쥐고 쓸 수 있는 vacuum [명] 진공청소기 inspire [동] 영감을 주다 extract [동] 추출하다 particle [명] 입자 below [전] ~ 아래에 surface [명] 표면 landing [명] 착륙 (land on ~에 착륙하다) mission [명] 임무 manufacturing [명] 제조 cordless [형] 무선의 purification [명] 정화 convert [동] 바꾸다 sweat [명] 땀

breath [명] 호흡 urine [명] 소변 drinking water 식수 a handful of 소수의, 한 움큼의 practical [형] 실용적인 incredible [형] 놀라운 [문제] astronaut [명] 우주비행사 oxygen [명] 산소 disgusting [형] 역겨운

구문

[4행] Originally, researchers designed it **to protect** test pilots during flights.
→ to protect 이하는 '~을 보호하기 위해'의 의미로, 〈목적〉을 나타내는 부사적 용법의 to부정사구이다.

[7행] Even your handheld vacuum **was inspired by** space research!
→ was inspired by는 「be + v-ed + by」 형태의 수동태로, '~에 의해 영감을 받다'의 의미이다.

[8행] NASA **wanted to extract** particles from below the surface of the Moon ... .
→ 동사 want는 to부정사(to extract)를 목적어로 취한다.

[12행] It can **convert** sweat, breath, and urine **into** clean drinking water.
→ convert A into B는 'A를 B로 바꾸다'의 의미이다.

[13행] In addition, the water from this system is actually **cleaner than** most of our planet's ... .
→ 「형용사 비교급 + than」은 '~보다 더 …한'의 의미이다.

● VOCABULARY INSIDE

Check Up 1 inspired 2 astronaut 3 vacuum 4 practical 5 individual 6 crime 7 guarantee 8 demanded

UNIT 11 | Food

pp. 67–72

READING 1 Measuring Fire

Mini Quiz
the Carolina Reaper

▶ **Reading Comprehension**
1 b 2 c 3 a 4 500

▶ **Grammar Inside Level 1**
Check Up c

해석

당신은 방금 낯선 고추 하나를 먹었다. 당신의 입은 불타는 듯하고, 당신은 땀을 흘리고 있다! 다음에, 어떤 낯선 고추를 먹기 전에 스코빌 매움 지수 척도를 확인해라! 미국인 과학자 Wilbur Scoville이 1912년에 이 척도를 만들어냈다. 그것은 고추의 매운 정도를 측정하기 위해 사용된다. 각각의 고추는 0부터 백만이 넘는 단위까지 특정한 숫자를 가진다. 더 큰 스코빌 수치의 고추가 더 맵다!

고추의 매운 정도를 시험하기 위해, 맛을 보는 사람들은 설탕물과 고추 추출물이 섞인 것을 마신다. 설탕물은 매운 맛이 사라질 때까지 더해진다. 설탕물에 대한 고추 추출물의 이 비율이 고추의 스코빌 수치이다. 예를 들어, 8,000은

가장 매운 할라페뇨의 스코빌 수치이다. 이것은 할라페뇨 추출물 1그램의 매운맛이 사라지기 전에 8,000그램의 설탕물이 필요하다는 것을 의미한다! 맛을 보는 사람들의 혀에 다행히도, 지금은 고추가 얼마나 매운지를 측정하기 위해 보통 기계가 사용된다.

2013년에, Carolina Reaper가 지구상에서 가장 매운 고추가 되었다. 이것의 스코빌 수치는 220만이다! 그것은 후추 스프레이보다 더 강력하다. 상상되는가?

어휘 measure [동] 측정하다, 재다 unfamiliar [형] 낯선, 익숙지 않은 pepper [명] 후추; *고추 on fire (몸의 일부가) 불타는 듯한[화끈거리는] sweat [동] 땀을 흘리다 heat [명] 열; *매움, 매운맛 scale [명] 규모; *척도 strange [형] 이상한; *낯선 spiciness [명] 매운 정도[맛] million [명] 100만 hot [형] 더운; *매운 test [동] 시험하다 taster [명] 맛을 보는 사람, 맛 감식가 mix [동] 섞다; [명] *혼합물 extract [명] 추출물 add [동] 더하다, 첨가하다 ratio [명] 비율 disappear [동] 사라지다 luckily [부] 다행히도 tongue [명] 혀 machine [명] 기계 on Earth 지구상에서 [문제] a variety of 다양한 (vary [동] 다양하다) rate [동] 등급을 매기다 represent [동] 나타내다

구문 [2행] Next time, check the Scoville Heat Unit Scale before [eating any strange peppers]!
→ [ ]는 전치사 before의 목적어 역할을 하는 동명사구이다.

[4행] It **is used** *to measure* the spiciness of peppers.
→ is used는 「be + v-ed」 형태의 수동태이다.
→ to measure 이하는 '~을 측정하기 위해'의 뜻으로, 〈목적〉을 나타내는 부사적 용법의 to부정사구이다.

[4행] **Each pepper has** a special number *from* zero *to* over a million units.
→ 「each + 단수명사」는 단수 취급하므로, 단수 동사인 has가 쓰였다.
→ from A to B는 'A에서 B까지'라는 의미이다.

[9행] This **ratio of** pepper extract **to** sugar water is the pepper's Scoville number.
→ ratio of A to B는 'B에 대한 A의 비율'의 의미이다.

[11행] This means [8,000 grams of sugar water is needed before *the heat from one gram of the jalapeño extract* disappears]!
→ [ ]는 동사 means의 목적어 역할을 하는 명사절로, 앞에 접속사 that이 생략되었다.
→ the heat ... extract는 접속사 before가 이끄는 부사절에서 주어 역할을 하는 명사구이다.

[12행] ..., machines are now often used to measure [how hot peppers are].
→ [ ]는 '~가 얼마나 …한지'의 의미인 「how + 형용사/부사 + 주어 + 동사」 형태의 간접의문문으로, to부정사 to measure의 목적어로 쓰였다.

READING 2 A Baker's Dozen

Mini Quiz
Usually "a baker's dozen" means 13 baked items

▶ **Reading Comprehension**
1 a 2 a 3 they received 13 instead 4 c

▶ **Grammar Inside Level 1**
[Check Up] much

빵집에 12개짜리 쿠키 한 묶음을 사러 간다고 상상해보라. 당신은 제빵사의 한 묶음을 가지고 돌아온다. 몇 개의 쿠키를 가지고 있는가? 답은 12개가 아니다. 13개이다. 그리고 훨씬 더 좋게도, 추가 쿠키는 무료이다!

'제빵사의 한 묶음'이라는 관용구는 어디서 온 것일까? 많은 사람들은 무게가 너무 적게 나가는 빵을 파는 것을 금하는 오래된 법에서 그것이 유래했다고 생각한다. 많은 나라에서, 제빵사가 표준보다 더 가벼운 빵 덩어리를 팔아서 고객들을 속이다 걸리면, 엄하게 처벌받을 수 있었다. 뜻하지 않게 누군가를 속이는 것을 피하고자, 영국의 제빵사들은 그들의 고객에게 추가 빵을 주었다. 고객들이 빵 12개 묶음을 요청하면, 그들은 대신 13개를 받았다. 그리고 결국에는 사람들이 이 풍습을 지칭하기 위해 '제빵사의 한 묶음'이라는 용어를 사용하기 시작했다.

이 관용구는 400여 년도 더 전에 처음으로 사용되었지만, 오늘날에도 여전히 잘 알려져 있다. 보통 '제빵사의 한 묶음'은 13개의 구워진 물품들을 의미하지만, 사람들은 때때로 13개의 무언가를 의미하기 위해 그것을 사용한다. 예를 들어, 당신은 다음번에 빵집에 갈 때 13명의 친구를 데리고 갈 수도 있다.

baker 몡 제빵사 (**bakery** 몡 빵집, 제과점) **bake** 동 (빵·과자 등을) 굽다 **dozen** 몡 12개짜리 한 묶음 **extra** 혱 추가의 **free** 혱 자유로운; *무료의 **phrase** 몡 [문법] (관용)구 **come from** ~에서 나오다[비롯되다] **originate** 동 유래하다 **ancient** 혱 고대의; *오래된 **law** 몡 법 **against** 전 ~에 반대하여; *~하지 않도록 **weigh** 동 무게가 ~이다 **cheat** 동 속이다, 사기 치다 **light** 혱 밝은; *가벼운 **normal** 혱 보통의; *표준의 **loaf** 몡 빵 한 덩이 **severely** 븿 엄하게, 심하게 **punish** 동 처벌하다 **customer** 몡 고객 **ask for** (물건 등을) 요청하다 **receive** 동 받다 **instead** 븿 대신에 **eventually** 븿 결국 **term** 몡 용어, 말 **refer to** ~을 지칭하다 **custom** 몡 풍습, 관습 **item** 몡 물품, 품목 [문제] **related to** ~와 관련된 **accidentally** 븿 뜻하지 않게, 우연히 **promote** 동 홍보하다 **persuade** 동 설득하다

1행 Imagine [that you go to a bakery *to buy* a dozen cookies].
→ [ ]는 동사 imagine의 목적어 역할을 하는 명사절이다.
→ to buy 이하는 '~을 사기 위해'의 의미로, 〈목적〉을 나타내는 부사적 용법의 to부정사구이다.

4행 ... it originated from ancient laws against [selling bread *that* weighed too little].
→ [ ]는 전치사 against의 목적어 역할을 하는 동명사구다.
→ that 이하는 선행사 bread를 수식하는 주격 관계대명사절이다.

6행 ..., if a baker **was caught cheating** his customers ..., he *could be* severely *punished*.
→ 「be caught + v-ing」는 '(옳지 못한 일을) 하다가 붙잡히다'의 의미이다.
→ could be punished는 조동사(could)가 들어간 수동태로, '~될 수 있었다'의 의미이다.

8행 To **avoid cheating** anyone accidentally, bakers in England *gave their customers extra bread*.
→ 동사 avoid는 목적어로 동명사(cheating)를 취한다.
→ 「give + 간접목적어 + 직접목적어」는 '~에게 …을 주다'의 의미이다.

10행 And eventually people began **to use** the term "a baker's dozen" *to refer* to the custom.
→ to use 이하는 동사 began의 목적어 역할을 하는 명사적 용법의 to부정사구이다.
→ to refer 이하는 '~을 지칭하기 위해'라는 의미로, 〈목적〉을 나타내는 to부정사구이다.

12행 **Although** this phrase *was* first *used* over 400 years ago, it *is* still well *known* today.
→ 접속사 although는 '(비록) ~이긴 하지만'의 의미이다.
→ was used와 is known은 「be + v-ed」 형태의 수동태이다.

14행 ..., you **could** take a baker's dozen of your friends with you *next time you go* to the bakery.
→ 조동사 could는 〈가능성〉을 의미하며 '~할 수 있다'의 의미이다.

→ 「next time + 주어 + 동사」는 '다음번에 ~가 …할 때'의 의미이다.

UNIT 12 | Places
pp. 73-78

READING 1   A Forbidden Palace

❷ Mini Quiz
yellow was the color of the emperor

▶ **Reading Comprehension**
   1 d   **2** b   **3** allowed to enter it without permission from the emperor   **4** a

▶ **Grammar Inside Level 2**
   Check Up My dog was named Fluffy by Mom.

해석   우리는 모두 어떤 일을 하는 것을 금지당한 적이 있다. 그런데 하나의 도시도 금지될 수 있을까? 그렇다, 가능하다! 자금성은 1406년부터 1420년까지 북경에 지어졌다. 이 중국의 황궁은 약 500년 동안 중국 정부의 중심이었다.

　당신은 이곳이 왜 '도시'라고 불리는지 궁금해할지도 모른다. 이 성은 단지 하나의 건물이 아니다. 거의 1,000개의 건물이 있어서, 그곳은 작은 도시만큼이나 크다. 그리고 황제의 허가 없이는 누구도 그곳에 들어갈 수 없었기 때문에 그곳은 '금지된'이라고 불린다. 사실 26피트 높이의 벽이 그것을 에워싸고 있었다!

　하지만 마지막 황제 Puyi가 1912년에 실각했을 때 모든 것이 바뀌었다. <u>그 후에 그것의 정치적 중심으로서의 역할은 끝났지만, 위대한 역사적 가치는 계속되었다.</u> 자금성은 1987년에 세계문화유산이 되었고, 지금은 고궁 박물원으로 알려져 있다. 그곳은 중국 전통 건축 양식의 아름다움을 볼 가장 좋은 장소 중 하나이다. 예를 들어, 노란색이 황제의 색이었기 때문에 모든 지붕은 노란색이다! 그뿐만 아니라, 그곳은 백만 개가 넘는 중국 유물과 예술품을 보유하고 있다!

어휘   forbidden 혱 금지된 (forbid 동 금지하다)   palace 명 성, 궁전   certain 혱 확실한; *어떤   build 동 (건물을) 짓다, 건설하다 (building 명 건물)   imperial 혱 제국의; *황제의   center 명 중심   government 명 정부, 정권   wonder 동 궁금하다   almost 부 거의   allow 동 허락[용납]하다   enter 동 들어가다   permission 명 허가, 허락   emperor 명 황제   surround 동 에워싸다, 둘러싸다   last 혱 마지막의   step down 실각하다, 물러나다   World Heritage Site 세계문화유산   known as ~로 알려진   traditional 혱 전통의   architecture 명 건축 양식   roof 명 지붕   furthermore 부 뿐만 아니라, 더욱이   hold 동 잡다; *보유하다   artifact 명 공예품; *유물   work of art 예술품, 미술품   [문제] political 혱 정치적인   cultural heritage 문화 유산   consist of ~로 구성되다   role 명 역할   historical 혱 역사(상)의   value 명 가치   continue 동 계속되다

1행 We **have** all **been forbidden** to do certain things.
→ 「have/has been + v-ed」의 현재완료 수동태이다. 이 문장에서 현재완료는 〈경험〉을 나타낸다.

5행 You might wonder [why it is called a "city]."
→ [ ]는 동사 might wonder의 목적어로 쓰인 「의문사 + 주어 + 동사」 어순의 간접의문문이다.

6행 There are almost 1,000 buildings, so it is **as big as** a small city.
→ 「as + 형용사 + as」는 '~만큼 …한'의 의미의 원급 비교 표현이다.

7행 And it **is called "forbidden"** because no one **was allowed to enter** it ... .
→ is called "forbidden"과 was allowed to enter는 둘 다 「동사 + 목적어 + 목적격 보어」를 수동태로 표현한 것이다.

12행 It is **one of the best places** *to see* the beauty of traditional Chinese architecture.
→ 「one of the + 최상급 + 복수명사」는 '가장 ~한 …들 중 하나'라는 의미이다.
→ to see 이하는 명사구 the best places를 수식하는 형용사적 용법의 to부정사구이다.

READING 2 Unique Homes

Ⓥ Mini Quiz
nomadic people from Central Asia, such as Mongolians

▶ **Reading Comprehension**
1 d 2 c 3 a 4 to withstand strong winds

▶ **Grammar Inside Level 2**
Check Up Your order will be shipped tomorrow (by them).

해석

당신은 광대한 왕국의 지배자이다. 당신의 영토를 살펴보기 위해 당신은 밖으로 나간다. 하지만 거대한 성 대신, 당신은 당신의 텐트를 떠난다! 그것은 몽골 제국의 황제, Genghis Khan이 했던 일이다. 그는 텐트의 일종인 유르트에서 살았다. 전통적으로 '게르'라고 알려져 있으며, 그것은 원형의 이동이 가능한 집이다. 그것의 뼈대는 강한 바람을 견디기 위해 구부릴 수 있는 나무로 만들어진다. 겉은 실내를 따뜻하게 유지하기 위해 펠트로 감쌌다. 다섯 명에서 열다섯 명의 사람들이 한 유르트에서 살 수 있다.

수천 년 동안, 이것은 몽골인과 같은 중앙아시아의 유목민들에게 주된 주거 형태였다. 그들은 매년 3번에서 4번 이동하곤 했다. 그들의 유르트는 쉽게 치워졌다가, 이동되고, 재조립될 수 있었다. 또한 그것들을 짓는 데는 30분에서 3시간밖에 걸리지 않았다.

유르트는 몽골 밖에서도 발견될 수 있다. Genghis Khan의 제국이 중앙아시아 밖으로 확장되면서, 유르트 문화도 그러했다. 유르트는 1970년대까지 터키에서 사용되었다. 심지어 지금도 헝가리의 시골 지역에서 그것들을 볼 수 있다.

어휘 unique 휑 독특한 ruler 몡 지배자, 통치자 vast 휑 광대한, 거대한 kingdom 몡 왕국 land 몡 땅 instead of ~ 대신에 huge 휑 거대한 castle 몡 성 emperor 몡 황제 Mongol 몡 몽골 (Mongolian 몡 몽골 사람) empire 몡 제국 traditionally 휊 전통적으로 round 휑 둥근 portable 휑 이동이 가능한, 휴대할 수 있는 frame 몡 틀, 액자; *뼈대 made of ~로 만들어진 bendable 휑 구부릴 수 있는 withstand 통 견디다, 이겨 내다 wrap 통 둘러싸다 main 휑 주된 take down (해체하여) 치우다, 분해하다 move 통 움직이다; *(집 등을) 옮기다, 이사하다 put ~ back together ~을 재조립하다 easily 휊 쉽게 expand 통 확장[확대]되다; 확장하다 countryside 몡 시골 지역 [문제] imaginary 휑 상상의 set up ~을 설치하다

1행 You go outside **to look at** your land.
→ to look at 이하는 '~을 보기 위해'의 의미로, 〈목적〉을 나타내는 부사적 용법의 to부정사구이다.

3행 That's [what Genghis Khan, emperor of the Mongol Empire, did].
→ [ ]는 선행사를 포함한 관계대명사 what이 이끄는 명사절로, 주격 보어 역할을 한다.

7행 Its frame is made of bendable wood **to withstand** strong winds.
→ to withstand 이하는 '~을 견디기 위해'의 의미로, 〈목적〉을 나타내는 부사적용법의 to부정사구이다.

9행 The outside **is wrapped** in felt to *keep the inside warm*.
→ is wrapped는 「be + v-ed」 형태의 수동태로, '~로 둘러싸이다'의 의미이다.
→ 「keep + 목적어 + 형용사」는 '~을 …하게 유지하다'의 의미이다. 동사 keep의 목적격 보어로 형용사 warm이 쓰였다.

12행 They **would move** three to four times every year.
→ 「would + 동사원형」은 '~하곤 했다'의 의미로, 과거에 자주 반복했던 일에 대해 말할 때 쓰인다.

13행 Their yurts could be **taken** down, **moved**, **and put** back together easily.
→ 등위접속사 and로 과거분사 taken, moved, put이 대등하게 연결되어 있다.

14행 **It** also **took** only thirty minutes to three hours **to build** them.
→ 「it takes + 시간 + to-v」는 '~하는 데 (…의 시간)이 걸리다'의 의미이다.

16행 **As** Genghis Khan's empire expanded outside of Central Asia, *so did yurt culture*.
→ 접속사 as는 '~하면서'의 의미이다.
→ 「so + do/does/did + 주어」는 '~도 그렇다'라는 의미의 도치 구문이다. 이 문장에서 did는 앞의 동사구 expanded outside of Central Asia를 받는 대동사이다.

● **VOCABULARY INSIDE**

Check Up　1 vast　2 permission　3 withstand　4 architecture　5 wonder　6 Portable
7 forbid　8 expand

UNIT 13 | Activities

pp. 79–84

READING 1　A Playground Favorite

◎ **Mini Quiz**
father

▶ **Reading Comprehension**
1 b　2 b　3 a　4 b

해석   정글짐은 대부분의 학교 운동장에서 발견될 수 있는 간단한 구조물이다. 그것들은 많은 공간이 필요하지 않고, 아이들을 즐겁게 하며, 심지어 수학을 가르치는 데 도움을 줄 수 있기 때문에 인기가 있다!

   최초의 공식 정글짐은 Sebastian Hinton에 의해 발명되었다. 그가 어렸을 때, 그의 아버지는 그에게 대나무 구조물을 만들어 주었다. 그 구조물은 3차원의 정육면체로 만들어졌고, 그의 아버지는 그것을 수학의 좌표계처럼 사용했다. 그는 수평 축의 한 세트를 X1, X2, 그리고 X3라고 불렀고, X축과 직각인 수평 축은 Y1, Y2, 그리고 Y3라고 불렀다. 마지막으로 그는 수직 축을 Z1, Z2, 그리고 Z3이라고 불렀다. 게임으로, 그는 "X1, Y3, Z2! 출발!"이라고 외치곤 했고, Sebastian은 그 정확한 지점에 도착하기 위해 쏜살같이 가곤 했다.

   1920년 어느 날, Sebastian은 일리노이주 위네카의 교육감에게 이 이야기를 들려주었다. 교육감은 그 아이디어에 관심이 있었고, 그래서 그들은 함께 그것에 착수했다. 그것이 최초의 공식적인 '정글짐'이 만들어진 방식이다. 그리고 곧, 그것들은 전국의 놀이터에 지어졌다.

어휘 **playground** 명 운동장, 놀이터 **simple** 형 단순한 **structure** 명 구조물, 건축물 **most** 형 대부분의 **popular** 형 인기 있는 **space** 명 공간 **entertaining** 형 즐겁게 하는 **math** 명 수학 (**mathematics** 명 수학) **official** 형 공식적인 **invent** 동 발명하다 **bamboo** 명 대나무 **made of** ~로 만들어진 **three-dimensional** 형 3차원의, 입체적인 **cube** 명 정육면체 **pole** 명 막대기; *축 **right angle** 직각 **yell out** 외치다, 소리치다 **race** 동 쏜살같이[급히] 가다 **correct** 형 정확한 **spot** 명 지점, 장소 **create** 동 만들다, 창조하다 [문제] **iron** 형 철의 **interested in** ~에 관심이 있는

구문 1행 Jungle gyms are simple structures [that *can be found* on most school playgrounds].
→ [ ]는 선행사 simple structures를 수식하는 주격 관계대명사절이다.
→ 조동사 can이 있는 수동태는 「can be + v-ed」로 나타내며, '~될 수 있다'의 의미이다.

6행 The first official jungle gym **was invented by** Sebastian Hinton.
→ was invented by는 「be + v-ed + by」 형태의 수동태로, '~에 의해 발명되다'의 의미이다.

11행 He **called one set of horizontal poles X1, X2, and X3**, ...
→ 「call + 목적어 + 목적격 보어」는 '~을 …라고 부르다'라는 의미이다. 이 문장에서 목적어는 one set of horizontal poles이며 목적격 보어는 X1, X2, and X3이다.

13행 ..., he **would yell** out "X1, Y3, Z2! Go!", and Sebastian **would race** *to get* ... .
→ 「would + 동사원형」은 '~하곤 했다'라는 의미로, 과거에 자주 반복했던 일에 대해 말할 때 쓰인다.
→ to get 이하는 '~에 도착하기 위해'의 의미로, 〈목적〉을 나타내는 부사적 용법의 to부정사구이다.

17행 That's [how the first official "jungle gym" was created].
→ 「how + 주어 + 동사」는 관계부사절로, '~가 …하는 방식(방법)'의 의미이다.

READING 2 The Ultimate Workout

Mini Quiz

- the 2nd paragraph: First, if you consistently train hard, you'll get in shape quickly.
- the 3rd paragraph: Secondly, martial arts help you reduce your stress levels.
- the 4th paragraph: Lastly, practicing martial arts will improve your memory.

▶ **Reading Comprehension**

1 d 2 burn, gain 3 recall 4 grow stronger

▶ **Grammar Inside Level 1**

[Check Up] 1 speaks 2 I don't remember you

해석 마음, 몸, 정신을 동시에 단련하고 싶은가? 무술에 시도해 보는 건 어떤가? 수천 년 동안, 사람들은 운동하고 그들 자신을 방어하기 위해 무술을 사용해왔다. 하지만 무술을 배워야 하는 다른 이유들이 있다.

첫째, 지속해서 열심히 훈련하면, 금방 좋은 몸 상태를 유지할 것이다. 당신은 유도나 태권도와 같은 무술에서 고강도 운동을 해서 칼로리를 줄이고 과도한 지방을 태울 수 있다. 게다가, 당신은 훈련하면서 근육을 키울 수 있다.

두 번째로, 무술은 스트레스 수준을 낮추는 데 도움을 준다. 그것은 발차기와 주먹으로 때리는 동작에서 분노를 풀어내도록 돕는다. 게다가, 태극권과 가라테와 같은 명상에 초점을 맞춘 무술은 당신이 진정하도록 도울 것이다.

마지막으로, 무술을 연습하는 것은 당신의 기억력을 향상할 것이다. 자연스럽고 효과적으로 동작을 결합하기 위해, 당신은 모든 행동을 기억해 내야 한다. 뇌의 신경 시냅스와 경로는 반복되는 각각의 움직임과 함께 더 강해지고, 이것은 더 나은 기억력으로 이어진다.

분명히, 무술은 환상적인 운동이다. 그러니 한번 시도해보는 게 어떤가?

어휘 ultimate [형] 궁극적인; *최고의 workout [명] 운동 (work out 단련하다, 운동하다) spirit [명] 정신 at the same time 동시에 martial art 무술 defend [동] 방어하다 reason [명] 이유, 원인 consistently [부] 지속해서 train [동] 훈련하다 get in shape 좋은 몸 상태를 유지하다 intensity [명] 강도, 세기 judo [명] [무술] 유도 burn [동] 태우다 excess [형] 과도한, 초과한 fat [명] 지방 in addition 게다가 gain [동] 얻다 muscle [명] 근육 reduce [동] 줄이다; *낮추다 let out 풀어내다, 내보내다 anger [명] 분노 meditation [명] 명상 tai chi 태극권 calm down 진정하다 improve [동] 향상하다 memory [명] 기억력 combine [동] 결합하다 movement [명] 동작, 움직임 naturally [부] 자연스럽게 effectively [부] 효과적으로 recall [동] 기억해 내다, 상기하다 action [명] 행동 pathway [명] 경로 repeated [형] 반복되는 lead to ~로 이어지다 give ~ a try ~을 한번 (시도)해보다 [문제] transform [동] 탈바꿈하다

구문

[2행] ..., people **have been using** martial arts *to exercise* and defend **themselves**.

→ 「have/has been + v-ing」는 '(계속) ~해오고 있다'의 의미인 현재완료 진행형이다.

→ to exercise 이하는 '운동하기 위해'의 의미로, 〈목적〉을 나타내는 부사적 용법의 to부정사구이다.

→ themselves는 '그들 자신'이라는 의미의 재귀대명사이다. 재귀대명사는 행위(defend)의 주체(people)가 행위의 대상과 동일할 때 쓰인다.

[4행] But there are other reasons **to learn** martial arts.

→ to learn 이하는 명사구 other reasons를 수식하는 형용사적 용법의 to부정사구이다.

[6행] **By doing** high-intensity workouts in martial arts such as judo or taekwondo, ...

→ 「by + v-ing」는 '~함으로써'라는 의미로 〈수단〉 및 〈방법〉을 나타낸다.

[9행] Secondly, martial arts **help you reduce** your stress levels.

→ 「help + 목적어 + 동사원형」은 '~가 …하는 것을 돕다'의 의미로, 동사 help는 목적격 보어로 동사원형(reduce)을 쓴다.

10행 ... martial arts like tai chi and karate will help you calm **yourself** down.
→ yourself는 '당신 자신'이라는 의미의 재귀대명사이다. 재귀대명사는 행위(calm down)의 주체(you)가 행위의 대상과 동일할 때 쓰인다.

15행 The brain's neural synapses and pathways **grow stronger** ... .
→ 「grow + 형용사」는 '~해지다'의 의미이다. 이때 형용사(stronger)는 주격 보어이다.

● **VOCABULARY INSIDE**

Check Up **1** structure **2** race **3** workout **4** spot **5** defend **6** entertaining
7 combine **8** memory

UNIT 14 | Senses
pp. 85–90

READING 1 How Insects Taste

Ⓥ Mini Quiz
1 F 2 F

▶ **Reading Comprehension**
1 a 2 d 3 make honey to survive 4 d

▶ **Grammar Inside Level 2**
Check Up brave enough to go

해석 거의 모든 동물들은 맛을 볼 수 있다. 이 감각은 음식을 먹고 찾는 데 도움이 되기 때문에, 생존을 위해 필수적이다.
미각은 인간과 곤충에게 다르게 작용한다. 인간보다 더 민감한 미뢰를 가진 곤충들이 있다. 꿀벌은 식물에서 나오는 당분의 낮은 농도를 감지할 수 있다. 게다가, 그들은 감미료가 인공적인지 아닌지를 알아낼 수 있다. 벌들은 생존하기 위해 꿀을 만들어야 한다. 그래서 그들은 꿀로 가공될 수 없는 감미료는 무시한다.
인간과 곤충은 또한 맛을 보기 위해 다른 신체 부위를 사용한다. 인간은 그들의 혀에 있는 수천 개의 미뢰로 맛을 본다. 곤충들은 맛을 보기 위해 확실히 그들의 입을 사용하긴 하지만, 그들은 또한 더듬이나 다리를 사용할 수도 있다. 예를 들어, 나비와 파리는 먹기 위해 그들의 관 모양의 입을 사용하기 전에 먼저 발로 무언가를 맛본다. 이 곤충들에게, 좋은 음식 위를 걷는 것은 그들의 식욕을 유발하기에 충분하다. 다시 말해서, 위에 서 있기에 충분히 좋은 음식은 먹기에도 충분히 좋다!

어휘 insect 명 곤충   taste 동 맛보다; 명 미각   sense 명 감각   essential 형 필수적인   survival 명 생존 (survive 동 생존하다)   work 동 일하다; *작용하다   human 명 인간, 사람   sensitive 형 민감한   honey bee 꿀벌   detect 동 감지[발견]하다   low 형 낮은   concentration 명 집중; *농도   sugar 명 설탕; *당분   plant 명 식물   figure out 알아내다   sweetener 명 감미료, 단 맛을 내는 것   artificial 형 인공적인   ignore 동 무시하다   process 동 가공[처리]하다   thousands of 수천의   tongue 명 혀   antennae 명 (곤충의) 더듬이   trigger 동 유발[촉발]하다   appetite 명 식욕   [문제] compare 동 비교하다

3행 There are insects with **more sensitive** taste buds **than** humans.
→ 「형용사 비교급＋than」은 '~보다 더 …한'의 의미이다.

4행 Honey bees **are able to detect** low concentrations of a sugar from plants.
→ 「be＋able＋to-v」는 '~할 수 있다'라는 의미로, 「can＋동사원형」과 바꾸어 쓸 수 있다.

5행 In addition, they can figure out [whether a sweetener is artificial].
→ [ ]는 '~인지 아닌지'의 의미인 접속사 whether가 이끄는 명사절로, figure out의 목적어로 쓰였다.

6행 The bees need **to make honey** *to survive*.
→ to make honey는 동사 need의 목적어 역할을 하는 명사적 용법의 to부정사구이다.
→ to survive는 '생존하기 위해'라는 의미로, 〈목적〉을 나타내는 부사적 용법의 to부정사이다.

7행 So they ignore any sweeteners [that *cannot be processed* into honey].
→ [ ]는 선행사 any sweeteners를 수식하는 주격 관계대명사절이다.
→ 조동사 cannot이 있는 수동태는 「cannot be＋v-ed」로 나타내며, '~될 수 없다'의 의미이다.

11행 **Although** insects *do use* their mouths for tasting, ...
→ 접속사 although는 '(비록) ~하지만'의 의미이다.
→ 조동사 do는 일반동사 use를 강조하며, '확실히', '정말', '꼭'이라는 의미이다.

12행 For these insects, [walking on good food] *is* **enough to trigger** their appetite.
→ [ ]는 주어로 쓰인 동명사구이다. 동명사구는 단수 취급하므로 동사는 3인칭 단수 be동사인 is가 쓰였다.
→ 「enough＋to-v」는 '~할 만큼 충분한'라는 의미이다.

13행 In other words, food [good enough to stand on] is good enough to eat!
→ [ ]는 명사 food를 수식하는 형용사구이다.

READING 2   A Pioneer for the Blind

ⓥ Mini Quiz
unpopular, death

▶ **Reading Comprehension**
1 c   2 b   3 a   4 1917

▶ **Grammar Inside Level 1**
Check Up 1 to help   2 to sell

해석   브라유 점자 덕분에 시각장애인들은 읽는 것이 가능하다. 그것은 Louis Braille에 의해 개발되었다. 그는 1809년에 프랑스에서 온전한 시력을 가지고 태어났다. 하지만 그는 세 살이었을 때, 눈을 다쳤고 감염이 그를 눈이 멀게 만들었다.

그럼에도 불구하고, 그는 똑똑한 학생이었고 10살에 국립 시각장애 청소년 협회에서 장학금을 받았다. <u>그해에 한 프랑스 군인이 양각의 12개 점으로 된 표기 체계를 만들었다.</u> 이 체계를 사용함으로써, 군인들은 말을 하지 않고도 밤에

의사소통을 할 수 있었다. 그 군인이 1822년에 Braille의 학교에서 연설했을 때, Braille은 그 체계가 시각장애인들을 위해 사용될 수 있다고 생각했다. 그래서 그는 그것을 개선하기로 결심했다.

Braille은 1837년에 6개의 점으로 된 표기 체계를 완성하고 발표했다. 그것을 읽기 위해, 하나의 손가락 끝이 양각의 점들을 가로질러 왼쪽에서 오른쪽으로 움직여진다. 그것은 사용하기 쉬웠지만, 폭넓은 수용은 더디게 다가왔다. 이 체계는 1852년에 그가 사망할 때까지 여전히 인기가 없었다. 미국이 브라유 표준으로 정한 것은 1917년이었고, 1932년에는 다른 영어권 국가들도 그것을 사용하기 시작했다.

어휘 pioneer 몡 선구자   blind 혱 눈이 먼   possible 혱 가능한   thanks to ~ 덕분에   develop 동 개발하다   perfect 혱 온전한, 완벽한   vision 몡 시력   infection 몡 감염   still 몡 아직(도); *그럼에도 불구하고   bright 혱 밝은; *똑똑한   scholarship 몡 장학금   national 혱 국립[국가]의   institute 몡 협회, 기관   system 몡 체계   soldier 몡 군인   communicate 동 의사소통하다   speak 동 말하다; 연설하다   decide 동 결심하다   improve 동 개선하다   complete 동 완성하다   publish 동 발표[공표]하다   dot 몡 점   writing 몡 쓰기; *표기   single 혱 단 하나의   fingertip 몡 손가락 끝   across 전 ~을 가로질러   raised 혱 솟아오른; *양각의   acceptance 몡 수용, 받아들임   remain 동 여전히[계속] ~이다   unpopular 혱 인기 없는   death 몡 사망, 죽음   settle on ~로 정하다   standard 몡 표준

구문

2행 But when he was three, he hurt his eye and infection **made him blind**.
→ 「make + 목적어 + 형용사」는 '~을 …하게 하다'의 의미이다. 동사 made의 목적격 보어로 형용사 blind가 쓰였다.

5행 **By using** the system, soldiers could communicate at night without speaking.
→ 「by + v-ing」는 '~함으로써'라는 의미로, 〈수단〉 및 〈방법〉을 나타낸다.

9행 **To read it**, a single fingertip *is moved* **from** left **to** right across raised dots.
→ to read it은 '그것을 읽기 위해'의 의미로, 〈목적〉을 나타내는 부사적 용법의 to부정사구이다.
→ is moved는 「be + v-ed」 형태의 수동태이다.
→ from A to B는 'A에서 B로'라는 의미이다.

11행 It was easy **to use**, but wide acceptance was slow in coming.
→ to use는 형용사 easy를 수식하는 부사적 용법의 to부정사이다.

11행 The system **remained unpopular** until his death in 1852.
→ 「remain + 형용사」는 '계속[여전히] ~이다'의 의미이다. 주격 보어로 형용사 unpopular가 쓰였다.

12행 **It was** in 1917 **that** the US settled on a Braille standard, and ... *started to use* it.
→ 「it + be ~ that ....」은 be동사와 접속사 that 사이의 단어나 구를 강조하는 표현으로, '…인 것은 (바로) ~이다'라는 의미이다.
→ 동사 start는 목적어로 to부정사(to use)와 동명사(using) 모두 취할 수 있다.

● VOCABULARY INSIDE

Check Up   1 survival   2 sense   3 trigger   4 acceptance   5 vision   6 ignore   7 completed   8 standard

UNIT 15 | Psychology

pp. 91–96

READING 1 The Sunk Cost Effect

Mini Quiz
c

▶ **Reading Comprehension**
1 d 2 a person has spent and can't get back 3 d 4 b

▶ **Grammar Inside Level 1**
[Check Up] It is interesting to learn new things.

해석 당신이 극장에서 영화를 보고 있다고 상상해봐라. 안타깝게도, 영화는 형편없다. 하지만 당신은 푯값을 지불했기 때문에 거기에 계속 앉아 있다. 당신은 매몰 비용 효과를 경험하고 있다.

이 효과를 이해하기 위해, 당신은 '매몰 비용'이라는 용어를 이해해야 한다. 매몰 비용은 어떤 사람이 소비했고 되찾을 수 없는 시간, 돈, 또는 노력을 말한다. 영화 푯값처럼 말이다. 이제, 한 남자가 식당을 매입하는데, 그것이 어떤 이익도 가져오지 않는다고 상상해보자. 그는 자신의 실패를 받아들이고 포기해야 한다. 하지만 그는 자신이 쓴 돈, 즉 '매몰 비용'을 낭비했다고 생각하고 싶지 않다. 그래서 그는 계속 식당에 돈을 쓴다. 결국, 형편없는 영화를 견디는 것이 시간 낭비인 것과 꼭 마찬가지로, 그것은 훨씬 더 많은 돈의 낭비이다. 이것이 매몰 비용 효과이다.

이는 누구에게나 발생할 수 있다. 당신은 당신의 노력이 낭비되는 것을 원치 않기 때문에 어떤 것에 성공하지 못했을 때 인정하기 힘들다. 하지만 손실을 받아들이고 더 나은 무언가로 넘어가는 것이 훨씬 더 현명하다.

어휘 sunk cost effect 매몰 비용 효과 imagine [동] 상상하다 theater [명] 극장, 공연장 unfortunately [부] 안타깝게도 terrible [형] 끔찍한; *형편없는 term [명] 용어, 말 effort [명] 노력, 수고 spend [동] (돈·시간·노력 등을) 소비하다, 쓰다 get back 되찾다 purchase [동] 매입[구매]하다 bring [동] 가져오다 profit [명] 이익, 수익 accept [동] 받아들이다 failure [명] 실패 give up 포기하다 waste [동] 낭비하다; [명] 낭비 happen [동] 발생하다, 일어나다 admit [동] 인정하다 unsuccessful [형] 성공하지 못한 wise [형] 현명한 loss [명] 분실; *손실, 손해 move on to ~로 넘어가다 [문제] investment [명] 투자 in the end 결국 endure [동] 견디다, 인내하다 fix [동] 고치다 consult [동] 상담하다

구문 [2행] But you **keep sitting** there because you paid for the ticket.
→ 「keep + v-ing」는 '계속 ~하다'의 의미로, 동사 keep은 목적어로 동명사(sitting)를 취한다.

[4행] **To understand the effect**, you *must understand* the term "sunk cost."
→ to understand the effect는 '이 효과를 이해하기 위해'라는 의미로, 〈목적〉을 나타내는 부사적 용법의 to부정사구이다.
→ 조동사 must는 '~해야 한다'라는 의미로, 〈의무〉를 나타낸다. 조동사 must 다음에는 반드시 동사원형(understand)이 온다.

[5행] A sunk cost is time, money, or effort [that a person has spent and can't get back ...].
→ [ ]는 선행사 time, money, or effort를 수식하는 목적격 관계대명사절이다.

[8행] But he doesn't **want to think** [that he wasted the money **he spent** — the "sunk cost."]
→ 동사 want는 to부정사(to think)를 목적어로 취한다.
→ [ ]는 to부정사 to think의 목적어 역할을 하는 명사절이다.

→ he spent는 선행사 the money를 수식하는 목적격 관계대명사절로, 앞에 that[which]이 생략되었다.

10행 In the end, it is a waste of **even more** money, just like [enduring a bad movie] is … .

→ 부사 even은 비교급 more를 강조하며, '훨씬'의 의미이다.

→ [ ]은 just like 이하의 부사절에서 주어 역할을 하는 동명사구이다.

11행 … unsuccessful at something because you **don't want your efforts _to be wasted_**.

→ 「want + 목적어 + to-v」는 '~가 …할 것을 원하다'라는 의미이다. 동사 want는 목적격 보어로 to부정사(to be wasted)를 취한다.

→ to be wasted는 '낭비되는 것'의 의미로, 「to be + v-ed」 형태의 to부정사의 수동태이다.

13행 But it is **much wiser** [to accept your losses] _and_ [move on to something better]!

→ 부사 much는 비교급 wiser를 강조하며, '훨씬'의 의미이다.

→ 등위접속사 and로 to accept your losses와 (to) move on 이하가 대등하게 연결되어 있다.

READING 2　The Salieri Complex

Ⓥ Mini Quiz
The Salieri Complex refers to the envy of ordinary people toward talented ones.

▶ Reading Comprehension
1 c　2 (1) F (2) F (3) T　3 a　4 with the release of the film _Amadeus_ in 1985

▶ Grammar Inside Level 1
Check Up 1 during　2 on

해석　살리에리 콤플렉스는 재능 있는 사람들을 향한 평범한 사람들의 질투를 가리킨다. 이 콤플렉스는 동시대의 아마데우스 모차르트를 매우 질투한 것으로 알려진 이탈리아 음악가 안토니오 살리에리의 이야기에서 비롯되었다. 하지만, 많은 사학자들은 현재 이러한 이야기들을 부정확한 것으로 믿고 있다.

　1750년, 살리에리는 이탈리아의 레냐고에서 태어났다. 그는 어린이 교회 성가대를 위해 베네치아에서 빈으로 이동했다. 그는 마침내 1774년에 그곳에서 궁정 작곡가가 되었다. 그의 경력 동안, 그는 40개의 오페라와 다양한 다른 작품들을 만들었다.

　아마도 살리에리가 모차르트만큼 재능이 있지는 않았지만, 그는 여전히 오스트리아에서 최고의 작곡가로 여겨졌다. 그의 음악에 대한 지식은 광범위했다. 그렇다면, 그 질투 이야기들은 어디에서 유래했을까? 그것들은 1985년에 영화 「아마데우스」의 개봉과 함께 시작되었을지도 모른다. 이 영화에서, 살리에리는 모차르트를 매우 질투하는 것으로 연기된다. 하지만, 이 영화는 허구이다. 그가 모차르트를 존경했을 가능성이 더 크다. 역사는 심지어 살리에리가 모차르트의 죽음을 애도했다는 것을 보여준다. 분명히, 모든 소문이 반드시 사실인 것은 아니다.

어휘　refer to ~을 가리키다[나타내다]　envy 몡 질투, 선망 (envious of ~을 부러워하는)　ordinary 혱 평범한, 보통의　talented 혱 (타고난) 재능이 있는 (talent 몡 재능)　originate 동 비롯되다, 유래하다　extremely 뷰 매우, 극도로　jealous of ~을 질투하는 (jealousy 몡 질투)　contemporary 혱 동시대의　historian 몡 사학자　inaccurate 혱 부정확한　choir 몡 합창단　eventually 뷰 마침내, 결국　court 몡 법정; *궁중　composer 몡 작곡가 (composition 몡 작곡; *작품)　career 몡 경력, 이력　consider 동 여기다　knowledge 몡 지식　comprehensive 혱 광범위한　tale 몡 이야기　release 몡 개봉, 출시　film 몡 영화　portray 동 묘사하다; *연기하다　fictional 혱 허구[소설]의　likely 혱 ~할 것 같은　respect 동 존경하다　mourn 동 애도하다, 슬퍼하다　passing 몡 죽음　clearly 뷰 분명히　rumor 몡 소문　necessarily 뷰 반드시

구문 3행 ... Antonio Salieri, an Italian musician [that *was said to be* extremely jealous of ...].
→ [ ]는 선행사 an Italian musician을 수식하는 주격 관계대명사절이다.
→ 「be + said + to-v」는 '~라고 알려지다'의 의미이다.

7행 However, many historians now **believe these stories to be inaccurate**.
→ 「believe + 목적어 + to-v」는 '~을 …한 것으로 믿다'의 의미로, 동사 believe는 목적격 보어로 to부정사(to be)를 취한다.

14행 ... **not as** talented **as** Mozart, he *was still considered* a top composer in Austria.
→ 「not as + 형용사의 원급 + as」는 '~만큼 …하지 않은'이라는 의미의 부정형 원급 비교 구문이다.
→ was still considered 이하는 'A를 B라고 여기다'의 의미인 consider A (to be) B를 수동태로 바꿔 쓴 형태이다.

17행 They **may have begun** with the release of the film *Amadeus* in 1985.
→ 「may have + v-ed」는 '~이었을지도 모른다'의 의미로, 〈과거의 일에 대한 약한 추측〉을 나타낸다.

19행 In the film, Salieri **is portrayed as** [being highly jealous of Mozart].
→ is portrayed as 이하는 'A를 B라고 연기하다'의 의미인 portray A as B를 수동태로 바꿔 쓴 형태이다.
→ [ ]는 전치사 as의 목적어 역할을 하는 동명사구이다.

21행 **It's** more **likely** he respected Mozart.
→ 「it is likely (that) + 주어 + 동사」는 '~가 …할 가능성이 크다', '~가 …할 것 같다'의 의미이다.

24행 Clearly, **not all** rumors are necessarily true.
→ every, all 등 〈전체〉를 의미하는 말과 〈부정〉을 의미하는 not이 함께 쓰이면 '모두 ~인 것은 아니다'라는 의미의 〈부분 부정〉을 나타낸다.

● **VOCABULARY INSIDE**

Check Up 1 envy 2 failure 3 endure 4 fictional 5 portray 6 profit
7 comprehensive 8 purchase

UNIT 16 | Light   pp. 97–102

READING 1 | Living Light

Ⓥ **Mini Quiz**
create light

▶ **Reading Comprehension**
1 b   2 d   3 (1) T (2) F   4 (1) prey (2) upper lip (3) attackers

▶ **Grammar Inside Level 1**
Check Up Traveling

무수히 많은 작은 빛으로 가득 찬 바다를 상상해보라. 상상의 세계처럼 들릴지 모르지만, 그것은 현실이다! 우리의 바닷속 깊은 곳에서, 많은 해양 생물들은 자신의 빛을 만들어낸다. (심해에는 알려지지 않은 생물체가 여전히 많이 있다.) 빛을 만드는 이 능력은 '생물 발광'이라 불린다.

생물 발광은 생물체의 몸 안의 루시페린이라 불리는 특수한 물질에 의해 일어난다. 이 물질은 산소에 노출될 때 빛을 만들어낸다. 발광 생물은 언제 빛을 만들지를 제어할 수 있고, 그들은 여러 다양한 목적으로 그것을 사용한다.

예를 들어, 아귀는 먹이를 유인하기 위해 머리 위의 불을 밝히는 공 모양의 부분을 이용한다. 더 작은 어류는 이 빛 뒤에 있는 위험을 알지 못하고 그것을 향해 헤엄쳐 간다. 짝을 유인하는 것과 더 큰 어류를 겁을 주어 쫓아내는 것은 생물 발광의 다른 용도이다. 작은 새우 같은 생물체인 오스트라코드는 윗입술에 빛을 밝혀서 짝을 유인한다. 어떤 심해 벌레들은 공격하는 자들을 혼란스럽게 하기 위해 생물 발광 탄알을 쏘기도 한다.

해양 생물의 생물 발광은 우리에게도 유익하다. 우리는 바다를 구경하며 수면 아래 깊은 곳의 아름다운 빛을 볼 수 있다.

어휘 **light** 형 빛 (**light up** (빛·색으로) 환하게[빛나게] 만들다) **ocean** 명 바다, 대양 **filled with** ~로 가득 찬 **millions of** 수백만의; *무수히 많은 **tiny** 형 아주 작은 **sound like** ~처럼 들리다 **fantasy** 명 상상의 산물, 공상 **reality** 명 현실 **deep** 부 깊은 곳에, 깊이; 형 깊은 **creature** 명 생물 **unknown** 형 알려지지 않은 **ability** 명 능력 **create** 동 만들다, 창조하다 **bioluminescence** 명 생물[생체] 발광 (**bioluminescent** 형 생물[생체] 발광의) **cause** 동 일으키다, 야기하다 **substance** 명 물질 **produce** 동 만들다, 생산하다 **expose** 동 노출시키다 **oxygen** 명 산소 **control** 동 제어[통제]하다 **purpose** 명 목적 **bulb** 명 전구; *공 모양의 부분 **attract** 동 유인하다, 마음을 끌다 **prey** 명 먹이, 사냥감 **danger** 명 위험 **toward** 전 ~을 향하여 **mate** 명 친구, 동료; *짝, 배우자 **frighten away** ~을 겁주어 쫓아내다 **shrimp-like** 형 작은 새우 같은 **upper lip** 윗입술 **worm** 명 벌레 **shoot** 동 쏘다 **bullet** 명 탄알, 총알 **confuse** 동 혼란시키다 **attacker** 명 공격자 **benefit** 동 유익하다 **look upon** ~을 구경하다[보다] **below** 전 ~ 아래에 **surface** 명 수면, 표면

구문

1행 Imagine an ocean [filled with millions of tiny lights].
→ [ ]는 명사 an ocean을 수식하는 과거분사구이다.

4행 This ability **to create light** *is called "bioluminescence."*
→ to create light는 명사구 this ability를 수식하는 형용사적 용법의 to부정사구이다.
→ is called "bioluminescence"는 'A를 B라고 부르다'의 의미인 call A B를 수동태로 바꿔 쓴 형태이다.

6행 Bioluminescence **is caused by** a special substance [called luciferin] **inside a creature's body**.
→ is caused by는 「be + v-ed + by」 형태의 수동태로, '~에 의해 야기되다'의 의미이다.
→ [ ]는 명사구 a special substance를 수식하는 과거분사구이다.

8행 Bioluminescent creatures can control [when they produce the light], and they use *it* for many different purposes.
→ [ ]는 「의문사 + 주어 + 동사」 어순의 간접의문문으로, 동사 can control의 목적어로 쓰였다.
→ 대명사 it은 앞문장의 명사 the light을 가리킨다.

10행 Anglerfish, for example, use a bulb on their head [that lights up] *to attract prey*.
→ [ ]는 선행사 a bulb on their head를 수식하는 주격 관계대명사절이다.
→ to attract prey는 '먹이를 유인하기 위해'의 의미로, 〈목적〉을 나타내는 부사적 용법의 to부정사구이다.

12행 [Attracting mates] and [frightening away bigger fish] are other uses of bioluminescence.
→ 등위접속사 and로 주어 역할을 하는 동명사구 attracting mates와 frightening ... fish가 대등하게 연결되어 있다.

13행 **Ostracods, small shrimp-like creatures**, attract mates *by lighting up* their upper lip.

→ small shrimp-like creatures는 명사 ostracods를 보충 설명하는 명사구로, 둘은 동격 관계이다.

→ by lighting up은 「by + v-ing」 형태로 '빛을 밝혀서'라는 의미이다.

READING 2   Small Dots, Big Vision

ⓥ Mini Quiz

The technique involved using tiny dots and various contrasting colors to portray the movement of light.

▶ **Reading Comprehension**

1 b   2 d   3 (1) F (2) F   4 d

▶ **Grammar Inside Level 2**

Check Up 1 sitting   2 left

해석   Georges Seurat는 19세기 화가였다. 그는 점묘법을 창시한 것으로 유명했다. 그 기법은 빛의 움직임을 묘사하기 위해 아주 작은 점과 대비되는 다양한 색을 사용하는 것을 포함했다.

이 양식은 대체로 과학적 이론에 기초했다. 그는 당대의 저명한 특정 화학자들과 물리학자들에 의해 영감을 받았다. 그는 인간의 뇌와 눈이 이 색들을 처리하는 방식에 특히 관심이 있었다. 이것이 그가 작은 점들을 사용한 이유이다. 그는 빛을 표현하기 위해 색을 섞거나 연속적인 선을 사용하지 않았다. 하지만, 사람들이 그의 작품을 멀리서 보면, 대부분은 아마도 그가 캔버스에 찍은 작은 점이 아니라 전체로만 그 그림을 볼 것이다.

그의 유명한 그림들 중 하나는 「아스니에르에서 멱 감는 사람들」이라고 불린다. 그 그림은 빛과 그림자의 대비를 보여주는 수많은 작은 점들로 이루어져 있다. 그것은 어느 여름날 강가의 풀로 덮인 둑에서 휴식을 취하고 있는 몇 명의 젊은 남자들을 묘사한다. 그것은 또한 나무들, 배들, 건물들, 그리고 위로 연기가 피어오르고 있는 공장들을 표현한다. 그것은 빛, 형태의 단순함, 대비, 그리고 구성의 완벽한 혼합을 보여주는 훌륭한 예이다.

어휘   dot 몡 점   vision 몡 시력; *시야   painter 몡 화가   famous for ~로 유명한   creation 몡 창시, 창조   pointillism 몡 점묘법(작은 색점들을 찍어서 표현하는 화법)   technique 몡 기법   involve 동 포함[수반]하다   tiny 혱 아주 작은   various 혱 다양한   contrasting 혱 대비되는, 대조적인 (contrast 몡 대비, 대조)   portray 동 묘사[표현]하다 (portrait 몡 초상(화))   movement 몡 움직임   inspire 동 영감을 주다   certain 혱 특정한, 어떤   renowned 혱 저명[유명]한, 명성 있는   chemist 몡 화학자   physicist 몡 물리학자   of one's time 당대의   interested in ~에 관심이 있는   process 동 처리하다   mix 동 섞다; 몡 혼합   continuous 혱 연속적인   express 동 표현하다   view 동 보다   at a distance 멀리서, 떨어져서   as a whole 전체로서   consist of ~로 이루어지다[구성되다]   relax 동 휴식을 취하다   grassy 혱 풀로 덮인   bank 몡 둑, 제방   depict 동 표현[묘사]하다   rise 동 오르다, 올라가다   shining 혱 빛나는; *훌륭한   simplicity 몡 단순함, 간단함   composition 몡 구성   [문제]   outdated 혱 구식의   characterize 동 특징 짓다   political 혱 정치적인   related to ~와 관련된   largely 뷔 대체로   based on ~에 기초한[근거하여]   theory 몡 이론

구문   **2행** The technique involved [using tiny ... colors] *to portray* the movement of light.

→ [ ]는 동사 involved의 목적어 역할을 하는 동명사구이다.

→ to portray 이하는 '~을 묘사하기 위해'의 의미로, 〈목적〉을 나타내는 부사적 용법의 to부정사구이다.

5행 He **was inspired by** certain renowned chemists and physicists of his time.

→ was inspired by는 「be + v-ed + by」 형태의 수동태로, '~에 의해 영감을 받다'의 의미이다.

6행 He was particularly interested in **how** the human brain and eyes process these colors.
→ how 이하는 〈방법〉을 나타내는 관계부사절로, '~하는 방식'이라는 의미이다.

9행 ... see the painting as a whole and not the small marks [he made on the canvas].
→ [ ]는 선행사 the small marks를 수식하는 목적격 관계대명사절로, 앞에 목적격 관계대명사 that[which]이 생략되었다.

12행 One of his famous paintings **is called Bathers at Asnières**.
→ is called *Bathers at Asnières*는 'A를 B라고 부르다'의 의미인 call A B를 수동태로 바꿔 쓴 형태이다.

14행 It portrays some young men [relaxing on a grassy bank by a river on a summer day].
→ [ ]는 명사구 some young men을 수식하는 현재분사구이다.

● **VOCABULARY INSIDE**

Check Up **1** Relax **2** rising **3** expose **4** substance **5** renowned **6** contrasting
7 confuse **8** purpose

READING
Inside
Workbook

LEVEL 1

UNIT 01 | Shapes

pp. 2–5

VOCABULARY TEST 1

01 덮다; 둘러싸다   02 건축가   03 만들다, 창조하다
04 삼각형   05 저장[보관]하다   06 특정한
07 용어, 말   08 육각형   09 어린 시절   10 음악의
11 선택하다, 고르다   12 감정   13 지역; 면적
14 특별[특수]한   15 나타내다   16 떠나다; 남기다
17 양   18 모양, 형태   19 권장[장려]하다   20 (소리가)
큰   21 형태   22 영향력 있는   23 폭발, 파열
24 space   25 efficient   26 impressive
27 secret   28 fit   29 honeycomb
30 silence   31 waste   32 square
33 produce   34 gap   35 communicate
36 ~로 가득 찬   37 ~와 비교하면   38 ~처럼 느끼다
39 다양한   40 ~에 따르면

VOCABULARY TEST 2

A ⓒ   B ⓑ   C 1 influential   2 loud   3 waste
4 produce   D 1 According to   2 a variety of
3 Compared to

GRAMMAR TEST

A 1 who   2 that   3 which   4 cannot
B 1 must not   2 must   3 cannot
C 1 who[that] teaches math
   2 who[that] made this necklace
   3 that[which] barks at strangers
   4 that[which] has a good camera

WRITING TEST

A 1 make you feel
   2 that is full of
   3 good at making honey
   4 named his works after
   5 that fit together without
B 1 hard to produce
   2 encouraged him to listen
   3 Compared to other shapes
   4 that[which] they produce
   5 who[that] viewed his paintings

UNIT 02 | Origins

pp. 6–9

VOCABULARY TEST 1

01 (용기를) 북돋우다, 격려하다   02 휴식을 취하다
03 경기, 시합   04 발명   05 몇몇(의)   06 거의
07 기초[기본]적인   08 다음에 나오는   09 맞은 편[쪽]의,
건너편의   10 ~의 너머[저편]에   11 다투다
12 패배시키다; 패배   13 용어, 말   14 ~인 것 같다;
나타나다   15 대단히, 크게   16 100년, 세기
17 형태, 판   18 일어나다, 발생하다   19 확대하다
20 완전히, 전적으로   21 관찰, 관측   22 인정하다
23 기구, 장치   24 telescope   25 expression
26 explain   27 enter   28 imagine   29 edge
30 opponent   31 apologize   32 unknown
33 traditionally   34 항복[포기]하다   35 패배를
인정하다, 항복하다   36 곤경에 처한, 궁지에 몰린
37 ~의 편에 있는   38 궁지에 몰린   39 ~ 이전에, ~에
앞서   40 약진[발전]하다

VOCABULARY TEST 2

A 1 ⓓ   B ⓐ   C 1 apologize   2 explain
3 encourage   4 opponent
D 1 in my corner   2 Prior to   3 give up

GRAMMAR TEST

A 1 because   2 travel   3 so   4 cook
B 1 because   2 so, that   3 so
C 1 attend   2 help   3 because
   4 experience   5 that

WRITING TEST

A 1 make things appear
   2 is on my side
   3 let them imagine what
   4 person to use a telescope
   5 Boxing was so popular that
B 1 decided to make
   2 means to be in trouble
   3 admitted defeat by throwing
   4 allowed him to magnify
   5 a boxer is driven

UNIT 03 | Sports pp. 10–13

VOCABULARY TEST 1

01 자국, 얼룩　02 녹초가 된, 기진맥진한
03 명확하게　04 체육관　05 (돈을) 쓰다; (시간을)
보내다　06 참석하다　07 금지하다　08 어두운
09 경쟁; 대회　10 (깜짝) 놀랄 만한　11 완벽한, 완전한
12 신체 단련, 건강　13 회전　14 편리한, 간편한
15 계단　16 (처)벌　17 지역　18 제공하다　19 땀
20 옷　21 강요하다, ~하게 만들다　22 전통
23 기구, 장비　24 experience　25 origin
26 interesting　27 strict　28 remain
29 early　30 consume　31 power　32 rule
33 cruel　34 wheel　35 popular　36 prison
37 개최되다, 일어나다　38 ~에 참여[참가]하다
39 ~을 응원하다　40 복귀하다

VOCABULARY TEST 2

A ⓑ　B ⓑ　C 1 consume　2 equipment
3 remain　4 stain　D 1 take part in　2 takes
place　3 cheer for

GRAMMAR TEST

A 1 fast　2 was drawn　3 painted　4 good
B 1 as heavy as Ron　2 as expensive as the
　 yellow hat[one]　3 as tall as her older sister
　 4 as old as my math teacher
C 1 was held
　 2 was baked by me
　 3 was visited by
　 4 The birds were observed by

WRITING TEST

A 1 was used to power
　 2 convenient way to exercise
　 3 as old as tennis itself
　 4 has been served since
　 5 for players to look
B 1 Running on a treadmill
　 2 to avoid looking
　 3 were banned for being
　 4 where it takes place
　 5 try taking part in

UNIT 04 | Jobs pp. 14–17

VOCABULARY TEST 1

01 조절[조정]하다　02 분석　03 상대[반대]측
04 (운동) 선수　05 복잡한　06 상태　07 전시하다,
내보이다　08 설명하다　09 미술품　10 습도
11 왼손잡이의　12 알아차리다　13 사진(술)
14 보수[수리]하다　15 복원[복구]하다　16 엉망으로
만들다　17 조각(품)　18 전공　19 힘; 강점, 장점
20 전술　21 치료, 처치　22 소중한, 귀중한
23 약화시키다　24 example　25 reward
26 skill　27 weakness　28 damage
29 pitcher　30 guard　31 cultural　32 expert
33 treatment　34 practice　35 identify
36 environment　37 ~ 덕분에　38 ~을 돌보다
39 ~와 같은　40 ~에 흥미가[관심이] 있는

VOCABULARY TEST 2

A 1 ⓒ　2 ⓐ　3 ⓑ　B ⓒ　C 1 adjust
2 treatment　3 damage　4 restore
D 1 Thanks to　2 such as　3 take care of

GRAMMAR TEST

A 1 bought him some flowers　2 asked the
　 witness questions　3 send me the files
B 1 일출을 보기 위해　2 약간의 음식을 사기 위해
　 3 이탈리아 요리를 배우기 위해
C 1 give me some advice　2 to ask a question
　 3 lent me several books

WRITING TEST

A 1 give me an example
　 2 be very interested in
　 3 added water to weaken
　 4 restored the painting by removing
　 5 so that they can
B 1 to create databases
　 2 safest ways to display
　 3 will be enjoyed
　 4 an expert at keeping
　 5 allows them to win

UNIT 05 | Solutions   pp. 18–21

VOCABULARY TEST 1

01 최신의   02 복잡한   03 조산의, 정상보다 이른
04 피할 수 없는   05 해소, 완화   06 감정
07 스트레스가 많은   08 사회   09 해결책, 해법
10 관점   11 격한   12 따뜻한   13 분리하다
14 기능   15 녹다; 녹이다   16 열정   17 기법
18 실험   19 (질)병   20 전력, 전기   21 실시하다
22 효과성   23 처리하다   24 situation   25 prove
26 major   27 prevent   28 decision
29 regulate   30 tiny   31 method
32 requirement   33 anger   34 improve
35 lower   36 ~을 찾다   37 ~에 따르면
38 한 번에   39 태어나다   40 ~로 이어지다

VOCABULARY TEST 2

A ⓐ   B ⓓ   C 1 prevent   2 emotions
3 cost   4 regulate   D 1 at a time   2 was
born   3 lead to

GRAMMAR TEST

A 1 sad   2 interesting   3 to play
   4 don't have to
B 1 safe   2 lucky   3 happy   4 can't[cannot]
   5 don't have to
C 1 leave the window open
   2 am able to help
   3 found the lecture difficult
   4 has to take

WRITING TEST

A 1 what incubators are for
   2 to keep them warm
   3 too small to regulate
   4 who used this method
   5 and hope they work
B 1 wanted to solve
   2 prevented by keeping
   3 prevent you from making
   4 a study conducted
   5 allows you to control

UNIT 06 | Future   pp. 22–25

VOCABULARY TEST 1

01 대기(권)   02 영향(력)   03 밝아지다; 밝히다
04 기후   05 현재, 지금   06 발달[성장]시키다
07 효율[능률]적으로   08 금지하다   09 점진적으로,
서서히   10 획기적인   11 열   12 감추다, 숨기다
13 역사적인   14 유지하다, 지키다   15 거대한
16 인구   17 예측[예견]하다   18 보존[보호]하다
19 빠르게 성장하는   20 특정한, 구체적인   21 온도,
기온   22 지하에   23 (위아래가) 뒤집힌
24 skyscraper   25 architect   26 dig
27 appearance   28 issue   29 structure
30 filter   31 heritage   32 suggest   33 prove
34 release   35 public   36 forehead
37 stage   38 ~을 (자세히) 살피다[검토하다]
39 게다가   40 예측하다

VOCABULARY TEST 2

A ⓓ   B ⓐ   C 1 massive   2 structure
3 prove   4 release   D 1 look at   2 In
addition   3 make a prediction

GRAMMAR TEST

A 1 comes   2 to watch   3 to store   4 don't
B 1 to drink   2 to spend   3 rains   4 wears
C 1 a vase   2 a dress   3 a lot of friends
   4 someone

WRITING TEST

A 1 population but little space
   2 larger foreheads than people
   3 would help them see
   4 will be able to design
B 1 will be hidden
   2 have been developing
   3 to deal with
   4 allow them to live
   5 keep rising

UNIT 07 | Environment pp. 26-29

01 상황   02 초기[최초]의   03 (유)독성의   04 형태
05 생산하다   06 오염시키다   07 화장품   08 아주
작은   09 부분적으로   10 배수관   11 치약
12 혁신   13 신발   14 유기농의   15 필요로 하다
16 환경적으로   17 방출하다   18 해양[바다]의
19 줄이다   20 천, 직물   21 대기   22 양
23 유해한, 해로운   24 including   25 build
26 chemical   27 oil   28 physical
29 consider   30 process   31 jersey
32 impact   33 fatal   34 habitat   35 practice
36 wisely   37 ~로 만들어진   38 ~에 의존[의지]하다
39 계속해서, 쉬지 않고   40 예를 들어

A ⓐ   B ⓑ   C 1 situation   2 amount
3 pollute   4 reduce   D 1 rely on   2 on and
on   3 for instance

A 1 used   2 sleeping   3 with whom   4 which
B 1 that   2 X   3 that   4 who
C 1 smiling   2 crying   3 shocking   4 broken

A 1 how jerseys are made
  2 are even smaller than
  3 we can do is buy
  4 from upcycled marine plastic
  5 the seafood we eat
B 1 rely on plastic to make
  2 must be processed
  3 making the situation even worse
  4 damaging CO_2 are released
  5 a jersey made partially

UNIT 08 | Health pp. 30-33

01 영향을 미치다   02 물리치다, 이기다   03 죽은
04 극히, 매우   05 발전[발달]하다   06 장치, 기구
07 (질)병   08 먹여주다   09 열   10 함유[포함]하다
11 독립적인   12 들어 올리다   13 식사, 끼니
14 기회   15 반대의, 다른 편의   16 과거   17 접시,
그릇   18 보호하다   19 감소하다   20 없애다, 제거하다
21 흔들다; 떨다, 떨리다   22 통제할 수 없이   23 위협
24 allow   25 infection   26 direction
27 cell   28 symptom   29 experience
30 defense   31 cough   32 record
33 effective   34 survive   35 invade
36 inject   37 ~와 같은   38 ~ 대신에   39 ~ 때문에
40 B와 같은 A

A 1 ⓓ   2 ⓐ   B 1 symptoms   2 lift
3 independent   4 opposite   C 1 the same, as
2 such as   3 because of

A 1 myself   2 himself   3 that   4 that
B 1 O   2 X   3 X   4 O
C 1 그가 우리에게 거짓말했다는 것   2 내일 비가 올
예정이라는 것   3 네가 행복하다는 것   4 Olivia가
그리스로 이사 갈 예정이라는 것

A 1 get symptoms such as
  2 an opportunity to spend
  3 for them to lift
  4 Jenner believed that surviving
  5 stop the hand from shaking
B 1 to feed themselves
  2 have to be fed
  3 how to beat
  4 causes people to shake
  5 will be able to make

UNIT 09 | Colors pp. 34-37

VOCABULARY TEST 1

01 감정의　02 옮기다, 나르다　03 마찬가지로
04 얻다　05 ~을 통해　06 상태　07 기법　08 무게
09 확인[확증]하다　10 나누다, 분리하다; 분리되다
11 심리, 마음　12 그림　13 벽　14 발견하다
15 퍼지다　16 무지개　17 속도　18 액체
19 오랜 (기간의), 장기(간)의　20 ~ 동안　21 ~을
따라　22 머무르다　23 표현하다　24 notice
25 sunlight　26 reflect　27 bedroom
28 pigment　29 original　30 work
31 investigation　32 apply　33 reveal
34 fade　35 light　36 ~로 알려진　37 결국 ~하게
되다　38 시간이 지나면서　39 서로　40 ~로 구성된

VOCABULARY TEST 2

A ⓓ　B ⓑ　C 1 express　2 Separate
3 notice　4 original　D 1 known as
2 composed of　3 over time

GRAMMAR TEST

A 1 great　2 sweet　3 helpful　4 until
　5 after
B 1 bad　2 nice　3 comfortable　4 beautiful
C 1 before　2 When　3 until　4 after

WRITING TEST

A 1 the room he stayed in
　2 separates the sunlight into all
　3 that looked darker and colder
　4 the time he painted them
　5 All you need is
　6 other pigments such as
B 1 has faded over time
　2 stops spreading
　3 hope to gain
　4 is composed of

UNIT 10 | Technology pp. 38-41

VOCABULARY TEST 1

01 우주비행사　02 보장하다　03 바꾸다　04 개별의
05 제조　06 임무　07 호흡　08 땀　09 열다
10 보호하다　11 전체의　12 장치　13 추출하다
14 표면　15 공격하다　16 부추기다　17 요구하다
18 영향; 영향을 끼치다　19 연구　20 성취[달성]하다
21 착륙　22 현지의　23 역겨운　24 inspire
25 expert　26 common　27 purification
28 security　29 particle　30 international
31 practical　32 warning　33 crime
34 ~을 되찾다　35 ~을 처리하다　36 결국
37 불쑥 나타나다　38 ~에 접속[접근]하다　39 최신의
40 소수의, 한 움큼의

VOCABULARY TEST 2

A ⓓ　B ⓒ　C 1 extract　2 achieve
3 encourage　4 convert　D 1 a handful of
2 deal with　3 get access to

GRAMMAR TEST

A 1 to open　2 to keep　3 have　4 worn
B 1 have lost　2 has, finished　3 allowed us
to come　4 advised him to drink
C 1 너는 바르셀로나를 방문한 적이 있니?
　2 엄마는 내가 내 방을 청소하기를 원하셨다.
　3 내 친구는 나에게 내 자전거를 가져와달라고 부탁했다.
　4 그들은 작년부터 호주에서 살아왔다.

WRITING TEST

A 1 have been attacked
　2 NASA has achieved much
　3 money to open the file
　4 get ready to work
　5 has saved many astronauts
B 1 encourages them to do
　2 use it to lock
　3 was inspired by
　4 wanted to extract particles
　5 caused the company to stop

UNIT 11 | Food

pp. 42-45

VOCABULARY TEST 1

01 뜻하지 않게, 우연히　02 더하다, 첨가하다
03 유래하다　04 (빵·과자 등을) 굽다　05 물품, 품목
06 12개짜리 한 묶음　07 결국　08 추가의　09 추출물
10 대신에　11 다행히도　12 기계　13 100만
14 처벌하다　15 낯선, 익숙지 않은　16 엄하게, 심하게
17 받다　18 이상한; 낯선　19 용어, 말　20 혀
21 사라지다　22 고객　23 무게가 ~이다
24 law　25 ratio　26 hot　27 pepper
28 scale　29 mix　30 cheat　31 test
32 custom　33 measure　34 ancient
35 sweat　36 (물건 등을) 요청하다　37 ~에서 나오다
[비롯되다]　38 ~와 관련된　39 (몸의 일부가) 불타는
듯한[화끈거리는]　40 ~을 지칭하다

VOCABULARY TEST 2

A ⓒ　B ⓓ　C 1 originate　2 weigh
3 accidentally　4 severely　D 1 refer to
2 comes from　3 ask for

GRAMMAR TEST

A 1 much　2 far　3 hottest　4 more
B 1 earlier　2 scariest　3 harder
C 1 the largest park　2 the smallest planet
　3 the best soccer player
D 1 이 뮤지컬은 지난번 것보다 훨씬 더 좋았다.
　2 겨울의 밤은 여름의 밤보다 훨씬 더 길다.
　3 너는 이 웹사이트에서 가장 저렴한 비행기 표를 찾을 수
　　있다.

WRITING TEST

A 1 use it to mean
　2 how hot peppers are
　3 When customers asked for
　4 eating any strange peppers
　5 selling bread that weighed
B 1 stronger than
　2 is used to measure
　3 To avoid cheating
　4 was caught cheating
　5 the hottest pepper

UNIT 12 | Places

pp. 46-49

VOCABULARY TEST 1

01 광대한, 거대한　02 허락[용납]하다　03 허가, 허락
04 금지하다　05 시골 지역　06 구부릴 수 있는
07 거대한　08 확장[확대]되다; 확장하다　09 제국의;
황제의　10 이동이 가능한, 휴대할 수 있는　11 마지막의
12 에워싸다, 둘러싸다　13 확실한; 어떤　14 황제
15 지붕　16 제국　17 역할　18 지배자, 통치자
19 견디다, 이겨 내다　20 건축양식　21 중심
22 둘러싸다　23 주된　24 political
25 historical　26 value　27 enter　28 hold
29 continue　30 unique　31 build
32 artifact　33 government　34 traditional
35 wonder　36 실각하다, 물러나다　37 ~로 알려진
38 ~ 대신에　39 (해체하여) 치우다, 분해하다　40 ~을
재조립하다

VOCABULARY TEST 2

A 1 ⓑ　2 ⓐ　3 ⓒ　B ⓑ　C 1 surround
2 expand　3 permission　4 forbid　D 1 known
as　2 put, back together　3 step down

GRAMMAR TEST

A 1 hurt　2 be kept　3 is called　4 finished
B 1 was told to stay longer　2 should be kept
　(by you)　3 will be delivered (by us)
C 1 must be completed
　2 will be finished
　3 is expected to come
　4 was made a superstar

WRITING TEST

A 1 It took thirty minutes to
　2 to look at your land
　3 been forbidden to do
　4 They would move
　5 the best places to see
B 1 as big as
　2 could be taken down
　3 allowed to enter
　4 why it is called
　5 so did yurt culture

UNIT 13 | Activities
pp. 50-53

VOCABULARY TEST 1

01 과도한, 초과한 02 대나무 03 줄이다; 낮추다
04 방어하다 05 결합하다 06 근육 07 막대기; 축
08 즐겁게 하는 09 운동 10 기억해 내다, 상기하다
11 얻다 12 정확한 13 지점, 장소 14 운동장,
놀이터 15 태우다 16 반복되는 17 만들다, 창조하다
18 동작, 움직임 19 정육면체 20 정신 21 분노
22 경로 23 이유, 원인 24 naturally 25 fat
26 intensity 27 most 28 official 29 simple
30 meditation 31 ultimate 32 structure
33 consistently 34 space 35 memory
36 좋은 몸 상태를 유지하다 37 외치다, 소리치다
38 동시에 39 ~에 관심이 있는 40 진정하다

VOCABULARY TEST 2

A ⓐ B ⓒ C 1 anger 2 correct 3 muscle
4 entertaining D 1 calm, down 2 yell out
3 at the same time

GRAMMAR TEST

A 1 to her 2 for 3 of 4 easily 5 Sadly
  6 late
B 1 happily 2 fast 3 Luckily 4 well
C 1 his phone to her
  2 an email to me
  3 a sandwich for me
  4 some questions of him

WRITING TEST

A 1 the first "jungle gym" was created
  2 a bamboo structure for him
  3 this story to the superintendent
  4 you reduce your stress levels
  5 you'll get in shape
B 1 to learn martial arts
  2 help you calm yourself
  3 have been using
  4 was invented by
  5 can be found

UNIT 14 | Senses
pp. 54-57

VOCABULARY TEST 1

01 완성하다 02 선구자 03 개발하다 04 수용,
받아들임 05 필수적인 06 비교하다 07 감지[발견]
하다 08 손가락 끝 09 단 하나의 10 감각
11 발표[공표]하다 12 눈이 먼 13 사망, 죽음
14 혀 15 유발[촉발]하다 16 여전히[계속] ~이다
17 무시하다 18 협회, 기관 19 시력 20 인기 없는
21 온전한, 완벽한 22 표준 23 의사소통하다
24 sensitive 25 bright 26 insect
27 artificial 28 scholarship 29 appetite
30 possible 31 survival 32 infection
33 taste 34 national 35 concentration
36 process 37 ~로 정하다 38 알아내다
39 ~ 덕분에 40 수천의

VOCABULARY TEST 2

A ⓑ B ⓐ C 1 complete 2 communicate
3 scholarship 4 infection D 1 Thanks to
2 figure out 3 Thousands of

GRAMMAR TEST

A 1 to be 2 to buy 3 to learn 4 to boil
B 1 seeing → to see 2 running → to run
  3 come → to come 4 receive → to receive
  5 enough tall → tall enough
C 1 expected to win
  2 decided to study
  3 too small to put
  4 smart enough to answer

WRITING TEST

A 1 made him blind
  2 It was in 1917 that
  3 figure out whether a sweetener
  4 could communicate without speaking
  5 from left to right
B 1 decided to improve
  2 enough to trigger
  3 good enough to eat
  4 cannot[can't] be processed into
  5 are able to detect

UNIT 15 | Psychology pp. 58–61

VOCABULARY TEST 1

01 묘사하다; 연기하다 02 매우, 극도로 03 분실; 손실, 손해 04 견디다, 인내하다 05 끔찍한; 형편없는 06 영화 07 상상하다 08 질투 09 현명한 10 부정확한 11 평범한, 보통의 12 이익, 수익 13 (타고난) 재능이 있는 14 용어, 말 15 광범위한 16 (돈·시간·노력 등을) 소비하다, 쓰다 17 인정하다 18 경력, 이력 19 매입[구매]하다 20 질투, 선망 21 존경하다 22 낭비하다; 낭비 23 이야기 24 contemporary 25 mourn 26 theater 27 fictional 28 historian 29 release 30 failure 31 knowledge 32 eventually 33 effort 34 composer 35 unsuccessful 36 originate 37 ~을 가리키다[나타내다] 38 결국 39 포기하다 40 ~로 넘어가다

VOCABULARY TEST 2

A ⓓ B ⓒ C 1 respect 2 terrible 3 comprehensive 4 effort D 1 give up 2 move on to 3 In the end

GRAMMAR TEST

A 1 in 2 to ride 3 It 4 on
B 1 in 2 on 3 for 4 at 5 during
C 1 It is important to keep
  2 It is hard to decide
  3 It is fun to play
  4 It is difficult to learn

WRITING TEST

A 1 It is more likely
  2 Enduring a bad movie is
  3 all rumors are necessarily
  4 wasted the money he spent
  5 not as talented as Mozart
B 1 You keep sitting
  2 much wiser to accept
  3 efforts to be wasted
  4 may have begun
  5 said to be jealous

UNIT 16 | Light pp. 62–65

VOCABULARY TEST 1

01 제어[통제]하다 02 저명[유명]한, 명성 있는 03 연속적인 04 풀로 덮인 05 아주 작은 06 생물 07 일으키다, 야기하다 08 물질 09 현실 10 표현[묘사]하다 11 움직임 12 유인하다, 마음을 끌다 13 점 14 노출시키다 15 능력 16 목적 17 쏘다 18 ~ 아래에 19 단순함, 간단함 20 먹이[사냥감] 21 화학자 22 기법 23 혼란시키다 24 benefit 25 physicist 26 surface 27 ocean 28 inspire 29 contrasting 30 mix 31 danger 32 deep 33 involve 34 ~로 가득 찬 35 수백만의; 무수히 많은 36 ~을 겁주어 쫓아내다 37 ~로 유명한 38 ~에 관심이 있는 39 멀리서, 떨어져서 40 전체로서

VOCABULARY TEST 2

A ⓑ B ⓓ C 1 imagine 2 danger 3 attract 4 ability D 1 interested in 2 at a distance 3 filled with

GRAMMAR TEST

A 1 riding 2 Eating 3 reading 4 climbing 5 hidden 6 standing
B 1 목적어 2 주어 3 주어 4 보어
C 1 named 2 made 3 wearing 4 barking

WRITING TEST

A 1 is caused by a substance
  2 The technique involved using tiny
  3 One of his famous paintings
  4 that lights up to attract
  5 was interested in how
B 1 by lighting up
  2 to create light
  3 was inspired by
  4 smoke rising above them
  5 young men relaxing

MEMO

READING Inside

Answer Key

A 4-level curriculum
integration reading course

- **A thematic reading program that integrates with school curriculum**
  중등 교육과정이 지향하는 문이과 통합 및 타교과 연계 반영한 독해서

- **Informative content with well-designed comprehension questions**
  정보성 있는 지문과 질 높은 다양한 유형의 문항 그리고 서술형 평가도 대비

- **Grammar points directly related to the *Grammar Inside* series**
  베스트셀러 Grammar Inside와 직접적으로 연계된 문법 항목 및 문항 제공

- **Exercises with useful, essential, and academic vocabulary**
  중등 필수 어휘 학습 코너 제공

- **A workbook for more vocabulary, grammar, and reading exercises**
  풍부한 양의 어휘, 문법, 그리고 쓰기 추가 문제 등을 수록한 워크북

Level	Grade	Words Limit
Reading Inside Starter	Low-Intermediate	140-160
Reading Inside Level 1	**Intermediate**	**160-180**
Reading Inside Level 2	Intermediate	180-200
Reading Inside Level 3	Low-Advanced	200-220

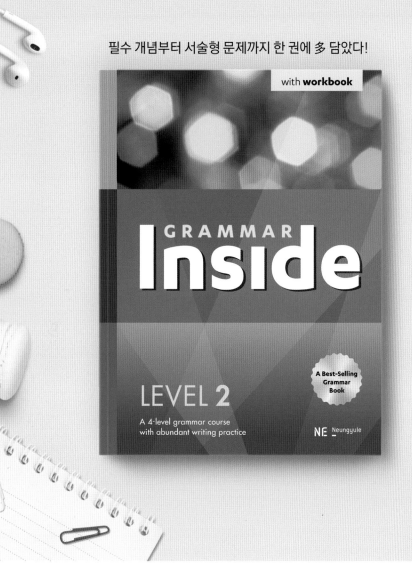

NE능률 교재 MAP

아래 교재 MAP을 참고하여 본인의 현재 혹은 목표 수준에 따라 교재를 선택하세요.
NE능률 교재들과 함께 영어실력을 쑥쑥~ 올려보세요!
MP3 등 교재 부가 학습 서비스 및 자세한 교재 정보는 www.nebooks.co.kr 에서 확인하세요.

초1-2	초3	초3-4	초4-5	초5-6
초등영어 리딩이 된다 Start 1	리딩버디 1	리딩버디 2	리딩버디 3	초등영어 리딩이 된다 Jump 1
초등영어 리딩이 된다 Start 2		초등영어 리딩이 된다 Basic 1	주니어 리딩튜터 스타터 1	초등영어 리딩이 된다 Jump 2
초등영어 리딩이 된다 Start 3		초등영어 리딩이 된다 Basic 2		초등영어 리딩이 된다 Jump 3
초등영어 리딩이 된다 Start 4		초등영어 리딩이 된다 Basic 3		초등영어 리딩이 된다 Jump 4
		초등영어 리딩이 된다 Basic 4		주니어 리딩튜터 스타터 2

초6-예비중	중1	중1-2	중2-3	중3
주니어 리딩튜터 1	1316 Reading 1	1316 Reading 2	1316 Reading 3	리딩튜터 입문
Junior Reading Expert 1	주니어 리딩튜터 2	주니어 리딩튜터 3	주니어 리딩튜터 4	정말 기특한 구문독해 완성
Reading Forward Basic 1	Junior Reading Expert 2	정말 기특한 구문독해 입문	정말 기특한 구문독해 기본	Reading Forward Advanced 1
	Reading Forward Basic 2	Junior Reading Expert 3	Junior Reading Expert 4	열중 16강 독해+문법 3
	열중 16강 독해+문법 1	Reading Forward Intermediate 1	Reading Forward Intermediate 2	Reading Inside 3
	Reading Inside Starter	열중 16강 독해+문법 2	Reading Inside 2	
		Reading Inside 1		

중3-예비고	고1	고1-2	고2-3, 수능 실전	고3 이상, 수능 고난도
Reading Expert 1	빠바 기초세우기	빠바 구문독해	빠바 유형독해	Reading Expert 5
리딩튜터 기본	리딩튜터 실력	리딩튜터 수능 PLUS	빠바 종합실전편	능률 고급영문독해
Reading Forward Advanced 2	Reading Expert 2	Reading Expert 3	Reading Expert 4	
	TEPS BY STEP G+R Basic		TEPS BY STEP G+R 1	

수능 이상/ 토플 80-89 · 텝스 600-699점	수능 이상/ 토플 90-99 · 텝스 700-799점	수능 이상/ 토플 100 · 텝스 800점 이상		
ADVANCED Reading Expert 1	ADVANCED Reading Expert 2	RADIX TOEFL Black Label Reading 2		
TEPS BY STEP G+R 2	RADIX TOEFL Black Label Reading 1	TEPS BY STEP G+R 3		
RADIX TOEFL Blue Label Reading 1, 2				

workbook

READING Inside

LEVEL 1

A 4-level curriculum
integration reading course

NE_ Neungyule

Workbook

READING
Inside

LEVEL 1

VOCABULARY TEST 1

반 / 이름:

[01–23] 다음 단어의 뜻을 쓰시오.

01 cover   _____

02 builder   _____

03 create   _____

04 triangle   _____

05 store   _____

06 specific   _____

07 term   _____

08 hexagon   _____

09 childhood   _____

10 musical   _____

11 choose   _____

12 emotion   _____

13 area   _____

14 special   _____

15 represent   _____

16 leave   _____

17 amount   _____

18 shape   _____

19 encourage   _____

20 loud   _____

21 form   _____

22 influential   _____

23 burst   _____

[24–35] 다음 뜻을 지닌 단어를 쓰시오.

24 공간, 자리   _____

25 효율적인   _____

26 인상적인, 인상 깊은   _____

27 비밀   _____

28 꼭 맞다   _____

29 벌집   _____

30 침묵   _____

31 낭비하다   _____

32 정사각형   _____

33 만들어내다, 생산하다   _____

34 틈, 간격   _____

35 의사소통하다; 전(달)하다   _____

[36–40] 다음 표현의 뜻을 쓰시오.

36 full of   _____

37 compared to   _____

38 feel like   _____

39 a variety of   _____

40 according to   _____

A 다음 영영 정의에 해당하는 단어를 고르시오.

admirable because it is very large, good, skillful, etc.

ⓐ efficient　　ⓑ specific　　ⓒ impressive　　ⓓ musical

B 다음 밑줄 친 단어와 비슷한 의미의 단어를 고르시오.

Some animals <u>store</u> food for the winter.

ⓐ find　　ⓑ save　　ⓒ break　　ⓓ catch

C 다음 빈칸에 알맞은 단어를 보기에서 골라 쓰시오.

보기　loud　produce　waste　influential

1 My uncle is a(n) _____ artist.

2 He spoke in a very _____ voice.

3 Don't _____ your money on useless things.

4 These factories _____ parts for cars and other vehicles.

D 다음 우리말과 일치하도록 빈칸에 알맞은 말을 쓰시오.

1 일기예보에 따르면, 곧 비가 올 것이다.
  ▶ A_____ t_____ the forecast, it'll rain soon.

2 그녀는 다양한 색으로 벽을 칠했다.
  ▶ She painted the wall with a v_____ o_____ colors.

3 작년 여름과 비교하면, 올 여름은 훨씬 더 덥다.
  ▶ C_____ t_____ last summer, this summer is much hotter.

A 다음 ( ) 안에서 알맞은 것을 고르시오.

1 I have a brother (who / which) is a teacher.

2 The person (which / that) called me was Jessica.

3 This is the book (who / which) is good for students.

4 Jennifer just started her project. She (must / cannot) be finished yet.

B 우리말과 일치하도록 **보기**에서 알맞은 말을 골라 문장을 완성하시오. (단, 한 번씩만 쓸 것)

보기	must	must not	cannot

1 너는 이 선을 넘어서는 안 된다.
▶ You _____ cross the line.

2 그녀는 일을 마친 후 피곤함이 틀림없다.
▶ She _____ be so tired after work.

3 그 소년은 John일 리가 없다. John은 지금 파리에 있다.
▶ The boy _____ be John. John is in Paris now.

C 우리말과 일치하도록 ( ) 안의 말과 관계대명사를 이용하여 문장을 완성하시오.

1 그는 수학을 가르치는 선생님이다. (teach, math)
▶ He is the teacher _____ _____ _____.

2 그녀는 이 목걸이를 만든 여자다. (make, this necklace)
▶ She is the woman _____ _____ _____ _____.

3 나는 낯선 사람들에게 짖는 개를 기른다. (bark, at strangers)
▶ I have a dog _____ _____ _____ _____.

4 나는 좋은 카메라가 있는 스마트폰을 샀다. (have, a good camera)
▶ I bought a smartphone _____ _____ _____ _____ _____.

A 우리말과 일치하도록 ( ) 안에 주어진 말을 바르게 배열하시오.

1 그것은 당신이 어떻게 느끼게 하는가? (you / feel / make)

▶ How does it _____ ?

2 그것은 모양들로 가득 찬 그림이다. (is / that / full / of)

▶ It is a painting _____ shapes.

3 벌은 꿀을 만드는 데만 능숙한 게 아닌 듯하다. (good / honey / at / making)

▶ It seems that bees are not only _____ .

4 그는 심지어 그의 작품들의 이름을 음악 용어들을 따서 지었다. (works / after / his / named)

▶ He even _____ musical terms.

5 공간을 남기지 않고 서로 딱 들어맞는 모양은 삼각형, 정사각형, 그리고 육각형이다.

(without / fit / together / that)

▶ The shapes _____ leaving spaces are the triangle,

the square, and the hexagon.

B 우리말과 일치하도록 ( ) 안의 말을 이용하여 문장을 완성하시오.

1 그 밀랍은 만들어내기 어렵다. (hard, produce)

▶ The wax is _____ _____ _____ .

2 그의 부모님은 그에게 음악을 듣도록 권장했다. (encourage, him, listen)

▶ His parents _____ _____ _____ _____ to music.

3 다른 모양들과 비교했을 때, 그것은 최소한의 둘레를 사용한다. (compare, other, shapes)

▶ _____ _____ _____ _____ , it uses the smallest perimeter.

4 벌은 그들의 몸에서 만들어내는 특별한 밀랍으로 서서히 벌집 칸들을 만든다. (they, produce)

▶ Bees gradually make cells from a special wax _____ _____ _____

from their bodies.

5 Kandinsky는 그의 그림을 보는 사람들이 음악을 듣고 있는 것처럼 느끼기를 원했다.

(view, his paintings)

▶ Kandinsky wanted people _____ _____ _____ _____ to feel

like they were listening to music.

[01–23] 다음 단어의 뜻을 쓰시오.

01 encourage _____

02 rest _____

03 match _____

04 invention _____

05 several _____

06 nearly _____

07 basic _____

08 following _____

09 opposite _____

10 beyond _____

11 argue _____

12 defeat _____

13 term _____

14 appear _____

15 greatly _____

16 century _____

17 version _____

18 happen _____

19 magnify _____

20 totally _____

21 observation _____

22 admit _____

23 device _____

[24–33] 다음 뜻을 지닌 단어를 쓰시오.

24 망원경 _____

25 표현 (어구) _____

26 설명하다 _____

27 들어오다, 들어가다 _____

28 상상하다 _____

29 가장자리, 모서리 _____

30 (게임 등의) 상대 _____

31 사과하다 _____

32 알려지지 않은, 미지의 _____

33 전통적으로 _____

[34–40] 다음 표현의 뜻을 쓰시오.

34 give up _____

35 throw in the towel _____

36 in trouble _____

37 in one's corner _____

38 on the ropes _____

39 prior to _____

40 take a leap forward _____

A 다음 단어의 영영 정의에 해당하는 단어를 고르시오.

> to relax oneself after doing something hard

ⓐ defeat   ⓑ argue   ⓒ happen   ⓓ rest

B 다음 밑줄 친 단어와 반대 의미의 단어를 고르시오.

> The real cause of the disease is <u>unknown</u>.

ⓐ famous   ⓑ boring   ⓒ near   ⓓ large

C 다음 빈칸에 알맞은 단어를 보기 에서 골라 쓰시오.

> 보기   explain   encourage   apologize   opponent

1 I want to _____. Please forgive me.

2 Can you please _____ what happened yesterday?

3 The stories of successful people always _____ me.

4 The boxer knocked his _____ down twice in just five minutes.

D 다음 우리말과 일치하도록 빈칸에 알맞은 말을 쓰시오.

1 항상 내편에 있어줘서 고마워.
   ▶ Thank you for always being i_____ m_____ c_____.

2 지불하기 이전에, 예약을 확인하시오.
   ▶ P_____ t_____ making a payment, check your reservation.

3 그녀는 춤 추는 방법을 배우는 것을 포기해야 했다.
   ▶ She had to g_____ u_____ learning how to dance.

A 다음 ( ) 안에서 알맞은 것을 고르시오.

1 There is nothing left (so / because) Joe ate it all.

2 My parents won't let me (traveling / travel) abroad by myself.

3 Taylor was exhausted, (because / so) she wanted to get some sleep.

4 My mother doesn't make me (cook / to cook) because I'm not good at it.

B 빈칸에 알맞은 말을 보기 에서 골라 두 문장을 연결하시오. (중복 사용 가능)

> 보기   because   so   that

1 Jenny couldn't go. The road was closed.

▶ Jenny couldn't go _____ the road was closed.

2 The class was very boring. Everyone fell asleep.

▶ The class was _____ boring _____ everyone fell asleep.

3 It was too noisy outside. He woke up in the middle of the night.

▶ It was too noisy outside, _____ he woke up in the middle of the night.

C 다음 문장에서 밑줄 친 부분을 바르게 고치시오.

1 My boss made me to attend the meeting.   _____

2 That box looks heavy. Let me helping you carry it.   _____

3 She didn't go to the museum so it was too far away.   _____

4 She has had her son experienced many different cultures.   _____

5 These products are so popular which they sold out quickly. _____

A 우리말과 일치하도록 ( ) 안에 주어진 말을 바르게 배열하시오.

1 그것은 사물을 겨우 세 배 더 크게 보이도록 할 수 있었다. (things / make / appear)

▶ It could only _____ three times bigger.

2 'in my corner'는 누군가가 나의 편에 있다는 것을 의미한다. (on / side / is / my)

▶ "In my corner" means that someone _____.

3 이것은 그들이 무슨 일이 일어나고 있는지 상상만 하게 했다. (them / what / imagine / let)

▶ This only _____ was happening.

4 그는 별을 연구하기 위해 망원경을 사용한 최초의 인물이었다. (person / a telescope / use / to)

▶ He was the first _____ to study the stars.

5 권투는 매우 인기가 있어서 몇몇 권투 용어가 영어에 들어오게 되었다.

(that / popular / was / so / boxing)

▶ _____ several boxing terms entered the English language.

B 우리말과 일치하도록 ( ) 안의 말을 이용하여 문장을 완성하시오.

1 Galileo는 자신만의 형태를 만들기로 결심했다. (decide, make)

▶ Galileo _____ _____ _____ his own version.

2 'on the ropes'는 곤경에 처했다는 의미이다. (mean, be, in trouble)

▶ "On the ropes" _____ _____ _____ _____.

3 코치들은 링 안으로 수건을 던짐으로써 패배를 인정했다. (admit, defeat, by, throw)

▶ The coaches _____ _____ _____ _____ a towel into the ring.

4 그것은 그가 사물을 서른 배까지 확대할 수 있게 했다. (allow, him, magnify)

▶ It _____ _____ _____ _____ things up to thirty times.

5 권투 선수가 상대편에 의해 로프로 몰리면, 그 선수는 거의 패배한 것이다. (a boxer, drive)

▶ When _____ _____ _____ _____ onto the ropes by the opponent, he or she is nearly defeated.

VOCABULARY TEST 1

반 / 이름:

[01–23] 다음 단어의 뜻을 쓰시오.

01 stain _____

02 exhausted _____

03 clearly _____

04 gym _____

05 spend _____

06 attend _____

07 ban _____

08 dark _____

09 competition _____

10 stunning _____

11 perfect _____

12 fitness _____

13 rotation _____

14 convenient _____

15 steps _____

16 punishment _____

17 area _____

18 serve _____

19 sweat _____

20 clothing _____

21 force _____

22 tradition _____

23 equipment _____

[24–36] 다음 뜻을 지닌 단어를 쓰시오.

24 경험하다 _____

25 기원 _____

26 재미있는, 흥미로운 _____

27 엄격한, 엄한 _____

28 여전히[계속] ~이다 _____

29 초창기의 _____

30 소비하다; 먹다 _____

31 동력을 공급하다 _____

32 규칙 _____

33 잔인한, 잔혹한 _____

34 바퀴 _____

35 인기 있는, 유명한 _____

36 감옥 _____

[37–40] 다음 표현의 뜻을 쓰시오.

37 take place _____

38 take part in _____

39 cheer for _____

40 make a comeback _____

A 다음 영영 정의에 해당하는 단어를 고르시오.

> to go to an event or a place

ⓐ force   ⓑ attend   ⓒ power   ⓓ begin

B 다음 밑줄 친 단어와 반대 의미의 단어를 고르시오.

> My parents had <u>strict</u> rules on computer games.

ⓐ full   ⓑ generous   ⓒ exciting   ⓓ short

C 다음 빈칸에 알맞은 단어를 보기에서 골라 쓰시오.

> 보기   equipment   stain   remain   consume

1 People all around the world _____ a lot of meat.

2 You should be careful when you deal with electrical _____.

3 Most stores will _____ closed during the Christmas season.

4 Sue spilled juice on herself. There is a big yellow _____ on her shirt.

D 다음 우리말과 일치하도록 빈칸에 알맞은 말을 쓰시오.

1 그녀는 다양한 교내 활동에 참여하는 것을 좋아한다.
   ▶ She likes to t_____ p_____ i_____ various school activities.

2 아카데미 시상식은 2월 또는 3월에 개최된다.
   ▶ The Academy Awards ceremony t_____ p_____ in February or March.

3 학생들은 교내 팀을 응원하기 위해 경기장에 갈 것이다.
   ▶ The students will go to the stadium to c_____ f_____ their school team.

A 다음 ( ) 안에서 알맞은 것을 고르시오.

1 Tommy can swim as (fast / faster) as Colin.

2 This picture (drew / was drawn) by Picasso.

3 The roof was (painting / painted) in red yesterday.

4 His new novel is as (good / best) as the previous one.

B 두 문장이 같은 의미가 되도록 ( ) 안의 말과 「as+형용사/부사+as」를 이용하여 문장을 완성하시오.

1 Tim is 63 kg. Ron is 63 kg too. (heavy)

▶ Tim is _____.

2 The green hat is $30. The yellow hat is $30 too. (expensive)

▶ The green hat is _____.

3 Amy is 164 cm tall. Her older sister is 164 cm tall too. (tall)

▶ Amy is _____.

4 My dad is 46 years old. My math teacher is 46 years old too. (old)

▶ My dad is _____.

C 우리말과 일치하도록 ( ) 안의 말을 이용하여 문장을 완성하시오.

1 그 축제는 서울에서 어제 개최되었다. (hold)

▶ The festival _____ _____ in Seoul yesterday.

2 그 애플 파이는 나에 의해 구워졌다. (bake, me)

▶ The apple pie _____ _____ _____ _____.

3 그 웹사이트는 많은 사람들에 의해 방문되었다. (visit)

▶ The website _____ _____ _____ many people.

4 그 새들은 과학자들에 의해 관찰되었다. (the birds, observe)

▶ _____ _____ _____ _____ _____ the scientists.

A 우리말과 일치하도록 ( ) 안에 주어진 말을 바르게 배열하시오.

1 바퀴의 회전은 방아에 동력을 공급하는 데 사용되었다. (to / was / power / used)
▶ The rotation of the wheel _____ a mill.

2 새로운 트레드밀은 운동하기에 쉽고 편리한 방법이었다. (exercise / way / to / convenient)
▶ The new treadmill was an easy and _____.

3 그들은 거의 테니스 그 자체만큼이나 오래된 행사에 참석할 것이다. (tennis / as / old / itself / as)
▶ They will attend an event almost _____.

4 딸기와 크림은 최초의 토너먼트 이후로 제공되어 왔다. (since / been / served / has)
▶ Strawberries and cream _____ the first tournament.

5 흰옷은 선수들이 팬들에게 더 잘 보이기 위한 방법이었다. (to / players / for / look)
▶ White clothes were a way _____ better for their fans.

B 우리말과 일치하도록 ( ) 안의 말을 이용하여 문장을 완성하시오.

1 트레드밀 위를 달리는 것은 힘든 일이다. (run, on, a treadmill)
▶ _____ _____ _____ _____ is hard work.

2 선수들은 땀에 젖어 보이는 것을 막기 위해 흰옷을 입었다. (avoid, look)
▶ The players wore white _____ _____ _____ sweaty.

3 1898년에, 그것은 너무 잔인하다는 이유로 금지되었다. (ban, for, be)
▶ In 1898, they _____ _____ _____ _____ too cruel.

4 그것은 개최되는 런던의 지역 이름을 따서 명명되었다. (it, take place)
▶ It is named after the area of London _____ _____ _____ _____.

5 윔블던을 볼 계획이라면, 한번 이 전통에 참여해봐라. (try, take part in)
▶ If you plan to watch Wimbledon, _____ _____ _____ _____
these traditions.

UNIT 04 | Jobs

반 / 이름:

[01–23] 다음 단어의 뜻을 쓰시오.

01 adjust _____

02 analysis _____

03 opposition _____

04 athlete _____

05 complex _____

06 condition _____

07 display _____

08 explain _____

09 artwork _____

10 humidity _____

11 left-handed _____

12 notice _____

13 photography _____

14 repair _____

15 restore _____

16 ruin _____

17 sculpture _____

18 specialty _____

19 strength _____

20 tactic _____

21 treatment _____

22 valuable _____

23 weaken _____

[24–36] 다음 뜻을 지닌 단어를 쓰시오.

24 예, 사례 _____

25 보상 _____

26 기량, 기술 _____

27 약함; 약점 _____

28 손상, 피해 _____

29 투수 _____

30 경비 요원 _____

31 문화의 _____

32 전문가 _____

33 치료, 처치 _____

34 연습, 실습 _____

35 (신원을) 확인하다; 찾다 _____

36 (주변의) 환경 _____

[37–40] 다음 표현의 뜻을 쓰시오.

37 thanks to _____

38 take care of _____

39 such as _____

40 interested in _____

A 다음 단어의 영영 정의를 바르게 연결하시오.

1 repair •   • ⓐ a positive feature

2 strength •   • ⓑ difficult to understand

3 complex •   • ⓒ to fix something damaged

B 다음 밑줄 친 단어와 비슷한 의미의 단어를 고르시오.

> I know that <u>athlete</u> who is stretching on the ground.

ⓐ actor   ⓑ teacher   ⓒ player   ⓓ artist

C 다음 빈칸에 알맞은 단어를 보기에서 골라 쓰시오.

> 보기 damage   adjust   treatment   restore

1 You can _____ the indoor temperature with this dial.

2 You need to get some proper _____ for your dental condition.

3 The huge snowstorm caused serious _____ to the town last year.

4 It's difficult to _____ the damaged artwork to its original condition.

D 다음 우리말과 일치하도록 빈칸에 알맞은 말을 쓰시오.

1 직업훈련센터 덕분에, Spencer 씨는 직업을 찾았다.

▶ T_____ t_____ the job training center, Mr. Spencer found a job.

2 그녀는 축구와 농구 같은 경기를 보는 것을 좋아한다.

▶ She loves watching sports s_____ a_____ soccer and basketball.

3 Henry가 휴가 동안 나의 고양이들을 돌봐줄 것이다.

▶ Henry will t_____ c_____ o_____ my cats during my vacation.

A 다음 두 문장의 의미가 일치하도록 보기와 같이 문장을 완성하시오.

> 보기 He showed his new smartphone to me.
> → He <u>showed me his new smartphone</u>.

1 I bought some flowers for him.

▶ I _____.

2 The detective asked questions of the witness.

▶ The detective _____.

3 Can you send the files to me by email?

▶ Can you _____ by email?

B 다음 문장의 밑줄 친 부분을 우리말로 옮기시오.

1 Mike woke up early <u>to see the sunrise</u>.

▶ _____

2 I visited a grocery store <u>to buy some food</u>.

▶ _____

3 Kelly went to Italy <u>to learn about Italian cuisine</u>.

▶ _____

C 우리말과 일치하도록 ( ) 안에 주어진 말을 바르게 배열하시오.

1 저에게 조언을 해주실 수 있나요? (me / advice / give / some)

▶ Can you _____?

2 나는 질문을 하기 위해 그녀에게 전화를 했다. (question / ask / a / to)

▶ I called her _____.

3 John은 지난 금요일에 여러 권의 책을 나에게 빌려주었다. (books / me / several / lent)

▶ John _____ last Friday.

A 우리말과 일치하도록 ( ) 안에 주어진 말을 바르게 배열하시오.

1 나에게 예를 들어줄 수 있는가? (an / me / give / example)

▶ Could you _____?

2 우선, 스포츠에 아주 흥미가 있어야 한다. (in / be / interested / very)

▶ First, you need to _____ sports.

3 경비 요원들은 산을 약화시키기 위해 재빨리 물을 더했다. (water / weaken / added / to)

▶ The guards quickly _____ the acid.

4 복원전문가들은 손상된 광택제를 제거함으로써 그 그림을 복원했다.

(the painting / by / restored / removing)

▶ Conservators _____ the damaged varnish.

5 우리는 전술을 바꿀 수 있도록 그들에게 이 정보를 말한다. (can / so / they / that)

▶ We tell them this information _____ change their tactics.

B 우리말과 일치하도록 ( ) 안의 말을 이용하여 문장을 완성하시오.

1 데이터베이스를 만들기 위해 뛰어난 분석 능력이 필요하다. (create, databases)

▶ You need excellent analytical skills _____ _____ _____.

2 그들은 각 재료들을 전시하는 가장 안전한 방법들을 안다. (safe, ways, display)

▶ They know the _____ _____ _____ _____ each material.

3 더 많은 해 동안 위대한 예술가들의 작품을 즐기게 될 것이다. (will, enjoy)

▶ The works of great artists _____ _____ _____ for many more years.

4 복원전문가는 예술품을 좋은 상태로 유지하는 데 전문가이다. (expert, at, keep)

▶ A conservator is _____ _____ _____ _____ artwork in good condition.

5 그들은 스포츠 팀이 그들이 이기도록 해주는 경기 전략을 세우는 것을 돕는다. (allow, them, win)

▶ They help sports teams make a game plan that _____ _____ _____ _____.

VOCABULARY TEST 1

반 / 이름:

[01–23] 다음 단어의 뜻을 쓰시오.

01 latest _____

02 complicated _____

03 premature _____

04 unavoidable _____

05 relief _____

06 emotion _____

07 stressful _____

08 society _____

09 solution _____

10 perspective _____

11 intense _____

12 warm _____

13 separate _____

14 function _____

15 melt _____

16 passion _____

17 technique _____

18 experiment _____

19 disease _____

20 electricity _____

21 conduct _____

22 effectiveness _____

23 handle _____

[24–35] 다음 뜻을 지닌 단어를 쓰시오.

24 상황 _____

25 입증[증명]하다 _____

26 중대한, 주요한 _____

27 예방하다, 막다 _____

28 결정 _____

29 규제하다; 조절하다 _____

30 아주 작은 _____

31 방법 _____

32 필수 요건 _____

33 분노 _____

34 향상되다 _____

35 낮추다 _____

[36–40] 다음 표현의 뜻을 쓰시오.

36 look for _____

37 according to _____

38 at a time _____

39 be born _____

40 lead to _____

A 다음 영영 정의에 해당하는 단어를 고르시오.

> very large or important

ⓐ major   ⓑ warm   ⓒ tiny   ⓓ stressful

B 다음 밑줄 친 단어와 비슷한 의미의 단어를 고르시오.

> She felt an <u>intense</u> pain in her arm.

ⓐ mild   ⓑ comfortable   ⓒ pleasant   ⓓ strong

C 다음 빈칸에 알맞은 단어를 보기에서 골라 쓰시오.

> 보기   cost   emotions   prevent   regulate

1 This exercise helps _____ weight gain.

2 Music has a big influence on my _____.

3 The _____ of living in a big city is expensive.

4 Use these buttons to _____ the temperature.

D 다음 우리말과 일치하도록 빈칸에 알맞은 말을 쓰시오.

1 한 번에 한 문제씩 풀어보자.
   ▶ Let's solve one problem a_____ a t_____.

2 그는 프랑스에서 태어났지만, 지금은 한국에 산다.
   ▶ He w_____ b_____ in France, but now he lives in Korea.

3 정크푸드를 너무 많이 먹는 것은 건강 문제로 이어질 수 있다.
   ▶ Eating too much junk food can l_____ t_____ health problems.

A 다음 ( ) 안에서 알맞은 것을 고르시오.

1 The music made her (sad / sadly).

2 I found the movie (interesting / interestingly).

3 He is not able (play / to play) the guitar very well.

4 We did the laundry yesterday. We (have to / don't have to) do it again.

B 다음 문장에서 밑줄 친 부분을 바르게 고치시오.

1 This helmet will keep you <u>safely</u>.   _____

2 You should consider yourself <u>luckily</u>.   _____

3 The flowers always made me <u>happily</u>.   _____

4 I <u>can</u> swim now because I hurt my legs.   _____

5 I <u>have to</u> go to school tomorrow because it's Saturday. _____

C 우리말과 일치하도록 ( ) 안에 주어진 말을 바르게 배열하시오.

1 창문을 연 채로 두세요. (leave / open / the window)
   ▶ Please _____.

2 나는 이제 너를 도울 수 있다. (to / able / help / am)
   ▶ I _____ you now.

3 그는 그 강의가 어렵다는 것을 알게 되었다. (found / difficult / the lecture)
   ▶ He _____.

4 그녀는 제시간에 도착하기 위해 택시를 타야 한다. (to / take / has)
   ▶ She _____ a taxi to get there in time.

A 우리말과 일치하도록 (   ) 안에 주어진 말을 바르게 배열하시오.

1 그것이 인큐베이터의 역할이다. (what / are / for / incubators)

▶ That's ＿＿＿＿＿＿＿＿＿＿＿＿＿＿＿＿＿＿＿.

2 그들은 자신을 따뜻하게 유지해주는 체지방이 거의 없다. (keep / warm / them / to)

▶ They have little body fat ＿＿＿＿＿＿＿＿＿＿＿＿＿＿＿＿.

3 그들은 너무 작아서 체온을 조절할 수 없다. (regulate / too / to / small)

▶ They are ＿＿＿＿＿＿＿＿＿＿＿＿＿＿＿＿ their body temperature.

4 이 방법을 사용한 참가자들은 그들의 분노를 줄일 수 있었다. (who / method / used / this)

▶ Participants ＿＿＿＿＿＿＿＿＿＿＿＿＿＿＿＿ were able to reduce their anger.

5 우리는 최신의 기법들을 찾고 그것들이 효과 있기를 바란다. (they / work / hope / and)

▶ We look for the latest techniques ＿＿＿＿＿＿＿＿＿＿＿＿＿＿＿＿.

B 우리말과 일치하도록 (   ) 안의 말을 이용하여 문장을 완성하시오.

1 Jane Chen은 이 문제를 해결하고 싶었다. (want, solve)

▶ Jane Chen ＿＿＿＿ ＿＿＿＿ ＿＿＿＿ this problem.

2 그러한 문제들은 그들을 따뜻하게 유지함으로써 막을 수 있다. (prevent, by, keep)

▶ Such problems can be ＿＿＿＿ ＿＿＿＿ ＿＿＿＿ them warm.

3 격한 감정은 차분하고 명확한 결정을 내리는 것을 방해한다. (prevent, you, from, make)

▶ Intense emotions ＿＿＿＿ ＿＿＿＿ ＿＿＿＿ ＿＿＿＿ calm, clear decisions.

4 오하이오 대학교에서 실시된 한 연구에 따르면, 스트레스를 해소하는 것은 꽤 간단하다. (a study, conduct)

▶ According to ＿＿＿＿ ＿＿＿＿ ＿＿＿＿ at Ohio University, relieving stress is quite simple.

5 외부의 관점을 갖는 것은 당신이 이러한 감정들을 통제하게 해준다. (allow, you, control)

▶ Having an outside perspective ＿＿＿＿ ＿＿＿＿ ＿＿＿＿ ＿＿＿＿ these emotions.

UNIT 06 | Future

반 / 이름:

[01–23] 다음 단어의 뜻을 쓰시오.

01 atmosphere _____

02 influence _____

03 brighten _____

04 climate _____

05 currently _____

06 develop _____

07 efficiently _____

08 forbid _____

09 gradually _____

10 groundbreaking _____

11 heat _____

12 hide _____

13 historical _____

14 maintain _____

15 massive _____

16 population _____

17 predict _____

18 preserve _____

19 fast-growing _____

20 specific _____

21 temperature _____

22 underground _____

23 upside-down _____

[24–37] 다음 뜻을 지닌 단어를 쓰시오.

24 고층 건물 _____

25 건축가 _____

26 파(내)다 _____

27 외모, (겉)모습 _____

28 쟁점, 사안; 문제 _____

29 건축물, 구조물 _____

30 정화 장치 _____

31 유산 _____

32 제안[제의]하다 _____

33 증명[입증]하다 _____

34 풀어 주다; 방출[발산]하다 _____

35 공공의, 대중을 위한 _____

36 이마 _____

37 단계, 시기 _____

[38–40] 다음 표현의 뜻을 쓰시오.

38 look at _____

39 in addition _____

40 make a prediction _____

A 다음 밑줄 친 단어와 비슷한 의미의 단어를 고르시오.

> The 3D printer is a groundbreaking invention in many ways.

ⓐ typical   ⓑ fixed   ⓒ real   ⓓ innovative

B 다음 밑줄 친 단어와 반대 의미의 단어를 고르시오.

> The professor explained the economic term by giving specific examples.

ⓐ general   ⓑ classic   ⓒ complex   ⓓ main

C 다음 빈칸에 알맞은 단어를 보기에서 골라 쓰시오.

> 보기   massive   prove   structure   release

1 The explosion left a _____ hole in the ground.

2 This _____ was designed to resist strong winds.

3 The evidence will _____ that the suspect is guilty.

4 Plants take in carbon dioxide and _____ oxygen into the atmosphere.

D 다음 우리말과 일치하도록 빈칸에 알맞은 말을 쓰시오.

1 나는 그 서류들을 검토할 시간이 없었다.
 ▶ I didn't have time to l_____ a_____ the papers.

2 그는 자상하다. 게다가, 그는 요리도 잘한다.
 ▶ He is kind. I_____ a_____, he is good at cooking too.

3 우리는 누가 대회에서 이길지 예측할 것을 요청받았다.
 ▶ We were asked to m_____ a p_____ who would win the contest.

GRAMMAR TEST

A 다음 ( ) 안에서 알맞은 것을 고르시오.

1 If he (comes / will come) to the party, we'll be very happy.

2 Summer is the best season (to watch / watching) horror movies.

3 The novelist needs an extra room (stores / to store) her books in.

4 If you (don't / will) wake up early tomorrow, you will miss the train.

B 보기 안의 동사를 이용하여 문장을 완성하시오.

보기 spend wear rain drink

1 I brought some juice _____.

2 Thailand is a good place _____ your vacation.

3 If it _____ tomorrow, I will stay home and watch TV.

4 If he _____ sunscreen, he will avoid getting a sunburn.

C 보기와 같이 밑줄 친 to부정사구가 꾸미는 말에 동그라미 하시오.

보기 Would you like (something) to drink?

1 I need a vase to put these flowers in.

2 I can't find a dress to wear to the wedding.

3 She has a lot of friends to invite to the party.

4 The scientist wants someone to help him with his research.

A 우리말과 일치하도록 ( ) 안에 주어진 말을 바르게 배열하시오.

1 멕시코는 빠르게 인구가 늘고 있지만 공간은 작다. (little / population / but / space)

▶ Mexico has a fast-growing _____.

2 미래 인간들은 오늘날의 인간들보다 더 넓은 이마를 가지게 될지도 모른다.

(than / foreheads / larger / people)

▶ Future people may have _____ today.

3 그것들은 태양으로부터 더 멀리 떨어진 행성에서 그들이 볼 수 있도록 도와줄 것이다.

(see / them / would / help)

▶ They _____ on planets farther from the Sun.

4 그들은 자신들의 아이들을 위한 건강한 신체를 디자인할 수 있을 것이다.

(be / design / able / will / to)

▶ They _____ healthy bodies for their children.

B 우리말과 일치하도록 ( ) 안의 말을 이용하여 문장을 완성하시오.

1 그것은 지하에 숨겨질 것이다. (will, hide)

▶ It _____ _____ _____ underground.

2 인간은 더 큰 뇌와 머리를 발달해오고 있다. (have, be, develop)

▶ Humans _____ _____ _____ larger brains and heads.

3 이러한 문제점들을 다루는 한 방법으로써, 건축가들은 소칼로 아래를 파낼 것을 제안했다. (deal with)

▶As a way _____ _____ _____ these issues, architects suggested

digging under Zócalo.

4 사람들은 그들이 다른 행성에서 살 수 있도록 해주는 기술을 만들지도 모른다. (allow, live)

▶ People might create technology that will _____ _____ _____

_____ on other planets.

5 만약 지구의 온도가 계속 오른다면, 사람들은 키가 더 크고 더 날씬한 신체를 가지게 될지도 모른다.

(keep, rise)

▶ If global temperatures _____ _____, people may have taller, thinner

bodies.

VOCABULARY TEST 1

반 / 이름:

[01–23] 다음 단어의 뜻을 쓰시오.

01 situation _____

02 initial _____

03 toxic _____

04 form _____

05 produce _____

06 pollute _____

07 cosmetics _____

08 tiny _____

09 partially _____

10 drain _____

11 toothpaste _____

12 innovation _____

13 footwear _____

14 organic _____

15 require _____

16 environmentally _____

17 release _____

18 marine _____

19 reduce _____

20 material _____

21 atmosphere _____

22 amount _____

23 harmful _____

[24–36] 다음 뜻을 지닌 단어를 쓰시오.

24 ~을 포함하여 _____

25 짓다; 축적하다 _____

26 화학 물질 _____

27 기름; 석유 _____

28 물리적인 _____

29 생각[고려]하다 _____

30 가공하다; 과정 _____

31 (운동 경기용) 셔츠 _____

32 영향 _____

33 치명적인 _____

34 서식지 _____

35 연습; 관행, 관례 _____

36 현명하게 _____

[37–40] 다음 표현의 뜻을 쓰시오.

37 made from _____

38 rely on _____

39 on and on _____

40 for instance _____

A 다음 영영 정의에 해당하는 단어를 고르시오.

> causing or ending in death

ⓐ fatal   ⓑ tiny   ⓒ organic   ⓓ marine

B 다음 밑줄 친 단어와 비슷한 의미의 단어를 고르시오.

> Sugary juice can be harmful to your teeth.

ⓐ complex   ⓑ dangerous   ⓒ safe   ⓓ useful

C 다음 빈칸에 알맞은 단어를 보기에서 골라 쓰시오.

> 보기   pollute   reduce   amount   situation

1 The _____ is getting worse and worse.

2 He spent a large _____ of money last year.

3 Using your car too much can _____ the air.

4 The aim of this campaign is to _____ car accidents.

D 다음 우리말과 일치하도록 빈칸에 알맞은 말을 쓰시오.

1 대부분의 자선 단체들은 기부금에 의존한다.
   ▶ Most charities r_____ o_____ donations.

2 그녀의 연설은 한 시간 넘는 동안 계속되었다.
   ▶ Her speech went o_____ a_____ o_____ for over an hour.

3 그들은 많은 종류의 과일을 재배하는데, 예를 들어 사과와 배이다.
   ▶ They grow many kinds of fruit; f_____ i_____ apples and pears.

반 / 이름:

A 다음 ( ) 안에서 알맞은 것을 고르시오.

1 He bought a (using / used) car last year.

2 The (sleeping / slept) baby looks so cute.

3 She is a doctor (with / with whom) I work.

4 Math is the subject (who / which) I like most.

B 다음 문장에서 생략할 수 있는 말에 동그라미 표시하고, 생략할 수 있는 말이 없으면 빈칸에 X를 쓰시오.

1 Jenny is the woman that he loves. _____

2 This is the restaurant at which I work. _____

3 The bag that I bought yesterday is quite big. _____

4 My parents are the people who I always rely on. _____

C 우리말과 일치하도록 보기 안의 말을 이용하여 문장을 완성하시오.

| 보기 | cry | smile | break | shock |

1 웃고 있는 아이들을 봐.
  ▶ Look at the _____ children.

2 저 울고 있는 소년은 내 남동생이다.
  ▶ That _____ boy is my brother.

3 나는 그 충격적인 소식을 Liam에게서 들었다.
  ▶ I heard the _____ news from Liam.

4 Betty는 그의 부서진 카메라를 고치고 싶어 한다.
  ▶ Betty wants to fix her _____ camera.

A 우리말과 일치하도록 ( ) 안에 주어진 말을 바르게 배열하시오.

1 셔츠가 어떻게 만들어지는지 생각해보라. (are / jerseys / how / made)

▶ Consider _____.

2 그것들은 모래보다 훨씬 더 작은 플라스틱 구슬이다. (smaller / even / are / than)

▶ They are plastic beads that _____ sand.

3 우리가 할 수 있는 한 가지 일은 제품을 더 현명하게 구매하는 것이다. (buy / is / can / we / do)

▶ One thing _____ products more wisely.

4 한 회사는 업사이클 된 해양 플라스틱으로 옷을 만들기 시작했다. (marine plastic / upcycled / from)

▶ A company started making clothing _____.

5 이런 화학 물질은 우리가 먹는 몇몇 해산물에서 발견될지도 모른다. (we / the / eat / seafood)

▶ These chemicals might be found in some of _____.

B 우리말과 일치하도록 ( ) 안의 말을 이용하여 문장을 완성하시오.

1 우리는 많은 것들을 만들기 위해 플라스틱에 의존한다. (rely, plastic, make)

▶ We _____ _____ _____ _____ _____ many things.

2 이는 석유가 폴리에스터로 가공되어야 한다는 것을 의미한다. (must, process)

▶ This means oil _____ _____ _____ into polyester.

3 마이크로비즈가 상황을 훨씬 더 악화하고 있다. (make, the situation, even, bad)

▶ Microbeads are _____ _____ _____ _____ _____.

4 매우 많은 양의 해로운 이산화탄소가 대기 중으로 방출된다. (damage, CO₂, release)

▶ Very large amounts of _____ _____ _____ _____ into the atmosphere.

5 영국의 한 축구 구단은 부분적으로 커피콩으로 만들어진 셔츠를 출시했다. (a jersey, make, partially)

▶ An English football club released _____ _____ _____ _____ from coffee beans.

UNIT 08 | Health

[01–23] 다음 단어의 뜻을 쓰시오.

01 affect   _____

02 beat   _____

03 dead   _____

04 extremely   _____

05 develop   _____

06 device   _____

07 disease   _____

08 feed   _____

09 fever   _____

10 contain   _____

11 independent   _____

12 lift   _____

13 meal   _____

14 opportunity   _____

15 opposite   _____

16 past   _____

17 plate   _____

18 protect   _____

19 reduce   _____

20 remove   _____

21 shake   _____

22 uncontrollably   _____

23 threat   _____

[24–36] 다음 뜻을 지닌 단어를 쓰시오.

24 허락하다, 가능하게 하다   _____

25 감염   _____

26 방향   _____

27 세포   _____

28 증상, 징후   _____

29 경험   _____

30 방어(물)   _____

31 기침   _____

32 기록하다   _____

33 효과적인   _____

34 살아남다; (고난 등을) 견디다   _____

35 침입하다   _____

36 주사[주입]하다   _____

[37–40] 다음 표현의 뜻을 쓰시오.

37 such as   _____

38 instead of   _____

39 because of   _____

40 the same A as B   _____

A 다음 영영 정의에 해당하는 단어를 고르시오.

> an activity or a situation that could cause danger or harm

ⓐ disease   ⓑ device   ⓒ cell   ⓓ threat

B 다음 밑줄 친 단어와 비슷한 의미의 단어를 고르시오.

> I think online shopping allows you to save time.

ⓐ enable   ⓑ remind   ⓒ stop   ⓓ encourage

C 다음 빈칸에 알맞은 단어를 보기에서 골라 쓰시오.

> 보기   lift   opposite   symptoms   independent

1 A high fever is one of early _____ of this disease.

2 This box is heavy, so I cannot _____ it by myself.

3 Traveling around the world alone made me more _____.

4 You are on the wrong bus. This bus goes in the _____ direction.

D 다음 우리말과 일치하도록 빈칸에 알맞은 말을 쓰시오.

1 그의 머리카락은 그녀의 것과 똑같은 색이다.
　▶ His hair is t_____ s_____ color a_____ hers.

2 나는 검은색과 갈색과 같은 어두운 색을 좋아한다.
　▶ I like dark colors s_____ a_____ black and brown.

3 그는 스트레스 때문에 악몽에 시달리고 있다.
　▶ He suffers from nightmares b_____ o_____ stress.

A 다음 (   ) 안에서 알맞은 것을 고르시오.

1 I looked at (me / myself) in the mirror.

2 Did he make all this food (him / himself)?

3 The bad news is (because / that) the match was canceled.

4 I know (it / that) you tried your best. So the result doesn't matter.

B 다음 밑줄 친 재귀대명사를 생략할 수 있으면 O, 없으면 X를 쓰시오.

1 I made the bracelet <u>myself</u>. _____

2 Can you tell me about <u>yourself</u>? _____

3 Emma passed the audition. She must be proud of <u>herself</u>! _____

4 The operation <u>itself</u> was a success, but the patient is not awake yet. _____

C 다음 밑줄 친 부분을 우리말로 옮기시오.

1 We don't believe <u>that he lied to us</u>.

   ▶ _____

2 I heard <u>that it is going to rain tomorrow</u>.

   ▶ _____

3 The important thing is <u>that you are happy</u>.

   ▶ _____

4 Is it true <u>that Olivia is going to move to Greece</u>?

   ▶ _____

A 우리말과 일치하도록 ( ) 안에 주어진 말을 바르게 배열하시오.

1 우리는 기침이나 열과 같은 증상을 얻는다. (as / get / such / symptoms)

▶ We _____ a cough or fever.

2 그것들은 친구나 가족과 시간을 보낼 기회이다. (to / spend / an opportunity)

▶ They are _____ time with friends or family.

3 이것은 그들이 접시에서 음식을 들어 올리는 것을 힘들게 만든다. (them / lift / to / for)

▶ This make it difficult _____ food from their plates.

4 Jenner는 그것을 견뎌내는 것이 천연두로부터 그 소년을 보호할 것이라고 믿었다.

(surviving / believed / Jenner / that)

▶ _____ it would protect the boy from smallpox.

5 손이 떨리는 것을 막으려 하는 것 대신, 그것은 숟가락 그 자체를 멈춘다.

(from / stop / the hand / shaking)

▶ Instead of trying to _____ , it stops the spoon itself.

B 우리말과 일치하도록 ( ) 안의 말을 이용하여 문장을 완성하시오.

1 Liftware는 그들이 자기 자신을 먹일 수 있도록 해준다. (feed, them)

▶ Liftware allows them _____ _____ _____.

2 그들은 보통 타인이 먹여줘야 한다. (have to, feed)

▶ They often _____ _____ _____ _____ by others.

3 면역 체계는 그것을 물리치는 방법을 기억한다. (how, beat)

▶ The immune system remembers _____ _____ _____ it.

4 그 병은 사람들이 통제할 수 없이 떨게 만든다. (cause, people, shake)

▶ The disease _____ _____ _____ _____ uncontrollably.

5 우리는 모든 위험한 바이러스에 대한 백신을 만들 수 있을 것이다. (will, able, make)

▶ We _____ _____ _____ _____ _____ vaccines for every dangerous virus.

VOCABULARY TEST 1

반 / 이름:

[01–23] 다음 단어의 뜻을 쓰시오.

01 emotional _____

02 carry _____

03 likewise _____

04 gain _____

05 through _____

06 state _____

07 technique _____

08 weight _____

09 confirm _____

10 separate _____

11 mind _____

12 painting _____

13 wall _____

14 discover _____

15 spread _____

16 rainbow _____

17 speed _____

18 liquid _____

19 long-term _____

20 during _____

21 along _____

22 stay _____

23 express _____

[24–35] 다음 뜻을 지닌 단어를 쓰시오.

24 알아차리다 _____

25 햇빛 _____

26 반영하다 _____

27 침실 _____

28 색소 _____

29 원래의 _____

30 일하다; 작용하다 _____

31 조사, 수사 _____

32 묻히다, 바르다 _____

33 드러내다 _____

34 바래다, 희미해지다 _____

35 (색 등이) 연한 _____

[36–40] 다음 표현의 뜻을 쓰시오.

36 known as _____

37 end up _____

38 over time _____

39 each other _____

40 composed of _____

A 다음 영영 정의에 해당하는 단어를 고르시오.

> an official examination of the facts about a situation, crime, etc.

ⓐ pigment   ⓑ sunlight   ⓒ technique   ⓓ investigation

B 다음 밑줄 친 단어와 비슷한 의미의 단어를 고르시오.

> Can you please <u>confirm</u> my reservation?

ⓐ cancel   ⓑ check   ⓒ create   ⓓ cause

C 다음 빈칸에 알맞은 단어를 보기에서 골라 쓰시오.

> 보기   original   notice   express   separate

1 I cannot _____ how happy I am now.

2 _____ the egg yolk from the egg white.

3 He didn't _____ that I was staring at him.

4 I think we should go back to our _____ plan.

D 다음 우리말과 일치하도록 빈칸에 알맞은 말을 쓰시오.

1 John은 유명한 예술가로 알려져 있다.

▶ John is k_____ a_____ a famous artist.

2 그 팀은 11명의 선수로 구성되어 있다.

▶ The team is c_____ o_____ eleven players.

3 그들의 관계는 시간이 지나면서 바뀌었다.

▶ Their relationship has changed o_____ t_____.

A 다음 ( ) 안에서 알맞은 것을 고르시오.

1 His voice sounds (great / greatly).

2 The pumpkin pie tastes (sweet / sweetly).

3 His advice sounds (helpful / helpfully) to me.

4 Let's stay inside (when / until) the rain stops.

5 She became healthier (after / before) she started exercising.

B 다음 문장의 밑줄 친 부분을 바르게 고치시오.

1 The fish tasted <u>badly</u>. _____

2 These muffins smell so <u>nicely</u>. _____

3 The cushion feels very <u>comfortably</u>. _____

4 Your wedding dress looks <u>beautifully</u>. _____

C 우리말과 일치하도록 빈칸에 알맞은 단어를 보기에서 골라 쓰시오.

| 보기 | until | when | after | before |

1 네가 그것을 잊기 전에 그것을 써라.
▶ Write it down _____ you forget it.

2 내가 여덟 살이었을 때, 나는 뉴욕에 살았다.
▶ _____ I was eight years old, I lived in New York.

3 네가 도착할 때까지 우리는 버스 정류장에서 기다릴 것이다.
▶ We will wait at the bus stop _____ you arrive.

4 집에 돌아온 후 손을 씻는 것을 잊지 마라.
▶ Don't forget to wash your hands _____ you come home.

A 우리말과 일치하도록 ( ) 안에 주어진 말을 바르게 배열하시오.

1 그것은 그가 머물렀던 방을 보여준다. (in / the / stayed / room / he)

▶ It shows _____.

2 프리즘은 햇빛을 무지개의 모든 색깔로 나눈다. (the sunlight / into / all / separates)

▶ The prism _____ of the colors in a rainbow.

3 그것은 더 어둡고 더 차가워 보이는 색으로 칠해졌다. (darker / looked / and / that / colder)

▶ It was painted in colors _____.

4 색은 그가 그것들을 그릴 당시의 심리 상태를 반영한다. (he / the time / them / painted)

▶ The colors reflect his state of mind at _____.

5 당신이 필요한 모든 것은 여과지, 검은 매직펜, 그리고 약간의 물이다. (is / you / need / all)

▶ _____ a filter paper, black markers, and some water.

6 검은색은 자홍색이나 청록색 같은 다른 색소로 분리될 것이다. (as / pigments / other / such)

▶ The black will separate into _____ magenta or cyan.

B 우리말과 일치하도록 ( ) 안의 말을 이용하여 문장을 완성하시오.

1 시간이 지나면서 페인트가 바래왔다. (have, fade, time)

▶ The paint _____ _____ _____ _____.

2 물이 퍼지는 것을 멈출 때까지 그 색에 어떤 일이 일어나는지 보아라. (stop, spread)

▶ Watch what happens to that color until the water _____ _____.

3 그들은 그의 감정 상태에 대한 더 명확한 이해를 얻기를 바란다. (hope, gain)

▶ They _____ _____ _____ a clearer understanding of his emotional state.

4 그들은 원래의 색깔이 어떤 색소로 구성되어 있는지를 발견할 수 있다. (compose, of)

▶ They can discover which pigments the original color _____ _____ _____.

VOCABULARY TEST 1

반 / 이름:

[01–23] 다음 단어의 뜻을 쓰시오.

01 astronaut _____

02 guarantee _____

03 convert _____

04 individual _____

05 manufacturing _____

06 mission _____

07 breath _____

08 sweat _____

09 unlock _____

10 protect _____

11 entire _____

12 device _____

13 extract _____

14 surface _____

15 attack _____

16 encourage _____

17 demand _____

18 impact _____

19 research _____

20 achieve _____

21 landing _____

22 local _____

23 disgusting _____

[24–33] 다음 뜻을 지닌 단어를 쓰시오.

24 영감을 주다 _____

25 전문가 _____

26 흔한 _____

27 정화 _____

28 보안 _____

29 입자 _____

30 국제적인 _____

31 실용적인 _____

32 경고 _____

33 범죄 _____

[34–40] 다음 표현의 뜻을 쓰시오.

34 get ~ back _____

35 deal with _____

36 in the end _____

37 pop up _____

38 get access to _____

39 up to date _____

40 a handful of _____

A 다음 영영 정의에 해당하는 단어를 고르시오.

> to give somebody the idea for something

ⓐ attack   ⓑ achieve   ⓒ protect   ⓓ inspire

B 다음 밑줄 친 단어와 비슷한 의미의 단어를 고르시오.

> They spent the <u>entire</u> day playing outside.

ⓐ partial   ⓑ unusual   ⓒ whole   ⓓ enjoyable

C 다음 빈칸에 알맞은 단어를 보기에서 골라 쓰시오.

> 보기 extract   encourage   achieve   convert

1 They _____ the juice from grapes.

2 She decided to start a business to _____ her goals.

3 Advertisements _____ people to buy things more often.

4 I want to _____ the small bedroom into a changing room.

D 다음 우리말과 일치하도록 빈칸에 알맞은 말을 쓰시오.

1 나는 단지 한 움큼의 쌀이 필요하다.
  ▶ I only need a h_____ o_____ rice.

2 그녀는 그 문제를 다룰 방법을 모른다.
  ▶ She doesn't know how to d_____ w_____ the problem.

3 당신은 그 프로그램에 접속하기 위해 비밀번호가 필요하다.
  ▶ You need a password to g_____ a_____ t_____ the program.

A 다음 ( ) 안에서 알맞은 것을 고르시오.

1 He told me (open / to open) the door.

2 I expect her (keep / to keep) the secret.

3 We (are / have) already repaired our car.

4 I have (wearing / worn) these glasses for two years.

B 우리말과 일치하도록 ( ) 안의 말을 이용하여 문장을 완성하시오.

1 나는 내 지갑을 잃어버렸다. (그래서 지금 지갑이 없다.) (lose)

▶ I _____ _____ my purse.

2 그녀는 책을 읽는 것을 막 끝마쳤다. (finish)

▶ She _____ just _____ reading the book.

3 그 남자는 우리가 그의 사무실에 들어오게 해줬다. (allow, us, come)

▶ The man _____ _____ _____ _____ into his office.

4 의사는 그가 더 많은 물을 마시기를 조언했다. (advise, him, drink)

▶ The doctor _____ _____ _____ _____ more water.

C 다음 문장을 우리말로 옮기시오.

1 Have you ever visited Barcelona?

▶ _____

2 Mom wanted me to clean my room.

▶ _____

3 My friend asked me to bring my own bike.

▶ _____

4 They have lived in Australia since last year.

▶ _____

A 우리말과 일치하도록 ( ) 안에 주어진 말을 바르게 배열하시오.

1 당신은 랜섬웨어에 의해 공격받았다. (have / attacked / been)

▶ You _____ by ransomware.

2 NASA는 우주에서 많은 것을 성취했다. (has / NASA / much / achieved)

▶ _____ in space.

3 그것은 파일을 열기 위해서 당신은 돈을 지불해야 한다고 말한다! (open / to / the file / money)

▶ It says you must pay _____!

4 당신은 컴퓨터를 시작하고 일할 준비를 한다. (to / get / work / ready)

▶ You start your computer and _____.

5 그것은 국제 우주 정거장의 많은 우주 비행사들을 구해왔다. (saved / many / has / astronauts)

▶ It _____ on the International Space Station.

B 우리말과 일치하도록 ( ) 안의 말을 이용하여 문장을 완성하시오.

1 해커들에게 돈을 지불하는 것은 그들이 그것을 다시 하도록 부추긴다. (encourage, them, do)

▶ Paying hackers _____ _____ _____ _____ it again.

2 사이버 범죄자들은 파일이나 시스템을 잠그기 위해 그것을 사용한다. (use, it, lock)

▶ Cybercriminals _____ _____ _____ _____ files or systems.

3 심지어 당신의 소형 진공청소기도 우주 연구에 의해 영감을 받았다! (be, inspire, by)

▶ Even your handheld vacuum _____ _____ _____ space research!

4 NASA는 달의 표면 아래로부터 입자를 추출하고 싶었다. (want, extract, particles)

▶ NASA _____ _____ _____ _____ from below the surface of the moon.

5 그것은 그 회사가 많은 공장에서 운영을 중단하도록 했다. (cause, the company, stop)

▶ It _____ _____ _____ _____ _____ operations at many of their plants.

UNIT 11 | Food

반 / 이름:

[01–23] 다음 단어의 뜻을 쓰시오.

01 accidentally _____

02 add _____

03 originate _____

04 bake _____

05 item _____

06 dozen _____

07 eventually _____

08 extra _____

09 extract _____

10 instead _____

11 luckily _____

12 machine _____

13 million _____

14 punish _____

15 unfamiliar _____

16 severely _____

17 receive _____

18 strange _____

19 term _____

20 tongue _____

21 disappear _____

22 customer _____

23 weigh _____

[24–35] 다음 뜻을 지닌 단어를 쓰시오.

24 법 _____

25 비율 _____

26 더운; 매운 _____

27 후추; 고추 _____

28 규모; 척도 _____

29 섞다; 혼합물 _____

30 속이다, 사기 치다 _____

31 시험하다 _____

32 풍습, 관습 _____

33 측정하다, 재다 _____

34 고대의; 오래된 _____

35 땀을 흘리다 _____

[36–40] 다음 표현의 뜻을 쓰시오.

36 ask for _____

37 come from _____

38 related to _____

39 on fire _____

40 refer to _____

반 / 이름:

A 다음 영영 정의에 해당하는 단어를 고르시오.

> to find out the size, length or amount of something

ⓐ bake   ⓑ receive   ⓒ measure   ⓓ disappear

B 다음 밑줄 친 단어와 비슷한 의미의 단어를 고르시오.

> We all should make an <u>extra</u> effort to save energy.

ⓐ proper   ⓑ recent   ⓒ basic   ⓓ additional

C 다음 빈칸에 알맞은 단어를 보기에서 골라 쓰시오.

> 보기   weigh   originate   severely   accidentally

1 Many English words _____ from Latin.

2 Your bags _____ more than 25 kg in total.

3 I _____ met my old school friend on the street.

4 The actor was _____ criticized because of his bad acting.

D 다음 우리말과 일치하도록 빈칸에 알맞은 말을 쓰시오.

1 'it'은 문단에서 무엇을 지칭합니까?
 ▶ What does "it" r_____ t_____ in the paragraph?

2 '피그말리온 효과'라는 말은 그리스 신화에서 나온다.
 ▶ The term "Pygmalion effect" c_____ f_____ a Greek myth.

3 만약 당신이 채식주의자라면, 특별 메뉴를 요청하세요.
 ▶ If you are a vegetarian, please a_____ f_____ a special menu.

A 다음 ( ) 안에서 알맞은 것을 고르시오.

1 China is (very / much) larger than Korea.

2 My hair is (far / more) longer than yours.

3 Today is the (hot / hottest) day of the year.

4 There are (more / most) important things than money.

B 다음 문장에서 밑줄 친 부분을 바르게 고치시오.

1 My sister woke up much <u>early</u> than me this morning.   _____

2 I think this movie is the <u>scarier</u> one I have ever seen.   _____

3 Playing the piano is <u>hardest</u> than playing the guitar for me.   _____

C 우리말과 일치하도록 ( ) 안의 말을 이용하여 문장을 완성하시오.

1 이곳은 우리 마을에서 가장 큰 공원이다. (large, park)
  ▶ This is _____ in my town.

2 수성은 태양계에서 가장 작은 행성이다. (small, planet)
  ▶ Mercury is _____ in the solar system.

3 나는 그가 이 세상에서 가장 뛰어난 축구 선수라고 생각한다. (good, soccer player)
  ▶ I think he is _____ in the world.

D 다음 문장을 우리말로 옮기시오.

1 This musical was a lot better than the last one.
  ▶ _____

2 Nights in winter are much longer than nights in summer.
  ▶ _____

3 You can find the cheapest plane tickets on this website.
  ▶ _____

A 우리말과 일치하도록 ( ) 안에 주어진 말을 바르게 배열하시오.

1 사람들은 때때로 13개의 무언가를 의미하기 위해 그것을 사용한다. (it / to / use / mean)
  ▶ Sometimes people _____ 13 of anything.

2 지금은 고추가 얼마나 매운지를 측정하기 위해 보통 기계가 사용된다. (are / hot / how / peppers)
  ▶ Machines are now often used to measure _____.

3 고객들이 빵 12개 묶음을 요청하면, 그들은 대신 13개를 받았다. (for / customers / asked / when)
  ▶ _____ a dozen loaves, they received 13 instead.

4 어떤 낯선 고추를 먹기 전에 스코빌 매움 지수 척도를 확인해라! (strange / any / eating / peppers)
  ▶ Check the Scoville Heat Unit Scale before _____!

5 그것은 무게가 너무 적게 나가는 빵을 파는 것을 금하는 오래된 법에서 유래됐다.
  (bread / weighed / that / selling)
  ▶ It originated from ancient laws against _____ too little.

B 우리말과 일치하도록 ( ) 안의 말을 이용하여 문장을 완성하시오.

1 그것은 후추 스프레이보다 더 강력하다. (strong)
  ▶ That is _____ _____ pepper spray.

2 그것은 고추의 매운 정도를 측정하기 위해 사용된다. (use, measure)
  ▶ It _____ _____ _____ _____ the spiciness of peppers.

3 누군가를 속이는 것을 피하고자, 제빵사들은 그들에게 추가 빵을 주었다. (avoid, cheat)
  ▶ _____ _____ _____ anyone, bakers gave them extra bread.

4 제빵사가 고객들을 속이다 걸리면, 처벌받을 수 있었다. (catch, cheat)
  ▶ If a baker _____ _____ _____ his customers, he could be punished.

5 2013년에, Carolina Reaper가 지구상에서 가장 매운 고추가 되었다. (the, hot, pepper)
  ▶ In 2013, the Carolina Reaper became _____ _____ _____ on Earth.

VOCABULARY TEST 1

반 / 이름:

[01–23] 다음 단어의 뜻을 쓰시오.

01 vast _____

02 allow _____

03 permission _____

04 forbid _____

05 countryside _____

06 bendable _____

07 huge _____

08 expand _____

09 imperial _____

10 portable _____

11 last _____

12 surround _____

13 certain _____

14 emperor _____

15 roof _____

16 empire _____

17 role _____

18 ruler _____

19 withstand _____

20 architecture _____

21 center _____

22 wrap _____

23 main _____

[24–35] 다음 뜻을 지닌 단어를 쓰시오.

24 정치적인 _____

25 역사(상)의 _____

26 가치 _____

27 들어가다 _____

28 잡다; 보유하다 _____

29 계속되다 _____

30 독특한 _____

31 짓다, 건설하다 _____

32 공예품; 유물 _____

33 정부 _____

34 전통의 _____

35 궁금하다 _____

[36–40] 다음 표현의 뜻을 쓰시오.

36 step down _____

37 known as _____

38 instead of _____

39 take down _____

40 put ~ back together _____

A 다음 단어의 영영 정의를 바르게 연결하시오.

1 huge   •   • ⓐ relating to government

2 political   •   • ⓑ very great in size or amount

3 architecture   •   • ⓒ the art of designing buildings

B 다음 밑줄 친 단어와 비슷한 의미의 단어를 고르시오

> This special glass can <u>withstand</u> strong impacts.

ⓐ prevent   ⓑ endure   ⓒ cause   ⓓ expect

C 다음 빈칸에 알맞은 단어를 보기에서 골라 쓰시오.

> 보기   forbid   expand   permission   surround

1 Tall trees _____ the park.

2 Mr. Harris is trying to _____ his business.

3 You cannot put posters on the wall without _____ from the city.

4 They made a policy to _____ people from smoking inside buildings.

D 다음 우리말과 일치하도록 빈칸에 알맞은 말을 쓰시오.

1 바흐는 '고전 음악의 아버지'로 알려져 있다.

▶ Bach is k_____ a_____ the "father of classical music."

2 그녀는 내가 책상을 재조립하는 것을 도와주었다.

▶ She helped me p_____ the desk b_____ t_____.

3 직원들은 회장이 즉각적으로 물러날 것을 요구했다.

▶ The employees asked the CEO to s_____ d_____ immediately.

A 다음 ( ) 안에서 알맞은 것을 고르시오.

1 He could be (hurting / hurt) by the nail.

2 What he said should (keep / be kept) secret.

3 He (call / is called) a tough guy by his friends.

4 The project must be (finished / finishing) on time.

B 다음 문장을 수동태로 바꾸어 쓰시오.

1 Jenny told me to stay longer.

▶ I _____ by Jenny.

2 You should keep milk in the refrigerator.

▶ Milk _____ in the refrigerator.

3 We will deliver the pizza in 30 minutes.

▶ The pizza _____ in 30 minutes.

C 우리말과 일치하도록 ( ) 안의 말을 이용하여 문장을 완성하시오.

1 그 프로젝트는 내일 완료되어야 한다. (must, complete)

▶ The project _____ _____ _____ tomorrow.

2 그 쇼는 20분 뒤에 끝날 것이다. (will, finish)

▶ The show _____ _____ _____ in 20 minutes.

3 Kevin은 파티에 올 것이라 예상된다. (expect, to come)

▶ Kevin _____ _____ _____ _____ to the party.

4 그 TV 시리즈로 그 여배우는 슈퍼스타가 되었다. (make, a superstar)

▶ The actress _____ _____ _____ _____ by that TV series.

A 우리말과 일치하도록 ( ) 안에 주어진 말을 바르게 배열하시오.

1 그것들을 짓는 데는 30분이 걸렸다. (it / to / took / thirty minutes)

▶ _____ build them.

2 당신의 영토를 살펴보기 위해 당신은 밖으로 나간다. (land / to / look at / your)

▶ You go outside _____.

3 우리는 모두 어떤 일을 하는 것을 금지당한 적이 있다. (forbidden / do / to / been)

▶ We have all _____ certain things.

4 그들은 매년 3번에서 4번 이동하곤 했다. (would / they / move)

▶ _____ three to four times every year.

5 그곳은 중국 전통 건축 양식의 아름다움을 볼 가장 좋은 장소 중 하나이다.

(the / to / see / places / best)

▶ It is one of _____ the beauty of traditional Chinese

architecture.

B 우리말과 일치하도록 ( ) 안의 말을 이용하여 문장을 완성하시오.

1 그곳은 작은 도시만큼이나 크다. (big)

▶ It is _____ _____ _____ a small city.

2 그들의 유르트는 쉽게 치워질 수 있었다. (could, take down)

▶ Their yurt _____ _____ _____ _____ easily.

3 허가 없이는 누구도 그곳에 들어갈 수 없었다. (allow, enter)

▶ No one was _____ _____ _____ it without permission.

4 당신은 이곳이 왜 '도시'라고 불리는지 궁금해할지도 모른다. (why, it, call)

▶ You might wonder _____ _____ _____ _____ a "city."

5 그의 제국이 중앙아시아 밖으로 확장되면서, 유르트 문화도 그러했다. (so, yurt culture)

▶ As his empire expanded outside of Central Asia, _____ _____ _____

_____.

UNIT 13 | Activities

반 / 이름:

[01-23] 다음 단어의 뜻을 쓰시오.

01 excess _____

02 bamboo _____

03 reduce _____

04 defend _____

05 combine _____

06 muscle _____

07 pole _____

08 entertaining _____

09 workout _____

10 recall _____

11 gain _____

12 correct _____

13 spot _____

14 playground _____

15 burn _____

16 repeated _____

17 create _____

18 movement _____

19 cube _____

20 spirit _____

21 anger _____

22 pathway _____

23 reason _____

[24-35] 다음 뜻을 지닌 단어를 쓰시오.

24 자연스럽게 _____

25 지방 _____

26 강도, 세기 _____

27 대부분의 _____

28 공식적인 _____

29 단순한 _____

30 명상 _____

31 궁극적인; 최고의 _____

32 구조물, 건축물 _____

33 지속해서 _____

34 공간 _____

35 기억력 _____

[36-40] 다음 표현의 뜻을 쓰시오.

36 get in shape _____

37 yell out _____

38 at the same time _____

39 interested in _____

40 calm down _____

A 다음 영영 정의에 해당하는 단어를 고르시오.

> more than is necessary, reasonable, or acceptable

ⓐ excess   ⓑ official   ⓒ ultimate   ⓓ simple

B 다음 밑줄 친 단어와 반대 의미의 단어를 고르시오.

> People should <u>combine</u> exercise with a healthy diet.

ⓐ increase   ⓑ prevent   ⓒ separate   ⓓ stop

C 다음 빈칸에 알맞은 단어를 보기에서 골라 쓰시오.

> 보기   anger   muscle   correct   entertaining

1 His face turned red with _____.

2 Nobody knows the _____ answer.

3 You need to exercise every day to gain more _____.

4 I saw an action movie in the theater. It was so _____.

D 다음 우리말과 일치하도록 빈칸에 알맞은 말을 쓰시오.

1 이 차는 당신을 진정해 줄 것이다.

▶ This tea will c_____ you d_____.

2 나는 화가 나서 소리치고 싶었지만, 참았다.

▶ I wanted to y_____ o_____ with anger, but I held back.

3 그는 일과 공부를 동시에 한다.

▶ He works and studies a_____ t_____ s_____ t_____.

A 다음 ( ) 안에서 알맞은 것을 고르시오.

1 I gave some flowers (her / to her).

2 He will buy a robot (to / for) his son.

3 She asked a favor (of / for) her friend.

4 I couldn't open the box (easily / easy).

5 (Sad / Sadly), I said goodbye to my family.

6 Heather came home (late / lately) last night.

B 다음 문장의 밑줄 친 부분을 바르게 고치시오.

1 My mom smiled <u>happy</u>.　　　　　_____

2 James drives very <u>fastly</u>.　　　　　_____

3 <u>Lucky</u>, I found my wallet.　　　　　_____

4 They slept <u>good</u> last night.　　　　　_____

C 다음 두 문장의 의미가 같도록 빈칸에 알맞은 말을 쓰시오.

1 He lent her his phone.

▶ He lent _____ _____ _____ _____.

2 My boss sent me an email.

▶ My boss sent _____ _____ _____ _____.

3 My mom made me a sandwich.

▶ My mom made _____ _____ _____ _____.

4 The reporter asked him some questions.

▶ The reporter asked _____ _____ _____ _____.

A 우리말과 일치하도록 ( ) 안에 주어진 말을 바르게 배열하시오.

1 그것이 최초의 '정글짐'이 만들어진 방식이다.

(created / the first "jungle gym" / was)

▶ That's how _____.

2 그의 아버지는 그에게 대나무 구조물을 만들어 주었다. (for / him / a bamboo structure)

▶ His father made _____.

3 Sebastian은 교육감에게 이 이야기를 들려주었다. (to / this story / the superintendent)

▶ Sebastian told _____.

4 무술은 당신이 스트레스 수준을 줄이는 데 도움을 준다. (your stress levels / you / reduce)

▶ Martial arts help _____.

5 지속적으로 열심히 훈련하면, 당신은 금방 좋은 몸 상태를 유지할 것이다. (in / you'll / shape / get)

▶ If you consistently train hard, _____ quickly.

B 우리말과 일치하도록 ( ) 안의 말을 이용하여 문장을 완성하시오.

1 무술을 배워야 하는 다른 이유들이 있다. (learn, martial arts)

▶ There are other reasons _____ _____ _____ _____.

2 태극권과 가라테는 당신이 자신을 진정하도록 도울 것이다. (help, you, calm, you)

▶ Tai chi and karate will _____ _____ _____ _____ down.

3 수천 년 동안, 사람들은 무술을 사용해왔다. (have, use)

▶ For thousands of years, people _____ _____ _____ martial arts.

4 최초의 공식 정글짐은 Sebastian Hinton에 의해 발명되었다. (invent, by)

▶ The first official jungle gym _____ _____ _____ Sebastian Hinton.

5 정글짐은 대부분의 학교 운동장에서 발견될 수 있는 간단한 구조물이다. (can, find)

▶ Jungle gyms are simple structures that _____ _____ _____ on most school playgrounds.

VOCABULARY TEST 1

반 / 이름:

[01–23] 다음 단어의 뜻을 쓰시오.

01 complete _____

02 pioneer _____

03 develop _____

04 acceptance _____

05 essential _____

06 compare _____

07 detect _____

08 fingertip _____

09 single _____

10 sense _____

11 publish _____

12 blind _____

13 death _____

14 tongue _____

15 trigger _____

16 remain _____

17 ignore _____

18 institute _____

19 vision _____

20 unpopular _____

21 perfect _____

22 standard _____

23 communicate _____

[24–36] 다음 뜻을 지닌 단어를 쓰시오.

24 민감한 _____

25 밝은; 똑똑한 _____

26 곤충 _____

27 인공적인 _____

28 장학금 _____

29 식욕 _____

30 가능한 _____

31 생존 _____

32 감염 _____

33 맛보다; 미각 _____

34 국립[국가]의 _____

35 집중; 농도 _____

36 가공[처리]하다 _____

[37–40] 다음 표현의 뜻을 쓰시오.

37 settle on _____

38 figure out _____

39 thanks to _____

40 thousands of _____

A 다음 영영 정의에 해당하는 단어를 고르시오.

to pay no attention to something

ⓐ taste   ⓑ ignore   ⓒ survive   ⓓ detect

B 다음 밑줄 친 단어와 비슷한 의미의 단어를 고르시오.

Money is not <u>essential</u> for happiness.

ⓐ necessary   ⓑ dangerous   ⓒ common   ⓓ unimportant

C 다음 빈칸에 알맞은 단어를 보기에서 골라 쓰시오.

보기   complete   infection   scholarship   communicate

1 Please _____ the form and submit it.

2 They _____ with each other by email.

3 He applied for the _____ at the university.

4 You should get a shot to avoid the _____.

D 다음 우리말과 일치하도록 빈칸에 알맞은 말을 쓰시오.

1 그의 기술 덕분에, 그는 직업을 구할 수 있었다.

▶ T_____ t_____ his skills, he could get a job.

2 나는 이 문제를 푸는 방법을 알아낼 수가 없다.

▶ I can't f_____ o_____ how to solve the problem.

3 시청 앞에 수천 명의 사람들이 모였다.

▶ T_____ o_____ people gathered in front of the city hall.

A 다음 ( ) 안에서 알맞은 것을 고르시오.

1 He wants (to be / being) a famous actor.

2 He is rich enough (buying / to buy) the car.

3 I'm planning (learning / to learn) a new language.

4 You need (boil / to boil) the water first to cook pasta.

B 다음 문장에서 <u>틀린</u> 부분을 찾아 바르게 고치시오.

1 I hope seeing you soon. _____

2 He was too weak running. _____

3 She promised come home early. _____

4 He played well enough receive the award. _____

5 The girl is enough tall to dunk the basketball. _____

C 우리말과 일치하도록 ( ) 안의 말을 이용하여 문장을 완성하시오.

1 그들은 경기에서 이기기를 기대했다. (expect, win)

▶ They _____ _____ _____ the game.

2 케이트는 프랑스에서 공부하기로 결정했다. (decide, study)

▶ Kate _____ _____ _____ in France.

3 그 상자는 너무 작아서 모든 것을 담을 수 없다. (too, small, put)

▶ The box is _____ _____ _____ _____ everything inside.

4 그녀는 그 모든 질문에 답할 만큼 충분히 똑똑했다. (smart, enough, answer)

▶ She was _____ _____ _____ _____ all the questions.

반 / 이름:

A 우리말과 일치하도록 ( ) 안에 주어진 말을 바르게 배열하시오.

1 그는 눈을 다쳤고 감염이 그를 눈이 멀게 만들었다. (him / blind / made)

▶ He hurt his eye and infection _____.

2 미국이 브라유 표준으로 정한 것은 1917년이었다. (was / it / in 1917 / that)

▶ _____ the US settled on a Braille standard.

3 그들은 감미료가 인공적인지 아닌지를 알아낼 수 있다. (figure / whether / a sweetener / out)

▶ They can _____ is artificial.

4 이 체계를 사용함으로써, 군인들은 말을 하지 않고도 의사소통을 할 수 있었다.

(speaking / communicate / could / without)

▶ By using the system, soldiers _____.

5 하나의 손가락 끝이 양각의 점들을 가로질러 왼쪽에서 오른쪽으로 움직여진다. (right / left / to / from)

▶ A single fingertip is moved _____ across raised

dots.

B 우리말과 일치하도록 ( ) 안의 말을 이용하여 문장을 완성하시오.

1 그는 그것을 개선하기로 결심했다. (decide, improve)

▶ He _____ _____ _____ it.

2 좋은 음식 위를 걷는 것은 그들의 식욕을 유발하기에 충분하다. (enough, trigger)

▶ Walking on good food is _____ _____ _____ their appetite.

3 위에 서 있기에 충분히 좋은 음식은 먹기에도 충분히 좋다. (good, enough, eat)

▶ Food good enough to stand on is_____ _____ _____ _____.

4 그들은 꿀로 가공될 수 없는 감미료는 무시한다. (can, be, process, into)

▶ They ignore any sweeteners that _____ _____ _____ _____

honey.

5 꿀벌은 식물에서 나오는 당분의 낮은 농도를 감지할 수 있다. (able, detect)

▶ Honey bees _____ _____ _____ _____ low concentrations of

a sugar from plants.

VOCABULARY TEST 1

반 / 이름:

[01–23] 다음 단어의 뜻을 쓰시오.

01 portray _____

02 extremely _____

03 loss _____

04 endure _____

05 terrible _____

06 film _____

07 imagine _____

08 jealousy _____

09 wise _____

10 inaccurate _____

11 ordinary _____

12 profit _____

13 talented _____

14 term _____

15 comprehensive _____

16 spend _____

17 admit _____

18 career _____

19 purchase _____

20 envy _____

21 respect _____

22 waste _____

23 tale _____

[24–36] 다음 뜻을 지닌 단어를 쓰시오.

24 동시대의 _____

25 애도하다, 슬퍼하다 _____

26 극장, 공연장 _____

27 허구[소설]의 _____

28 사학자 _____

29 개봉, 출시 _____

30 실패 _____

31 지식 _____

32 마침내, 결국 _____

33 노력, 수고 _____

34 작곡가 _____

35 성공하지 못한 _____

36 비롯되다, 유래하다 _____

[37–40] 다음 표현의 뜻을 쓰시오.

37 refer to _____

38 in the end _____

39 give up _____

40 move on to _____

A 다음 영영 정의에 해당하는 단어를 고르시오.

> to show great sadness because someone has died

ⓐ portray   ⓑ waste   ⓒ consider   ⓓ mourn

B 다음 밑줄 친 단어와 비슷한 의미의 단어를 고르시오.

> She is a very <u>talented</u> pianist.

ⓐ clever   ⓑ strict   ⓒ gifted   ⓓ cheerful

C 다음 빈칸에 알맞은 단어를 보기에서 골라 쓰시오.

> 보기   effort   comprehensive   respect   terrible

1 I _____ my grandparents.

2 I got a(n) _____ grade on my math test.

3 They provide a(n) _____ range of goods.

4 We should put more _____ into the project.

D 다음 우리말과 일치하도록 빈칸에 알맞은 말을 쓰시오.

1 네가 성공할 때까지 포기하지 마라.

▶ Don't g_____ u_____ until you succeed.

2 다음 주제로 넘어갑시다.

▶ Let's m_____ o_____ t_____ the next topic.

3 결국, 그는 그 대학에 가기로 선택했다.

▶ I_____ t_____ e_____, he chose to go to that college.

A 다음 ( ) 안에서 알맞은 것을 고르시오.

1 I drink coffee (in / on) the morning.

2 It is scary (ride / to ride) a roller coaster.

3 (It / That) is interesting to learn about insects.

4 We always have a party (at / on) Christmas Day.

B 다음 빈칸에 알맞은 단어를 보기에서 골라 쓰시오.

보기	in	at	on	for	during

1 My sister was born _____ 2020.

2 We will go on a picnic _____ Sunday.

3 She watched a movie _____ two hours.

4 They have lunch _____ 12:30 every day.

5 I'm going to travel around London _____ this vacation.

C 우리말과 일치하도록 ( ) 안의 말을 이용하여 문장을 완성하시오.

1 약속을 지키는 것은 중요하다. (important, keep)

▶ _____ _____ _____ _____ _____ a promise.

2 무엇을 살지 결정하는 것은 어렵다. (hard, decide)

▶ _____ _____ _____ _____ what to buy.

3 내 친구들과 노는 것은 재밌다. (fun, play)

▶ _____ _____ _____ _____ with my friends.

4 외국어를 배우는 것은 어렵다. (difficult, learn)

▶ _____ _____ _____ _____ _____ foreign languages.

A 우리말과 일치하도록 ( ) 안에 주어진 말을 바르게 배열하시오.

1 그가 모차르트를 존경했을 가능성이 더 크다. (more / likely / is / it)

▶ _____ he respected Mozart.

2 형편없는 영화를 견디는 것은 시간 낭비이다. (a bad movie / enduring / is)

▶ _____ a waste of your time.

3 분명히, 모든 소문이 반드시 사실인 것은 아니다. (necessarily / rumors / all / are)

▶ Clearly, not _____ true.

4 그는 자신이 쓴 돈을 낭비했다고 생각하고 싶지 않다. (the money / spent / he / wasted)

▶ He doesn't want to think that he _____.

5 살리에리는 아마도 모차르트만큼 재능이 있지는 않았다. (as / as / not / talented / Mozart)

▶ Salieri was probably _____.

B 우리말과 일치하도록 ( ) 안의 말을 이용하여 문장을 완성하시오.

1 당신은 거기에 계속 앉아 있다. (you, keep, sit)

▶ _____ _____ _____ there.

2 손실을 받아들이는 것이 훨씬 더 현명하다. (much, wise, accept)

▶ It is _____ _____ _____ _____ your losses.

3 당신은 당신의 노력들이 낭비되는 것을 원하지 않는다. (efforts, waste)

▶ You don't want your _____ _____ _____ _____.

4 그것들은 그 영화의 개봉과 함께 시작되었을지도 모른다. (may, begin)

▶ They _____ _____ _____ with the release of the film.

5 그는 아마데우스 모차르트를 질투한 것으로 알려졌다. (say, to, jealous)

▶ He was _____ _____ _____ _____ of Amadeus Mozart.

VOCABULARY TEST 1

반 / 이름:

[01-23] 다음 단어의 뜻을 쓰시오.

01 control _____

02 renowned _____

03 continuous _____

04 grassy _____

05 tiny _____

06 creature _____

07 cause _____

08 substance _____

09 reality _____

10 depict _____

11 movement _____

12 attract _____

13 dot _____

14 expose _____

15 ability _____

16 purpose _____

17 shoot _____

18 below _____

19 simplicity _____

20 prey _____

21 chemist _____

22 technique _____

23 confuse _____

[24-33] 다음 뜻을 지닌 단어를 쓰시오.

24 유익하다 _____

25 물리학자 _____

26 수면, 표면 _____

27 바다, 대양 _____

28 영감을 주다 _____

29 대비되는, 대조적인 _____

30 섞다; 혼합 _____

31 위험 _____

32 깊은 곳에, 깊이; 깊은 _____

33 포함[수반]하다 _____

[34-40] 다음 표현의 뜻을 쓰시오.

34 filled with _____

35 millions of _____

36 frighten away _____

37 famous for _____

38 interested in _____

39 at a distance _____

40 as a whole _____

A 다음 영영 정의에 해당하는 단어를 고르시오.

> the reason why something is done

ⓐ surface   ⓑ purpose   ⓒ creature   ⓓ simplicity

B 다음 밑줄 친 단어와 비슷한 의미의 단어를 고르시오.

> The computer can <u>process</u> many tasks at the same time.

ⓐ affect   ⓑ create   ⓒ fail   ⓓ handle

C 다음 빈칸에 알맞은 단어를 보기에서 골라 쓰시오.

> 보기   attract   imagine   ability   danger

1 I can't _____ life without my smartphone.

2 Many people are in _____ of losing their jobs.

3 This event will _____ people from around the city.

4 She lost her _____ to communicate due to the accident.

D 다음 우리말과 일치하도록 빈칸에 알맞은 말을 쓰시오.

1 내 남동생은 테니스에 관심이 있다.
  ▶ My brother is i_____ i_____ tennis.

2 나는 직장에서 떨어진 곳에 살고 있다.
  ▶ I live a_____ a d_____ from my work.

3 그들은 크림으로 가득 찬 도넛을 먹고 있다.
  ▶ They are eating doughnuts f_____ w_____ cream.

A 다음 ( ) 안에서 알맞은 것을 고르시오.

1 He is good at (rides / riding) a bicycle.

2 (Eat / Eating) healthy food is important.

3 The man (read / reading) a book is my brother.

4 Look at that koala (climbed / climbing) the tree.

5 I found a small box (hidden / hiding) under the bed.

6 She was talking to a man (stood / standing) at the gate.

B 다음 문장에서 밑줄 친 동명사(구)의 역할을 주어, 목적어, 보어 중 골라 쓰시오.

1 Thank you for inviting me. _____

2 Reading books is my hobby. _____

3 Saving energy is very important. _____

4 My favorite activity is swimming. _____

C 다음 빈칸에 알맞은 단어를 보기에서 골라 알맞은 형태로 쓰시오.

보기	wear	make	bark	name

1 I know a boy _____ Michael.

2 She has a bag _____ in Italy.

3 Can you see the woman _____ a scarf?

4 I was scared of the dog _____ in the yard.

A 우리말과 일치하도록 ( ) 안에 주어진 말을 바르게 배열하시오.

1 생물 발광은 루시페린이라 불리는 물질에 의해 일어난다. (by / is / caused / a substance)
   ▶ Bioluminescence _____ called luciferin.

2 그 기법은 아주 작은 점을 사용하는 것을 포함했다. (tiny / involved / the technique / using)
   ▶ _____ dots.

3 그의 유명한 그림들 중 하나는 「아스니에르에서 멱 감는 사람들」이라고 불린다.
   (his famous / one / paintings / of)
   ▶ _____ is called *Bathers at Asnières*.

4 아귀는 먹이를 유인하기 위해 머리 위의 불을 밝히는 공 모양의 부분을 이용한다.
   (that / attract / to / lights up)
   ▶ Anglerfish use a bulb on their head _____ prey.

5 그는 인간의 뇌와 눈이 이 색들을 처리하는 방식에 관심이 있었다. (how / in / was / interested)
   ▶ He _____ the human brain and eyes process these
   colors.

B 우리말과 일치하도록 ( ) 안의 말을 이용하여 문장을 완성하시오.

1 오스트라코드는 윗입술에 빛을 밝혀서 짝을 유인한다. (by, light up)
   ▶ Ostracods attract mates _____ _____ _____ their upper lip.

2 빛을 만드는 이 능력은 '생물 발광'이라 불린다. (create, light)
   ▶ This ability _____ _____ _____ is called "bioluminescence."

3 그는 당대의 저명한 특정 물리학자들에 의해 영감을 받았다. (inspire, by)
   ▶ He _____ _____ _____ certain renowned physicists of his time.

4 그것은 또한 위로 연기가 피어오르고 있는 공장들을 표현한다. (smoke, rise, above them)
   ▶ It also depicts factories with _____ _____ _____ _____.

5 그것은 어느 여름날 강가의 풀로 덮인 둑에서 휴식을 취하고 있는 몇 명의 젊은 남자들을 묘사한다.
   (young men, relax)
   ▶ It portrays some _____ _____ _____ on a grassy bank.

MEMO

MEMO

READING
Inside

workbook

A 4-level curriculum
integration reading course

- **A thematic reading program that integrates with school curriculum**
중등 교육과정이 지향하는 문이과 통합 및 타교과 연계 반영한 독해서

- **Informative content with well-designed comprehension questions**
정보성 있는 지문과 질 높은 다양한 유형의 문항 그리고 서술형 평가도 대비

- **Grammar points directly related to the *Grammar Inside* series**
베스트셀러 Grammar Inside와 직접적으로 연계된 문법 항목 및 문항 제공

- **Exercises with useful, essential, and academic vocabulary**
중등 필수 어휘 학습 코너 제공

- **A workbook for more vocabulary, grammar, and reading exercises**
풍부한 양의 어휘, 문법, 그리고 쓰기 추가 문제 등을 수록한 워크북

Level	Grade	Words Limit
Reading Inside Starter	Low-Intermediate	140-160
Reading Inside Level 1	**Intermediate**	**160-180**
Reading Inside Level 2	Intermediate	180-200
Reading Inside Level 3	Low-Advanced	200-220